"This book pioneers a new spiritual approach to coaching informed by transpersonal theory, depth psychology, and the wisdom of astrology. Alba Carod shows that the interpretation of dreams coupled with study of astrological symbolism creates meaningful emotional resonances for her clients. Her luminous paintings of dream images enhance the text and demonstrate the process of creative dialogue with dreams. Alba's work unites intuition, meditation, and active imagination with practical strategies for change."

Greg Bogart, PhD, *author of* Dreamwork and Self-Healing

"Carod takes transpersonal coaching to a whole new level through creatively integrating astrology, dream work, and active imagination. Carod's seminal ideas, helpful examples, and illustrative case stories show the harmonious blending and collaboration of astrology and dream work to create an impactful and cohesive approach in transpersonal coaching. I wholeheartedly recommend this book to my transpersonal coaching students and supervisees."

Jevon Dängeli, *transpersonal coach and educator at Alef Trust*

I0092217

Archetypal Coaching

Archetypal Coaching offers a transformative approach to personal growth, blending ancient Greek astrological foundations and dream work with modern coaching techniques, somatic awareness, and Jungian active imagination.

Astrological archetypes illuminate the roots of struggles and highlight potential resources, while dreams act as a focused lens, bringing attention to issues that require immediate exploration. The approach explored within this book emphasizes interactive dialogue with archetypes and symbols, using embodied imagination and somatic awareness to guide clients in creating a personal symbol that embodies their inner process and potential, echoing Jung's concept of the transcendent function. Supported by six in-depth case studies and numerous examples, the author outlines a holistic framework for integrating astrology and dream work into coaching, emphasizing personal growth and treating archetypes as dynamic tools for creativity and self-discovery.

This book will appeal to established coaches, counselors, and therapists interested in integrating archetypal work into their practice, as well as students of Jungian psychology, coaching, art therapy, astrology, and related fields.

Alba Carod is a transpersonal coach and psychology teacher for higher education from Barcelona. A certified astrologer with a master's in transpersonal psychology, she has developed a unique coaching method integrating astrological archetypes and dream work to foster self-awareness and transformation.

Archetypal Coaching

Creating Synergies Through Astrology and Dream Work

Alba Carod

Routledge
Taylor & Francis Group

LONDON AND NEW YORK

Designed cover image: From The New York Public Library. "The dispute between Athena and Poseidon over sovereignty of Attica" New York Public Library Digital Collections. https://digitalcollections.nypl.org/items/510d47e4-1a1d-a3d9-e040-e00a18064a99

First published 2026
by Routledge
4 Park Square, Milton Park, Abingdon, Oxon, OX14 4RN

and by Routledge
605 Third Avenue, New York, NY 10158

Routledge is an imprint of the Taylor & Francis Group, an informa business

© 2026 Alba Carod

British Library Cataloguing-in-Publication Data
A catalogue record for this book is available from the British Library

ISBN: 978-1-041-04191-7 (hbk)
ISBN: 978-1-041-04190-0 (pbk)
ISBN: 978-1-003-62725-8 (ebk)

DOI: 10.4324/9781003627258

Typeset in Times New Roman
by codeMantra

Contents

About the Author

Alba Carod, a transpersonal coach and psychology teacher for higher education, hails from Barcelona and resides in the northeast of Spain, nestled by the shores of the Mediterranean Sea. Since a young age, she has been captivated by the profound symbolic language of archetypes. Her fascination with astrology has persisted throughout her youth and adulthood, leading her to become a certified astrologer accredited by the Astrological Faculty of London. A passion for understanding the human mind further motivated her to pursue a degree in psychology.

In her first steps working as a counselor, she combined archetypal knowledge with counseling. With time, she realized that although clients experienced insights through the archetypes, they were not committed to action, probably because they sensed a lack of agency.

It was during her participation in the master's in Transpersonal Psychology with Alef Trust (Liverpool John Moores University) in 2020 that Alba found her inspiration to integrate archetypal work into a transpersonal coaching framework.

Drawing upon her knowledge and experience in psychology, coaching, astrology, and dreams, Alba has developed a comprehensive coaching method firmly rooted in self-awareness. Through her innovative approach, she combines astrological archetypes and dream work to support individuals in their transformative journeys.

This approach lays the foundation for a new model of transpersonal coaching grounded in participatory archetypal exploration.

For more information about her work and services, visit her website at https://astrodreamcoachingwithalba.com/.

Acknowledgments

I wish to express my deepest gratitude to Jevon Dängeli, my tutor and teacher for the Transpersonal Coaching Psychology module and certificate, for his inspiration and wholehearted trust in my approach during my master's studies.

I also wish to express my sincere appreciation to my research participants and clients for their invaluable contributions.

Preface

This book is for coaches, counselors, and therapists who are open to the possibility of including archetypal work in their practice.

Archetypal coaching brings awareness to dream symbols and to the inner dynamics reflected by the natal chart archetypes that are related to the client's trigger. Dreams and astrological archetypes together provide a profound framework for exploring the psyche. Dreams reflect the current state of the unconscious through symbolic imagery, while astrological archetypes offer a symbolic map of the psyche, revealing potentialities and shedding light on the roots of emotional triggers.

Greek Theurgic practices, Jungian active imagination and the transcendent function, Assagioli's subpersonalities, Hillman's imaginal psychology, Bogart's questioning method, and Dängeli's transpersonal coaching have all served as sources of inspiration. "Archetypal Coaching" recovers the Platonic and Theurgic astrological foundations from ancient Greece as a participatory interactive tool with the archetypes and dream symbols. It applies coaching techniques, somatic awareness, and Jungian active imagination to facilitate deep self-reflection and personal growth.

Synergy, from the Greek *syn* ("together") and *ergon* ("work"), means "working together" or "cooperation." Archetypal coaching cultivates transformative synergies by engaging in dialogue with archetypes and dream symbols. This process acknowledges fragmented parts of the psyche, fostering their integration and unlocking their higher potential. An archetypal coach helps individuals navigate the universal catalog of archetypes and symbols, choosing beneficial expressions to harmonize fragmented energies into a cohesive whole. By working with both dream symbols and archetypes, individuals enter a transformative field where the ego dissolves into collective awareness.

Active imagination is essential for integrating these elements, as it engages the mind in bridging conscious and unconscious thoughts. Clients are encouraged to observe and interact with images that arise in the liminal space, enabling symbols to intuitively shape the psyche. This approach supports gentle and progressive transformation without excessive reliance on intellectual analysis.

By transcending cognitive understanding, this process fosters an experiential connection with archetypal energies. Through creativity and exploration, individuals gain fresh perspectives, deepen self-awareness, and cultivate a stronger sense of agency.

Some critics argue that astrology restricts human freedom. However, this coaching approach engages with archetypes in a participatory manner. Instead of interpreting astrological and dream configurations, it presents symbolic scenarios, empowering clients to select those that align with their goals or vision. This approach draws on the diverse possibilities of archetypal expression. Our inner "archetypal catalog" contains a vast array of potential roles and qualities we can embody. By consciously choosing which archetypal attributes to cultivate and express, we enhance our agency, actively shaping our reality and personal growth.

For my master's dissertation (Carod, 2021), I evaluated the effectiveness of this system for coaching using organic inquiry, a transpersonal qualitative research method developed over the past two decades at the Institute of Transpersonal Psychology.

I recruited six women from diverse cultural and geographical backgrounds, all with an interest in archetypal work. Their ages ranged from 35 to 65, and each had pursued professional careers and master's-level education. Over the course of the study, participants engaged in five coaching sessions followed by a semi-structured interview. To ensure their anonymity, they chose pseudonyms, and their stories were shared with them for feedback and consent.

To prepare for this work, I engaged in somatic meditative practices, reviewed relevant literature, and creatively explored my own dreams. This process deepened my ability to support and facilitate the liminal experiences of my clients. I also painted and dialogued with recurring dream images to uncover their symbolic significance. To structure and interpret these dream puzzles, I intuitively selected a guiding archetype as a central framework for exploration.

Drawing from my own experience, I encouraged research participants to select or create symbols that represented their higher potential. In their final responses to my research question on the impact of archetypal work in their lives, four out of six participants used the terms "coherence" and "centeredness." The sense of belonging to a universal pattern or order may have been what brought coherence and meaning to the coaching sessions. By creating their own symbol, participants embodied Jung's concept of the transcendent function, which suggests that integrating conscious and unconscious elements fosters a sense of wholeness and purpose.

In the painting in Figure 0.1, Pandora is seen digging inside the box of dream symbols, which seem eager to emerge from the darkness. The small blue bird perched on her right hand symbolizes intuitive messages and guidance from my unconscious mind. The star above the blue bird represents hope for the future – the one element said to remain after Pandora released the illnesses sealed within the collective unconscious.

According to myth, Pandora was created as a punishment for humanity after the Titan Prometheus stole fire from the gods to empower humans. She was given a box containing all the evils of the world and warned never to open it. However, an alternative perspective suggests that Pandora was liberating humanity from their unconscious contents, challenging the conventional belief that her act of opening the box was the source of human suffering.

Figure 0.1 Pandora opening the box of dream symbols. Illustration by the author

Reference

Carod, A. (2021). *The transformative experiences of coaching using archetypal imagery within a participatory framework: An organic inquiry*. Alef Trust, John Moores University.

Introduction

This book invites readers on a journey into the transformative potential of dream symbols and astrological archetypes within coaching and personal development. Drawing on the foundational theories of transpersonal psychology, it blends coaching practices with archetypal insights to foster meaningful change, expanded awareness, and personal empowerment.

Chapter 1 introduces the **Archetypal Foundations of Transpersonal Psychology**, identifying personal potentials through myth and metaphor, connecting individual experience to a broader field of consciousness. It begins with an exploration of the unconscious and Jungian principles of *Individuation*, the path to self-realization and the practice of active imagination. Frameworks like *Psychosynthesis* and *Archetypal Psychology* provide pathways for understanding the symbolic language of the psyche.

Chapter 2 transitions into **Archetypal Dynamics in Coaching Practice,** exploring how archetypes shape the human psyche and influence self-discovery. This chapter explores the origins and foundational principles of coaching, from Socratic questioning to psychodynamic techniques that reveal the interplay between subpersonalities and archetypes. Techniques such as rewriting personal myths and using *Archetypal Anchors* help clients expand their internal "reality map," opening up new choices and directions in life. By blending archetypal insights with modern coaching, this chapter demonstrates how deeply rooted patterns can be transformed into constructive pathways.

Chapter 3, Coaching in the Liminal Space, introduces the liminal space as a gateway for transformation, where clients can shift their state of consciousness and gain insights through mindful awareness, participatory engagement, and somatic grounding.

In **Chapter 4, Coaching with Dream Symbols**, readers delve into the world of dreams as profound symbols of the unconscious. By tracing ancient traditions and modern perspectives, this chapter explores how dreams serve as creative, transformative expressions of the psyche. Techniques for interpreting dreams, connecting dream symbols to archetypes, and utilizing dreams as tools for emotional balance and self-regulation are presented, allowing clients to find synchronicities between their dreams and waking lives for a deepened understanding of self.

DOI: 10.4324/9781003627258-1

Chapter 5 examines **astrology's role in coaching**, tracing its roots from ancient Sumeria through the Greek Platonic Cosmos, which envisioned the universe as a living, archetypal order. This chapter highlights astrology's links to Theurgy – neoplatonic ritual practices for divine connection – the influence of Renaissance thinker Marsilio Ficino, who revived the concept of *Anima Mundi*, or world soul, and Jung's approach to astrology. This chapter provides a comprehensive look at how astrology's rich symbolic language can deepen the coaching framework, enabling clients to explore their inner landscape with curiosity and depth. Practical examples illustrate how astrological symbols offer insights into personal dynamics and how questioning can reveal archetypal patterns. Topics include working with archetypal potentials, attachment styles, timing, and personal development.

Chapter 6 delves into **the experiences of six women** grappling with fears and issues surrounding self-esteem. Spring found herself overwhelmed by the academic demands of her master's degree, expressing her apprehensions about losing her boundaries through her dreams. Following an accident, Roshani found herself in a vulnerable state, prompting her to confront her deepest fears. Marguerite recognized the importance of overcoming her fear of revealing herself to the world. Mary explored themes of self-protection and the fear of rejection through her dreams. Susanne grappled with self-criticism and excessive rumination. Lastly, Rose's dream about consuming spoiled food prompted her to address her self-esteem issues. These narratives highlight how the integration of astrology and dream work provided profound insights for these women, shedding light on potential qualities and behaviors worth exploring further.

The **Appendices** offer practical exercises and structured approaches that guide readers through each coaching process.

Chapter 1

The Archetypal Foundations
of Transpersonal Psychology

Myths: Our Divine Origins

Myths are traditional stories or legends that often feature supernatural beings or events. They serve to explain natural phenomena, customs, or cultural beliefs while embodying traits that define human nature, such as will, primal impulses, intellect, emotions, and intuition. In societies, myths provide reassurance and help reduce uncertainty.

In his book *Myth and Reality*, Professor Mircea Eliade (1963, p. 11) emphasizes that "myth is a sacred history that narrates the origin of reality, whether it's the entire Cosmos or a fragment." Eliade posits that the "sacred," the first appearance of something, holds value, and myths, considered sacred and significant stories in archaic societies, are valuable assets due to their role in the evolution of humans into mortal, sexed, and cultural beings.

In Mesopotamia, the story of Gilgamesh, a powerful king, unfolds as he confronts profound sadness and seeks immortality after the death of his friend, god Enkidu. His journey across distant lands explores themes of mortality, wisdom, and purpose, leaving a legacy of heroism and introspection. Similarly, in Chinese folklore, Mulan exemplifies courage and resilience, disguising herself as a man to take her father's place in battle. Her story challenges traditional gender roles and celebrates bravery.

Greek mythology offers a vast array of narratives that have profoundly shaped Western culture. Hesiod's *Theogony* provides a comprehensive genealogy of the Olympian gods, beginning with Chaos and the emergence of Gaea, Uranus, and their offspring, including the Titans and Aphrodite. This epic details the cosmic drama of Uranus casting his children into the abyss, the rise of Chronos (Saturn), and the eventual overthrow of Chronos by his son Zeus (Jupiter), who liberates his siblings and establishes a new divine order. It also introduces figures like Prometheus, credited with the creation of humanity, and Pandora, whose story reflects themes of temptation and divine justice. Hesiod's *Works and Days* complements these tales, emphasizing moral and practical wisdom rooted in justice, symbolized by Zeus's daughter Athena.

DOI: 10.4324/9781003627258-2

Homer's *Iliad* and *Odyssey* explore themes of wrath, heroism, and resilience, with Achilles' defiance during the Trojan War and Odysseus' resourceful journey home forming two of the most enduring epics in literary history. Ovid's *Metamorphoses* adds a Roman perspective, weaving together tales of transformation that range from human to animal, plant, or constellation. Through these narratives, Ovid elevates human emotions and desires, often subverting traditional divine hierarchies and presenting love, embodied by Amor (Cupid), as the driving force of change and conflict.

Myths have historically served as mirrors of the human experience, weaving action and reaction to reflect universal truths. They provide frameworks for understanding emotions, challenges, and aspirations, offering insights into human nature and cultural values. These stories have transcended time, inspiring works of art like Botticelli's paintings, Shakespeare's plays, and modern adaptations in operas, films, comics, and digital media. Contemporary portrayals often adapt archetypal traits to suit current narratives, demonstrating the timeless relevance of myth.

Philosophical perspectives have also shaped the interpretation of myths. Plato emphasized their revelatory power, suggesting that understanding myths requires intuition and a reliance on the insights of great poets like Homer and Hesiod. This contrasts with the logical, reasoned approach favored by modern Western philosophy. Yet both rational analysis and intuitive interpretation illuminate the enduring relevance of myth, enabling individuals to connect deeply with its symbolic elements.

In coaching, the integration of myth enhances self-awareness and personal growth. Myths, rich with archetypal symbolism, serve as tools to explore the depths of the psyche, offering clients profound insights into their own lives. By blending rational understanding with the intuitive flashes evoked by myth's revelatory qualities, coaching sessions can guide individuals toward clarity, resilience, and transformation. Mythology, as a reflection of the human journey, continues to inspire and provide meaning, bridging the ancient and the contemporary in a dialogue that speaks to the soul.

The Sacred Dimension of the Psyche

It is interesting to note that the word "psychology" was formed by combining the Greek word *psychē* (breath, life, soul) with *logia*, from the Greek logos (speech, word, reason).

In ancient Greek philosophy, *psychē* was not merely a term for the mind but encompassed the essence of life, breath, and soul. The Greeks saw the soul as the seat of reason, emotion, and character, which influenced their understanding of human behaviors and mental processes. Hence, in its origin, psychology came into being as the reasoning or speech of the soul.

The concept of psychology as the reasoning of the soul suggests that our thoughts, emotions, and behaviors are deeply interconnected with our inner essence or soul. This perspective encourages a holistic approach to mental health and well-being, where nurturing the soul and understanding its needs are as important as addressing cognitive and behavioral aspects.

Diving deeper into the connection between ancient Greek philosophy, psychology, and spirituality reveals a rich tapestry of thought that integrates the mind, body, and soul. Ancient Greek philosophers like Socrates, Plato, and Aristotle explored concepts that are foundational to modern psychology and spirituality.

Socrates (in Plato's *Apology*) emphasized the importance of self-knowledge and introspection, famously stating, "Know thyself." He believed that understanding one's inner self was key to achieving wisdom and virtue (Cooper & Hutchinson, 1997). Plato viewed the soul as immortal and central to human existence. In his theory of forms, he suggested that the soul connects with a higher realm of truth and knowledge, influencing our understanding of reality (Phaedo). Aristotle introduced the concept of the soul as the "form" of a living being, integrating it with the body and influencing behavior and thought ("De Anima"). His work laid the groundwork for the study of psychology as a scientific discipline. Integrating these ancient philosophical insights with modern psychological practices can deepen our understanding of the human experience. It highlights the importance of nurturing the soul, fostering inner growth, and recognizing the interconnectedness of all life. By honoring the energy of the universe within us, we can cultivate a richer, more meaningful perspective on life, aligning our actions with the deeper currents of existence and promoting holistic well-being.

The word *transpersonal* ("beyond or through the personal") refers to experiences, processes, and events in which one transcends one's usual self-conscious awareness and experiences a connection to or participation in a larger, more meaningful reality (Daniels, 2005). Transpersonal psychology posits that the self extends beyond a solitary ego, including others, nature, and the entirety of space and time. This comprehensive self-concept, associated with non-ordinary states of consciousness, forms the basis for comprehending and promoting human transformation (Friedman & Hartelius, 2013).

In the late 1960s, a group in California, drawing from humanistic, existential psychology and spiritual traditions, established transpersonal psychology to encompass the full spectrum of human experience. Over the past 50 years, transpersonal psychology has broadened its investigation and understanding of transformation through theories, subjective experiences, healing, and transcendence (Daniels, 2013).

In psychology, this type of transformative process has been called individuation by Carl Jung (1960a, 1960b) and self-realization by Roberto Assagioli (1965). Esoteric and new spiritual practices emphasize a psychospiritual self-change process, seen in self-realization (psychosynthesis) and individualization (Jungian depth psychology).

Both Jung and Assagioli made a vital distinction between the sacred dimension of the psyche – what they referred to as the "transpersonal" or "higher self" – and the more surface level of consciousness, the "ego-consciousness." This distinction is central to their understanding of the psyche's complexity. The ego-consciousness, the center of everyday awareness and identity, operates within the realm of personal experience. It is concerned with the practicalities of life, self-preservation, and navigating social roles.

On the other hand, the transpersonal or higher self encompasses a deeper connection to the spiritual and universal aspects of the psyche, which Jung understood as part of the collective unconscious and the archetypal realm. Psychotherapeutic work, as envisioned by both Jung and Assagioli, is not merely about resolving personal conflicts or easing psychological symptoms. It is viewed as a sacred journey, one that can lead to the transformation of consciousness. This journey allows the individual to transcend the limitations of the ego, opening up to the greater wisdom and unity found in the transpersonal realm.

The Unconscious

The term "unconscious" was first introduced in Europe by German philosopher Friedrich Schelling (1800) in the late 18th century. He used the term in the context of his philosophical work to refer to aspects of the mind that operate outside of conscious awareness. Later, the concept was further developed by other thinkers, including Eduard von Hartmann, who wrote *Philosophy of the Unconscious* in 1869.

However, it was Sigmund Freud (1856–1939), the founder of psychoanalysis who brought the idea of the unconscious into the field of psychology, creating a systematic theory that explored the unconscious mind's influence on behavior, followed by Carl Jung, who expanded the idea with his concepts of the collective unconscious and archetypes.

Freud (Assagioli, 1965, p. 12) demonstrated that various physical symptoms and psychological disturbances are due to instincts, drives, phantasies, buried in the unconscious and retained there by resistances and defense mechanisms of various kinds. He also found that many manifestations of our normal life, such as dreams, fancies, forgetting, mistakes and lapses of behavior, and even some kinds of artistic and literary production, are due to the same psychological mechanisms.

Freud believed that the unconscious was the product of personal experiences and referred to "God" as a projection of the mind that could be analyzed. While Freud did not acknowledge any connection between humans and the sacred, Jung believed people have a natural and automatic tendency toward things that are considered sacred or holy, even if they are not consciously aware of it.

Jung claimed that the unconscious was inherited from the past collective experience of humanity. The collective unconscious, he believed, is made up of archetypal and numinous forces (a collection of knowledge and imagery) that every person is born with and that are shared by all human beings due to ancestral experience. Jung goes so far to say that "the whole of mythology could be taken as a sort of projection of the collective unconscious" (Jung, 1960b, p. 152).

Jung remained agnostic about the possibility of a "God" or "Spirit" as an objective reality, since for him it could not be demonstrated (Assagioli, 1965). The Jungian notion of "God" is the "Self."

According to Jung (1976, para. 789), the Self encompasses all psychic phenomena in the human being, expressing the unity and totality of the personality, although it can only be partially perceived. As a transcendental entity, the Self incorporates both conscious and unconscious aspects, manifesting itself in dreams, myths, and stories as a figure of higher order, such as a king, hero, or prophet, or as a symbol of wholeness such as the circle or the cross. Although conceptually it represents the unity of opposites, it can also appear as a unified duality, such as the Tao. Its symbols often have significant luminosity, such as the mandala, standing out as a central archetypal representation (para. 790).

Jung uses the image of the mandala to reflect this union and its central point, around which everything else is organized. The center point is the Self, surrounded by all the other opposites. Jung initially used the mandala symbol to represent the Greek term for order and harmony in reference to the cosmos. He later referred to the astrological map as the mandala, representing the potential of the psyche as indicated by the archetypal configurations. Each person has a center that contains their unique being. This center tries to express itself, but the competing voices of the complexes, archetypes, and even the ego frequently drown it out.

For Jung, the unconscious encompasses all psychic processes that are neither conscious nor perceptually related to the Self. These contents, submerged below the threshold of consciousness, are not lost and can emerge in appropriate circumstances, such as in sleep, in hypnosis, or through associations with forgotten content (1976, para. 837).

"The Shadow is a living part of the personality and therefore wants to live with it in some form" (Jung, 1968, 9i, para. 44). This concept suggests that the Shadow, as a repressed aspect of the Self, seeks integration rather than suppression. In the words of C. G. Jung, "Until you make the unconscious conscious, it will direct your life and you will call it fate." This profound statement encapsulates Jung's perspective on fate and determinism which suggests that what you deny subdues you, while what you accept transforms you. Often, we try to deny aspects of our life, believing that they will disappear, but in reality, this denial reinforces what we are trying to avoid. He highlighted the role of the unconscious mind in shaping our experiences and influencing our choices.

The unconscious is projected and played out until it is brought into conscious awareness and worked through. The issue at hand is how to interact with it so that we encourage the change in energy that leads to transformation. By acknowledging and addressing our unconscious projections, we open the door to understanding their origins and implications. However, intellectual comprehension alone does not bring about change; true alchemical transformation within the psyche can only occur via the symbol-making process (see Chapter 4). This creative symbolic process facilitates a deeper integration of unconscious material, allowing for growth and self-awareness that transcend mere intellectual insight.

The unconscious operates with its own agenda, facilitating the integration of specific aspects of our personality. This facilitation usually happens through crises and periods of suffering, which act as transformative catalysts. True transformation only occurs when we fully accept what we face, taking responsibility and finding ways to live it in a positive way. From this premise, various therapeutic approaches have emerged that work with the contents of the unconscious such as Psychoanalysis, Psychosynthesis, Archetypal Psychology, and Imaginal Psychology.

Individuation

In Jung's analytical psychology, the fundamental goal of human life is individuation, which is essentially a psychospiritual quest for full humanness and psychological integration, representing the realization of the archetype of the Self.

The word "individuality," derived from the Latin *individuus*, translates as "undivided" or "total," referring to the condition of being an "undivided being" or an "unfragmented being." We achieve individuation by integrating all the psychic parts of ourselves, both semi-conscious and totally unconscious, into a conscious whole.

Jung viewed psychology as a modern expression of the same archetypal forces that have shaped human consciousness throughout history. In *Collected Works* (9i), Jung suggests that psychology, like myth, operates with ideas derived from archetypal structures, translating the ancient language of myth into a modern form. He states, "Psychology... operates with ideas which in their turn are derived from archetypal structures and thus generate a somewhat more abstract kind of myth" (CW 9i, para. 302). Jung fused psychology with ancient knowledge, incorporating classical mythology, Gnosticism, and Alchemy.

The Gnostic worldview posits a higher realm to which the human soul will eventually return.[1] Underlying this apparent dualism is the acknowledgment of a deeper tension inherent in humanity's existence – the reflection of the divine and earthly realms. Based on Gnostic mythical schemas, Jung identified the objectively oriented consciousness with the material or "fleshly" part of humankind, bound up in the cosmic cycle of generation and decay. This leads to a personality and sense of self that is dependent on temporal existence, resulting in anxieties and a lack of permanence. The true self, according to Jung and the Gnostics, is the supreme consciousness existing and persisting beyond all space and time, called the pure consciousness or Self. This is different from the temporally constructed "ego consciousness," which is the temporally constructed form of a discrete existent. The pure or true Self is associated with Spirit (pneuma), the mind relieved of its temporal contacts and context (Segal, 1992).

Alchemy occupies a central place in Jung's collective unconscious hypothesis, where he draws analogies between alchemy, symbolism, and the analytic process. Jung (1969) emphasizes the dual nature of alchemy, which involves both a chemical process and a mystical component. The Greek roots of alchemy refer to the processes of extracting juice (*chemeia*) and separating metals from gold (*chimia*). For both types, the transmutative process entails transforming a given substance into a higher one, defining alchemy as the art of transmutation. Jung discusses the insights that alchemy provides into individuation and the transcendent nature of the psyche.

In his book *Jung and the Alchemical Imagination*, Jeffrey Raff (2000, p. 68) compares the alchemical process to the Jungian transcendent function. The transcendent function is based on the union of opposites through a symbol, with one of the characteristics of the self being its ability to integrate dualities such as good and bad, masculine and feminine, spiritual and material.

For Jung, individuation is a lifelong journey characterized by the interplay between opposites, primarily the conscious and unconscious. This process entails bringing together all components of one's psyche, including the shadow, self, and anima/animus.

Carl Jung discusses the tension between the persona and the inner self in *Collected Works of C. G. Jung*, Volume 7. He explains that the persona, while necessary for social adaptation, can lead to psychological issues when over-identified with. The person may neglect important aspects of their inner life, resulting in neurosis. Jung writes:

> Every individual has both a social role (the persona) and a deeper, private self. When a person overly identifies with their social role at the expense of their inner values and deeper needs, the resulting disconnection can lead to psychological distress. (CW 7, para. 244)

Jung argued that repressing parts of the self, including traits that may be considered socially undesirable or negative, causes them to form part of the shadow – hidden aspects of the personality. Failing to integrate these repressed parts into consciousness can result in psychological distress, including anxiety and depression, as the neglected elements continue to influence behavior unconsciously. To fully individuate, a person must confront and embrace the shadow, allowing for the integration of these fragmented parts and achieving personal transformation (Jung, CW 9i, para. 99). By embracing and resolving these opposing energies inside oneself, one might acquire a sense of wholeness and self-realization – in other words, a better knowledge of one's true identity and life's purpose.

According to Jung, conflicts between the conscious and unconscious mind can give rise to psychological problems (complexes), and individuation involves integrating these aspects into consciousness through the Self, the psychic totality, integrating both personal and transpersonal consciousness.

In *The Structure and Dynamics of the Psyche*, Jung (CW 8, para. 408) describes psychic processes as "a scale that slides along the instinctual and spiritual consciousness." According to Jung, the one-sidedness of this sliding consciousness can be overcome by the acceptance of the shadow. During the Jungian process of individuation, the focus of identity is transferred from the ego (the center of consciousness whose role is to analyze through cognition) to a deeper existential center (the Self), an entity that includes the conscious and unconscious dimensions of the psyche: masculine and feminine, rational and irrational, light and shadow.

The manifestation of the Jungian-realized Self implies an alternative mode of being, more mature and authentic than the ordinary self of everyday existence.

It is illustrated in various ways in the myths of many religions: as soul, spirit, and atman, as a state of enlightenment, etc. (Daniels, 2005).

For this journey to be transformative, it is essential to move beyond intellectual analysis and embrace a global, integral, and expanded consciousness.

There are several transformative practices for exploring the unconscious mind and engaging with symbolic representations within the psyche, including dream work, astrology, active imagination, symbolic exploration, and meditative practices. Psychotherapy modalities, such as Jungian analysis and psychodynamic therapy, offer structured frameworks for this exploration.

Carl Jung emphasized the need to apply dream insights to waking life. He described individuation as the process of identifying unconscious content in dreams and integrating it consciously. Actively engaging with dreams – keeping a journal, reflecting on recurring themes or symbols, and exploring the emotions evoked – deepens self-awareness and facilitates psychological integration.

Active Imagination, a technique developed by Jung, involves consciously dialoguing with different aspects of the psyche through visualization. By engaging directly with archetypes and symbols from dreams or mythology, clients gain profound insights, revealing hidden motivations, conflicts, and potential healing pathways. This practice is a dynamic method for accessing deeper layers of the psyche.

The exploration of symbolic meanings embedded in myths, archetypes, fairy tales, art, and cultural narratives offers profound insights into universal themes and archetypal patterns. Reflecting on these symbols in relation to one's life fosters personal growth and a deeper connection to collective wisdom. Jung synthesized psychology with ancient knowledge, such as mythology and alchemy, drawing symbolic maps like the horoscope to reveal the unfolding of the psyche over time. Although he did not formally recognize astrology, Jung secretly consulted his clients' natal charts, viewing planetary placements as psychological complexes, such as the anima and animus (Greene, 2018, p. 16). He saw this dynamic relationship with archetypal forces as the path to psychospiritual development.

In *Psychology and Alchemy* (1957), Jung stated: "If modern psychotherapy thus returns to hit upon the vivified archetypes of the collective unconscious, this means a repetition of that phenomenon which can often be observed in times of great religious change" (p. 49).

Addressing archetypes and unconscious motives helps clients recognize psychic dynamics without judgment. Jungian psychiatrist Edward Whitman (1970) noted that astrological techniques are as valuable as dream interpretation, as they offer information on personality traits and unconscious dynamics.

Understanding planetary influences helps therapists comprehend the client's inner world. For example, a strong Mars placement may signal tendencies toward aggression or impulsivity, guiding the therapist to discuss healthier ways to channel assertiveness. Similarly, identifying the Moon sign sheds light on emotional needs and attachment styles, helping therapists and coaches support clients in building secure relationships.

Active Imagination

Active imagination is a process that involves consciously engaging with the unconscious mind to bring its contents into awareness. Jung first introduced this concept in his work *The Transcendent Function*, where he explained the dynamic process within the psyche that unites opposing forces, creating a new symbolic perspective (1960a, pp. 67–91).

Active imagination involves a specific form of meditation that requires deep concentration and emotional engagement with images arising from dreams, reveries, emotional surges, waking fantasies, or deliberately induced altered states of consciousness. Its aim is not to serve as material for intellectual analysis of repressed conflicts but to let the unknown express itself in its own symbolic language – the language of images. Imagination serves as a threshold or gateway to psychic realms that are ordinarily inaccessible (Greene, 2018, p. 74).

The inclusion of archetypes connected to dream symbols in active imagination dialogues generates profound effects. By engaging both dream symbols and archetypes, active imagination allows for a dynamic interaction between conscious and unconscious elements of the psyche. This process enables the individual to access deeper layers of psychic content, encouraging integration and personal transformation through the symbolic interplay of these forces.

In *Inner Work: Using Dreams and Active Imagination for Personal Growth*, Jungian author Robert Johnson (2009, p. 138) emphasizes the distinctive quality of awareness in active imagination.

> Essentially, Active Imagination is a dialogue that you enter into with the different parts of yourself that live in the unconscious. In some ways it is similar to dreaming, except that you are fully awake and conscious during the experience. This, in fact, is what gives this technique its distinctive quality. Instead of going into a dream, you go into your imagination while you are awake.

While the transcendent function refers to both a psychological process and a method, active imagination specifically refers to the method of interacting with the unconscious. This function helps mediate between conflicting inner states, transforming "either/or" choices into "both/and" solutions, leading to a new level of being (Chodorow & Jung, 2015).

It involves two key stages: first, letting the unconscious rise up by focusing on a mood, image, or fantasy; and second, consciously engaging with what emerges, often through dialogue or creative expression such as painting, writing, or movement. By actively participating in this process, individuals can clarify unconscious emotions and impulses, transforming raw psychic material into something that can be integrated into conscious awareness (Chodorow & Jung, 2015, pp. 5–12).

Jung, in his discussion of the transcendent function, stresses the necessity of relinquishing control and engaging with unconscious processes. He explains that to integrate these processes, we must allow ourselves to "merge" with them, stating that we can "gain possession of them by allowing them to possess" us (Jung, 1966, CW 7, p. 368). This echoes the importance of surrendering control, aligning with Johnson's emphasis on allowing the unconscious to actively shape our conscious experience.

This relationship between conscious awareness and unconscious material is essential for understanding the deeper layers of the psyche. Jung also identified the symbol formation process as a key mechanism for energy transformation. Symbols carry emotional significance and a charge of libidinal energy, distinguishing them from mere signs. Symbols are the vital clues to psychic development and the transformative shifts in energy.

Liz Greene (2018, p. 82) explains that, according to both Neoplatonic philosophers and Jung, true symbols are not human-made social constructs but rather *discovered* because they embody divine realities or, in Jungian terms, archetypal realms. These symbols, such as myths, were not invented but "happened" spontaneously. For Jung, symbols also act as gateways, facilitating movement into a "liminal zone," a space where the conscious and unconscious interact. This liminal zone can be likened to the hypnagogic state, a transitional phase between wakefulness and sleep, where the subconscious and conscious mind engage and communicate through symbolic imagery.

In this state, symbols serve as mediators, opening pathways to deeper layers of the psyche, allowing for direct experience of archetypal forces. By facilitating access to the hypnagogic or liminal space, symbols enable a person to connect with underlying truths that are otherwise hidden in the unconscious. As these symbols embody divine or archetypal energies, engaging with them through active imagination or dream work becomes a method for deeper psychological integration and self-awareness.

Jungian theorists like Marie-Louise von Franz and Robert Johnson (2009) have further refined the process into specific stages. For example, von Franz (1997) outlines a process that includes emptying the ego, allowing an unconscious image to arise, giving it form, and confronting it ethically. Similarly, Johnson's approach involves inviting the unconscious, engaging in dialogue, applying ethical values, and solidifying the experience through rituals. In *Inner Work* (2009), Robert Johnson emphasizes the importance of physically integrating dream insights into waking life. After attempting to understand a dream mentally, Johnson suggests taking a physical action that affirms the dream's message. This step could be practical, such as paying bills on time or resolving a confused relationship, or symbolic, like performing a ritual that reinforces the dream's meaning. These structured stages provide a way to not only engage with the unconscious but also integrate its insights into daily life.

While active imagination, developed by Carl Jung, shares similarities with theurgical practices in its emphasis on inner exploration and interaction with symbolic images, it differs in its psychological focus and therapeutic applications. In the practice of active imagination, the mind participates consciously in the events that take place on the imaginative level, which is neither conscious nor unconscious and creates a life experience that combines the elements of both (Johnson, 2009).

Jung (1968, CW9, paras. 101, 262) differentiated active imagination, where images work independently from conscious will and desire, from fantasy, which is very much focused on our expectations.

The distinction between active imagination and fantasy emphasizes the importance of giving up control in order to access a more authentic source of creativity. To achieve this state of surrendering or letting go, one must be willing to embrace uncertainty and vulnerability. We can start by practicing somatic awareness and meditation techniques to quiet the mind and open ourselves up to new possibilities.

In Active Imagination, fantasy images gain autonomy, much like the *theia phantasia* in Iamblichean theurgy, where they come to the soul from an external source. Hillman (in Shaw, 2024, p. 273) argues that this externalization is essential for healing the psyche. The author draws from the tradition of Greek Dionysian theater – where the audience is moved beyond themselves, identifies with the actors, and experiences catharsis – healing involves a psychological dismemberment and release from rigid literal fixations.

In a passage of *De mysteriis*, Iamblichus (in Shaw, 1985, p. 10) asserts that:

Intellectual understanding does not connect theurgists with divine beings.... In fact, these very symbols by themselves perform their own work, without our thinking.

This concept shares a resemblance with Hillman's suggestion to allow images to articulate themselves without imposing interpretations. Hillman bases its therapeutic approach on the exploration of images rather than on their explanation (1975).

Hillman revives Iamblichus's view of the soul and aligns it with Jung's concept of Active Imagination. In this process, fantasies initially appear as passive "scenes in a theater," to be merely observed. However, the individual eventually realizes that "his own drama is being performed on this inner stage" – a direct communication from the unconscious, according to Jung. These fantasies are not random but are created by the unconscious, bringing images and scenarios to life before the viewer (Shaw, 2024, p. 273).

To avoid relying solely on fantasy, coaches and therapists may guide clients toward an embodied state, fostering presence and connection to bodily sensations while exploring their inner world. Clients engage with archetypes and dream symbols, allowing unexpected symbols and emotions to naturally arise, rather than controlling outcomes based on conscious desires. The work with archetypes in active imagination fosters an interactive position with the gods (archetypes) wherein the client gains the ability to dialoguing with his archetypes and dream symbols in an expanded state of mind, adopting a creative approach in relation to their circumstances.

Surrendering control and staying connected to bodily sensations facilitate deeper creativity and insight. Allowing moments of silence in the process enables awareness of how images relate to body sensations, fostering a fertile interaction with archetypes and dream images.

To reach this expanded state of body and consciousness, I guide the client to a somatic-centered meditation (Dängeli, 2022, p. 62). In the process of active imagination, we guide our clients to interact with archetypes and symbols. By focusing on the sensations and emotions within the body, one can tap into the deeper layers of the unconscious mind where archetypal imagery resides.

Psychosynthesis

Roberto Assagioli (1888–1974) was an Italian psychiatrist and pioneer in the fields of humanistic and transpersonal psychology. Assagioli sought to integrate depth psychology with the modernized expression of the occult, Platonic-Hindu approach to man and God. His approach in Psychosynthesis is deeply influenced by both Western psychology and Eastern spiritual traditions, particularly the Theosophical concept of the "permanent atom." This idea refers to an indestructible spiritual essence or core of the human being, which persists beyond the limitations of the physical and psychological self.

His intention was to create a holistic model of human development, incorporating the wisdom of both Western and Eastern traditions, and to encourage the direct experience of these deeper dimensions of the Self beyond historical, cultural, or religious constraints. Assagioli's work on synthesizing Eastern and Western spiritual traditions includes practical techniques such as meditation and visualization, which are essential for transpersonal exploration and integration. By fostering a connection with the Self, individuals can navigate developmental stages and harmonize their personalities, ultimately finding a deeper meaning and direction (Assagioli, 2007). His work attempts to universalize spiritual growth by drawing on a wide range of influences, including contemporary psychologists like William James, Carl Jung, Viktor Frankl, Abraham Maslow, and others, bridging psychology and spirituality (Assagioli, 2007, pp. 8–9).

Psychosynthesis, as developed by Assagioli, seeks to integrate psychoanalysis with spiritual understanding. Assagioli aimed to demonstrate that human development extends beyond childhood traumas, emphasizing the potential for growth in a healthy individual, which Maslow later referred to as "self-actualization." However, Assagioli delved deeper into the subject, exploring the idea that human potential extends beyond the ordinary and encompasses spiritual and transpersonal experiences.

Assagioli claimed that Carl Jung, "of all modern psychotherapists, is the closest in theory and practice to psychosynthesis" and further expanded on the similarities between his own and Jung's views (Keen, 1974, p. 3):

> We regard man as a fundamentally healthy organism in which there may be temporary malfunctioning. Nature is always trying to re-establish harmony, and within the psyche the principle of synthesis is dominant. Irreconcilable opposites do not exist. The task of therapy is to aid the individual in transforming the personality and integrating apparent contradictions. Both Jung

and myself have stressed the need for a person to develop the higher psychic functions, the spiritual dimension.

Assagioli emphasizes that self-realization is not merely a psychological process but a spiritual one, where individuals can access higher states of consciousness through practices such as meditation, visualization, affirmation, dis-identification, substitution, and the ideal model between others.

In his lecture *Jung and Psychosynthesis* (1966), Assagioli discusses how psychosynthesis both draws upon and diverges from Jungian psychology. While he acknowledges the valuable contributions Jung made, particularly with the concept of the collective unconscious and archetypes, Assagioli differentiates between the conscious self (the "I") and the ever-changing psychological contents we experience, such as sensations, thoughts, and feelings. He explains that while people often confuse the self with these contents, they are actually distinct. The self is a stable point of pure self-awareness, akin to a lighted screen onto which various psychological experiences are projected. This self remains constant even though it may seem submerged or to disappear during sleep, anesthesia, or hypnosis, only to reappear mysteriously when consciousness is regained. Assagioli emphasizes that this points to the existence of a permanent, higher Self beyond the temporary fluctuations of the conscious ego (1966, pp. 18–19).

Assagioli critiqued Jung's concept of the collective unconscious for lacking a clear distinction between the higher, middle, and lower levels of the unconscious. Psychosynthesis places a particular emphasis on the exploration of these realms, particularly the higher unconscious, which is regarded as the source of mystical experiences and higher intuitions (Assagioli, 1965, 1991).

> Processes of "psychological osmosis" are going on all the time, both with other human beings and with the general psychic environment. The latter corresponds to what Jung has called the "collective unconscious"; but he has not clearly defined this term, in which he includes elements of different, even opposite natures, namely primitive archaic structures and higher, forward-directed activities of a superconscious character. In psychosynthesis, self-realization is seen as a dynamic relationship and growing alignment with the Self, without merging entirely with it, as such a union would entail a boundless state of awareness encompassing the cosmos. (Assagioli, 1965, p. 19)

This perspective is central to psychosynthesis, which seeks to integrate the conscious self with the higher Self, guiding individuals toward greater self-awareness and alignment.

By exploring this concept of a stable "I" separate from transient experiences, psychosynthesis supports individuals in connecting with a stable sense of self beyond fleeting experiences, using techniques like visualization, meditation, and introspection. Assagioli emphasizes that psychosynthesis aims for the harmonious integration of all aspects of the personality, including unconscious subpersonalities, into a unified Self. This integration is facilitated by the framework of identification, disidentification, and self-identification. Freedom, in the context of psychosynthesis, emerges when we release our identifications with the various roles, beliefs, and emotions that we mistakenly associate with who we are. Firman (in Nocelli, 2021, p. 1) clarifies that this process involves gradually disidentifying from the contents of the mind, body, and feelings to reveal our core as a center of pure consciousness and will. This movement toward Self-realization parallels the Buddhist concept of enlightenment and is a progressive awakening to deeper truths beyond the surface of our thoughts and emotions.

Self-identification allows individuals to recognize that their true identity lies in the conscious awareness that observes, makes choices, and creates meaning in life. This deeper realization enables people to live more authentically and intentionally, anchored in their true Self rather than in fleeting identifications. By cultivating self-awareness, one can become aware of these personality identifications and disidentify from them, creating space for a more authentic connection to the will, which plays a critical role in personal development. The will acts as the guiding force, helping individuals navigate psychological processes toward their true purpose. Assagioli (1965, p. 125) stresses that the will is directly linked to the Self, and it helps regulate unconscious motivations. As a previous step, before engaging the will, one must explore and bring unconscious drives to light, rationalizing them so that they work harmoniously toward a goal.

Assagioli defines the will as a multifaceted process involving six stages: purpose, deliberation, decision, affirmation, planning, and execution (1965, pp. 7–8). Purpose is the first stage, and it involves recognizing the inner "call of Self." This call is not an external imposition but a resonance with one's values, meanings, and transpersonal qualities. Deliberation follows, allowing the individual to weigh various possibilities for manifesting this purpose. Importantly, deliberation requires disidentification from limiting factors such as family expectations, cultural pressures, and subpersonalities so that the individual can move freely to the next stage – choice. Affirmation, or the act of committing to live one's truth, strengthens the decision and ensures alignment with one's deeper purpose, free from external attachments.

Planning, the fifth stage, also requires disidentification. Without this, the planning process may unconsciously revert to old stories or societal pressures. Firman (in Nocelli, 2021, p. 5) further explains that the process of self-identification involves discerning between core elements of the Self – such as purpose, meaning, and values – and external identifications like societal roles, family pressures, or subpersonality agendas. For example, planning might be unconsciously influenced by the desire to meet others' expectations, even when this doesn't align with the true Self. When planning is guided by the Self, it remains free from external identifications and serves the genuine purpose of the individual. The final stage, manifestation, brings the plan into action, allowing the individual to remain connected to their purpose and ensure that their choices are grounded in an authentic expression of their will.

Psychosynthesis also highlights methods to enhance self-awareness and integrate the personality. These include cathartic methods, projective techniques like the Rorschach or Thematic Apperception Tests, and creative outlets like art, writing, or music, which serve as bridges between the conscious and unconscious mind. Writing biographies or keeping diaries allows clients to reflect on their life events and uncover unconscious material more easily, contributing to self-awareness and psychological growth.

A central practice in psychosynthesis is dis-identification, which encourages individuals to detach from different aspects of their personality, acknowledging that while they experience thoughts, desires, and emotions, these are not the essence of their true self. Assagioli (1965, p. 172) emphasizes that the self is the stable and constant center of awareness, while the contents of the psyche – thoughts, feelings, and behaviors – are ever-shifting and temporary. For example, labeling unconscious feelings as external forces (e.g., "A wave of discouragement is trying to submerge me" rather than "I am discouraged") helps individuals resist being overtaken by these impulses (Assagioli, 1965, p. 21). Disidentification fosters a healthy separation between the Self and the ever-changing aspects of the psyche, allowing the individual to maintain clarity and focus on their true goals.

This idea can be paralleled in work with astrological archetypes. When a client is experiencing a particular lack or emotional imbalance, identifying the archetypal energy that is currently unbalanced or missing from their life can be transformative. When individuals realize that they are under the influence of a repressed or unbalanced archetype, they can disidentify from its limiting effects through identifying with the higher, more balanced expressions of the same archetype, similar to Assagioli's "ideal model" (see Chapter 2 on subpersonalities).[2] For instance, someone under Saturn's influence may feel constrained by structure. However, recognizing its higher, more balanced manifestations, such as discipline and responsibility, allows for disidentification from Saturn's limiting aspects and aligns with the individual's purpose.

Subpersonalities are recognized, integrated, and balanced within the individual, rather than being seen as the entirety of the Self. The key lies in identifying with the higher Self, which unites and directs these different parts toward harmonious integration. Counselors working within the psychosynthesis framework help clients understand that subpersonalities represent only aspects of their full identity, encouraging the development of a more unified, coherent self-image (Assagioli, 1991, p. 51). Recognizing subpersonalities in the context of these ideal models creates a psychological distance that opens up space for creative and adaptive responses. This detachment allows individuals to accept these parts of themselves and integrate them in a healthy way, using the ideal as a compass for personal development.

Assagioli's Ideal Model technique can be extended to the realm of archetypes. Like Jung, Assagioli was also secretly investigating astrology, though it remained less overt in his public work. In 2012, in an office at the Psychosynthesis Institute in Florence, boxes labeled "Spiritual Astrology" containing all of Assagioli's astrology papers were found. In the box were the charts of family and friends. A valuable resource for understanding investigations in this area is the book by psychosynthesis psychotherapist Will Parfitt (2022), *Astrological Psychology and Roberto Assagioli*. While Assagioli did not explicitly frame his work in terms of archetypes, his method offers a pathway to recognizing how subpersonalities influence personal development.[3]

When comparing this with Jung's work, both psychologists recognize the importance of integrating unconscious content and highlight the value of symbolic representations in navigating the complexity of the human psyche. However, Jung emphasizes the emergence of symbols that unite opposites in the individuation process, acting as natural expressions of psychic wholeness, while Assagioli works more consciously with the ideal model, visualizing it as a dynamic force guiding personal evolution.

Archetypal Psychology

> Psychology is ultimately mythology, the study of the stories of the soul. (Hillman, 1972, p. 16)

Archetypal psychology incorporates culture, history, and pluralistic Greek myth archetypes. Unlike Jung's individuation, Hillman prioritizes soul-making through interactions with inner images, rejecting the consolidation of the Self archetype (Hillman & Moore, 1989).

For Hillman (1972, p. 52), soul-making, which evokes the sense of the presence of psyche and anima, implies the steering of an emotional and living factor of overwhelming importance:

> A psychology whose name is soul making strikes holy different chords in the soul itself, than does the ego psychology. Depth psychology, as it was originally named in German, leads eventually to the recognition of the soul as the inward downward factor in personality, the factor which gives depth.

Embracing a polytheistic stance, Hillman encourages exploration of diverse beliefs, myths, and gods for a profound understanding of the soul. In this context, archetypal psychology does not confine itself to Western archetypes but acknowledges universal patterns across cultures and historical periods.

Hillman called for the rescue of images that are capable of releasing startling new insights (Hillman & Moore, 1989, p. 25). His concept of archetypal images emphasizes their dynamic, experiential nature as they actively interact with the soul, influencing us in ways that extend beyond mere intellectual understanding. These images possess an active presence, shaping our experiences on a deeper level. In connection with this, Tarnas (2006, p. 70) refers to what Hillman has termed "an archetypal eye" – an imaginative intelligence, inherent in all of us, that allows us to recognize and discern the rich multiplicity of archetypal patterns not only in the intimate microcosm of our personal lives but also in the significant events of history and culture. This ability to perceive archetypal images bridges the individual and collective realms, offering profound insights into both personal experience and broader human narratives.

Much like the theurgic symbols in Iamblichus's philosophy, which penetrate the soul and exert their influence independently of our conscious thought, for Hillman, archetypal images work on us without requiring interpretation.

Archetypal psychology, according to James Hillman, derives from the Neoplatonic tradition of Plotinus, Porphyry, Iamblichus, and Proclus. The Neoplatonists had both direct and indirect influence on C. G. Jung, whom Hillman regards as the "first immediate father" of archetypal psychology. If Jung's psychology may be seen as a kind of Christian (monotheistic) Neoplatonism, archetypal psychology recognizes itself as more polytheistic, drawing more directly on the ideas of Plotinus and other non-Christian Neoplatonists (Shaw, 2016).

With archetypal psychology, Hillman follows a trajectory of Neoplatonists. Plotinus's thought was developed by Iamblichus into theurgy: the recognition that the soul in the body is fragmented and needs to recover itself not by withdrawal, introspection, and escape but by creating proper receptacles to contain the gods, to give these deepest impulses of the soul a divine shape (Shaw, 2016, 338).

In *The Myth of Analysis* (1972, p. 3), Hillman introduces the concept of "the transformation of psyche into life" as:

> ... freeing the psychic phenomena from the curse of the analytical mind. Psychology has become a subtle system for distorting the psyche into a belief that there is something wrong with it and for analyzing its imagination into diagnostic categories.

Neoplatonist Iamblichus (in Shaw, 1995) believed that our illnesses are not just physical ailments but signs of our failure to properly receive and contain the gods' influences. Hillman (1975) echoes this idea, advocating for the creation of "appropriate receptacles" to better contain these divine influxes.

In the context of active imagination and spiritual practice, these receptacles could take the form of personalized symbols that we create and engage with intentionally. By crafting a symbol during an active imagination session and then using it in ritual, we essentially build a container for these archetypal energies, allowing us to integrate and channel archetypal influences more effectively into our lives. The melting of the ego state into collective awareness prepares the ground from which a potential archetypal awareness and change can be cultivated.

Imaginal Psychology

Since ancient times, people have deliberately used their imagination to create the reality they want for themselves. For example, ancient civilizations like the Egyptians and Greeks believed in powerful gods and goddesses who controlled aspects of their lives, leading them to build temples and make offerings in hopes of influencing their favor. Indigenous cultures around the world often incorporate imagination into spiritual rituals and ceremonies. Shamans may journey into alternate realms through visionary experiences to commune with spirits or gain insights for healing and guidance.

This belief in the power of imagination to shape reality is still evident today in practices like visualization, meditation and positive affirmations. Concepts like maya (illusion) and samsara (cycle of birth and rebirth) in Hinduism and Buddhism emphasize the idea that perception shapes reality. In order to speed up their spiritual growth and inner change, Tibetan monks imagine themselves as already enlightened beings while they meditate.

Hillman's imaginal psychology underscores the profound impact of the imaginal world on our well-being, attributing autonomy to images that shape emotions, thoughts, and behaviors (Hillman, 1975; Hillman & Moore, 1989). This branch of archetypal psychology focuses on soul-making, engaging meaningfully with images in a realm between body and spirit, fostering imagination, fantasy, and reflection.

For Hillman (1975), the gods personify the archetypes in consciousness according to our capacity to imagine. This provides a sense of personal meaning, as it acknowledges the soul's ability to relate to and interact with the gods, as was recognized in ancient Greece.

> Suppose the fantasies, feelings, and behavior arising from the imaginal part of ourselves are archetypal in their sickness and natural. Perhaps the unconscious and psychodynamics are fantasies that could be replaced with better ones. (Hillman 72, p. 4)

Imaginal psychology encourages practices like active imagination, dream analysis, and mythological studies to establish a connection with this creative realm.

Whereas Jung's psychology focuses on the analysis of psychic dynamics and their constellations (the ego or personality, the anima and animus, as well as the shadow as unconscious aspects), Hillman's therapeutic approach recognizes the images and symbols that spontaneously emerge from the individual, such as those found in dreams.

James Hillman takes a more imaginative and metaphorical approach to myths. For example in the myth of Eros and Psyche, he focuses on soul-making, where the journey of Psyche symbolizes not merely a path to individuation but a deeper participation in the imaginal world.[4] Psyche's journey from innocence through suffering and eventual transformation into an immortal represents the soul's path to self-realization, echoing themes of love, sacrifice, and spiritual awakening. The myth is also referred to in Plato's "Symposium," where Eros is discussed as a powerful force that connects mortals to the divine, helping the soul transcend earthly limitations. For Hillman, the myth evokes the soul's movement toward depth and complexity. He views the anima (as represented by Psyche) not as something to be integrated into consciousness but rather as a way of engaging with the soul's depths. Hillman emphasizes Eros as the connecting force – what binds and unifies opposites through love and emotional intensity. He argues that imaginative involvement is essential for transformation, contrasting it with Jung's reflective consciousness (Hillman, 1972, pp. 85–87).

Hillman asserts that soul-making requires not just reflection but emotional engagement, particularly through practices like active imagination, which connect us to archetypal symbols in profound ways. He argues that symbols and archetypes facilitate transformation by opening up liminal spaces – the threshold between conscious and unconscious mind. These symbols, such as those seen in dreams or mythic imagery, are not constructs but are discovered and act as gateways to deeper psychic realities, allowing access to the soul's language and mysteries (Hillman, 1972, pp. 90–92). This tale has been used symbolically to represent the challenges the human soul (Psyche) faces in its quest for union with the divine (Eros), emphasizing the transformational power of love.

Archetypal coaching draws inspiration from the ancient Greek theurgist Iamblichus (in Shaw, 1995), who believed that intellectual understanding alone does not connect the practitioner with divine beings or forces. Instead, the archetypal symbols themselves perform their own transformative work. This aligns with my focus on the practical engagement with symbols, prioritizing experiential and symbolic work over purely intellectual interpretation. It is through this embodied, imaginal practice that true transformation can occur, moving beyond theoretical analysis to an active encounter with the deeper layers of the psyche. Although I follow Jung with respect to holding a dynamic relationship with the archetypes in active imagination and the creation of a unifying symbol, the archetypal coaching approach that I propose does not focus on an individuation process or on developmental stages. As Hillman suggests, we look for an engagement with images and archetypes and a personification of the archetypes in consciousness according to our capacity to imagine.

Engaging in coaching offers a unique opportunity for individuals to take an empowered role in their journey. Coaches facilitate self-discovery by asking powerful questions, eliciting insights, and supporting clients in setting and achieving meaningful goals. Archetypal coaching encourages clients to explore their unconscious mind, engage with symbolic representations, and integrate new awareness into their daily lives.

While clients are introduced to the basic concept of archetypes, they are encouraged to explore the images freely, without imposing predetermined interpretations. Instead of directing the process toward a specific developmental or individuation goal, this method encourages participants to engage with images, archetypes, and symbols through a dialogue with these images, allowing them to reveal their meaning in a non-linear, open-ended process, rather than forcing them into a strict framework of personal development or progress.

In the context of coaching or therapy, particularly when engaging with archetypes, a goal-oriented mindset often focuses on achieving specific outcomes or resolving issues within a predetermined framework. While goals can provide direction and structure, they may inadvertently limit the depth and spontaneity of the process. Shifting toward curiosity and wonder opens up the exploration of archetypes to a broader spectrum of possibilities.

Curiosity invites therapists and clients alike to approach archetypes and dream symbols with an open mind and a willingness to explore the unknown aspects of the psyche. It encourages a deeper inquiry into the symbolic meanings and emotional resonances that archetypes evoke, rather than rushing toward predefined solutions or conclusions. By embracing curiosity, therapists create a supportive environment where clients feel empowered to delve into their inner landscapes without the pressure of achieving immediate results.

Wonder, however, allows for awe and reverence toward the archetypal energies that emerge during therapy. It acknowledges the profound mysteries of the human psyche and the transformative potential inherent in archetypal exploration.

Authentic exploration of archetypes involves allowing clients the freedom to engage with these symbolic energies in a way that is true to their own experiences and inner wisdom. It emphasizes the process of discovery over predefined outcomes, recognizing that each client's journey with archetypes is unique and unfolds at its own pace.

By avoiding the imposition of predetermined expectations, therapists and coaches create a space where clients can authentically connect with the archetypes that resonate most deeply with their current life circumstances. This approach encourages clients to explore the multifaceted dimensions of archetypes, embracing both their light and shadow aspects without judgment or fear.

Personifying the Metaphor

Personification began with Greek and Roman sanctuaries and altars where gods were worshipped. Ancient Greeks practiced rituals honoring gods and goddesses to influence their destinies and create purpose. For example, the festival of Eleusis in Ancient Greece was a highly revered ritual that honored Demeter and Persephone, celebrating the cycle of death and rebirth. Participants believed that by partaking in the rituals and living a virtuous life, they could connect with the divine and gain a deeper understanding of the world around them. These rituals reconnected individuals with myth, empowering them to shape their reality, liberate from stagnant moments, and instill confidence in rebuilding their world.

Eliade (1963, p. 18) highlights the value of experiencing the myth through rituals to influence external events:

> The fact that myth tells how something came into existence, or how a pattern of behavior, an institution, a manner of working were established, is the reason why myths constitute the paradigms for all significant human acts; by knowing the myth one knows the "origin" of things and hence can control and manipulate them at will; this is not an "external," "abstract knowledge" but a knowledge that one experiences ritually, either "by ceremonially recounting the myth, or by performing the ritual.

By engaging in these ancient practices, people were able to transcend the limitations of their individual experiences and find common ground with others. Through the power of storytelling and ritual, ancient societies were able to pass down their wisdom and knowledge from generation to generation, ensuring that their legacy would live on and continue to inspire future explorers of the human experience.

Campbell (1976)[5] and Hillman (1975), among other authors with a Jungian orientation, consider the therapeutic role of myths and how they promote a meaningful life. Our personal characteristics and behaviors reflect the dynamics of powerful archetypal principles, which we enact in our everyday life. These principles, portrayed in ancient times as immortal gods and goddesses, are as relevant today as they were then, for they represent dynamic principles of the human psyche.

For Jungian analyst Robert A. Johnson (2009), our ability to engage mythic sensibility enables spiritual experiences. Johnson introduced the concept that myths are polyvalent and polyfunctional, meaning that different people from different cultures and times may interpret them in different ways. Additionally, their importance will change depending on where a person is in life. Mythological tales may not contain a corpus of abstract truth that is just waiting to be unearthed, but they do include a complex exposition of meaning and significance.

All facets of existence can be interpreted figuratively. In truth, symbolic life enables us to transcend the regrets, disappointments, and limitations, resulting in meaning and fulfillment.

In my own coaching approach, I am integrating the Jungian technique of active imagination with Hillman's more creative perspective. Archetypal psychologist James Hillman (1975) challenges conventional perspectives by advocating for a psychology that acknowledges multiple forces within the psyche.[6] Hillman suggests that when the metaphor lacks personification, it can lead to excessive self-idealization, overreliance on others, excessive ambition, or the development of addictive behaviors.

Theurgists like Iamblichus (c. 245–c. 325) and Ficino (1433–1499) could diagnose psychic imbalances and prescribe rituals to realign the soul with its guiding deity because they had access to gods, rituals, and shrines as containers for the soul's pathologies. Iamblichus would tell us that our illnesses are not themselves the gods but indicate our failure to receive and contain the gods properly (Shaw, 1995). As Shaw (2016) notes, these containers provided a way to manage the imbalances of the soul. In contrast, we lack such external containers today. However, as Hillman suggests, this absence can serve a purpose. The debilitating experience of having "gods as diseases" strips the ego of its illusion of control. Hillman argues that it is primarily through the wounds of human life that the gods enter, not necessarily through overtly sacred or mystical experiences. Pathology, then, becomes a tangible way to witness powers beyond egoic control, highlighting the insufficiency of the ego's limited perspective (1975, p. 339).

One example is the myth of Narcissus, which warns about the dangers of excessive self-love and the idealization of oneself. In contemporary culture, there's a prevalent emphasis on self-absorption and vanity, as well as the idolization of others through social media and advertising. These self-centered tendencies echo the narrative of Narcissus. In this myth, Narcissus is so obsessed with his reflection on the water that he wastes away and dies. The myth shows that when people focus too much on an image or idea, they may lose touch with reality and the world. This can lead to harmful behaviors and bad outcomes, like what happened to Narcissus.

According to the American Psychiatric Association (2022),[7] the narcissistic personality disorder (NPD) is defined as a pervasive pattern of grandiosity (sense of superiority in fantasy or behavior), need for admiration, and lack of empathy, beginning by early adulthood and occurring in a variety of contexts. Often undiagnosed, individuals with NPD may not recognize their condition, as they are excessively goal-focused in ways that enhance self-image and struggle to redirect their attention (Ronningstam & Baskin-Sommers, in O'Brien & O'Brien, 2021, p. 184). This intense focus on goals, especially in leadership positions, can worsen the disorder.

Jung himself often pointed out that when these gods do not have their own proper place and due recognition, they can become sources of illness. Unrecognized archetypal energies can be the root cause of mental and emotional pathologies. Jung explains that:

> there are as many archetypes as there are typical situations in life. Endless repetition has engraved these experiences into our psychic constitution, not in the form of images filled with content, but at first only as forms without content, representing merely the possibility of a certain type of perception and action. (Jung, CW 9i, para. 99)

When a situation arises that corresponds to a particular archetype, that archetype becomes activated, often giving rise to a compulsive force that overrides reason and will. If this force is not consciously recognized, it can lead to inner conflicts or even pathological manifestations such as neurosis (Jung, CW 9i, para. 99).

Research shows that unconscious fears, along with shame, rage, and low self-esteem, disrupt an individual's sense of self-agency and impair decision-making. Such disturbances often trace back to early developmental injuries that leave narcissistic wounds – deep, unresolved feelings of inadequacy that block one's ability to experience self-worth or love. These wounds often form into complexes with a powerful archetype at their core, experienced negatively by the ego. In such cases, feedback from others can be perceived as personal attacks, as the ego struggles to defend itself against these overwhelming archetypal forces. Thus, cultivating awareness of the Shadow and these complexes is crucial in defending against the unconscious forces that disrupt psychological health (O'Brien & O'Brien, 2021, p. 187).

The story of Narcissus reminds us to stay connected to the world outside ourselves. By attributing human qualities to metaphorical images, hidden psychological forces are made more accessible. Examining various interpretations of the Narcissus myth in literature, art, and culture illuminates real-life instances of self-love's adverse effects.

Exploring the archetypal forces within a client's natal chart can shed light on the Shadow aspects of narcissism, revealing hidden impulses and offering insights on how to bring them into balance. However, true balance can only be achieved through conscious engagement with these archetypes. As Jung noted, "a complex can be really overcome only if it is lived out to the full" (CW 9i, para. 184). Personal transformation involves not just recognizing unconscious patterns but also fully engaging with the emotional energy embedded in them. This process can be enhanced by active imagination, dream work, and the creation of symbols through various artistic expressions – whether through painting, writing, movement, or working with materials like clay. By interacting with symbols or archetypes in these ways, individuals can work through unconscious material and foster deeper psychological integration.

When, for example, we face resistance to significant change or must adapt to unexpected changes, personifying the myth of Prometheus can offer valuable assistance. Prometheus symbolizes the impulse toward progress, compelling us to explore uncharted aspects of ourselves. Athena, by teaching him astronomy, mathematics, and architecture, contributed to turning Prometheus into a sage. This myth reflects the transmission of wisdom to humanity, as Prometheus considered it unjust that only the gods possessed it. In retaliation, Zeus chained him to a rock on Mount Caucasus, where a vulture daily devoured his liver. In this context, Zeus represents internal resistance to change, demanding a price for our growth and evolution, such as feelings of guilt or fear of the repercussions that a certain change in our lives might entail.

Transforming the myth's negative impact on the unconscious requires shedding light on it and revealing its specific meaning. In the case of Prometheus, the personalization of the myth through the planet Uranus in our natal chart can provide clues on how to express ourselves differently. In a dialogue of active imagination (which can be either in automatic writing or in a guided meditative state), we can invite the archetype of Uranus to provide greater clarity on the issue that concerns us.

In the case of Spring (see Chapter 6), the archetype of Uranus has a close aspect (geometric configuration between planets based on the distance between them) to her Mercury (the planet governing mental processes and communication). Her need for authentic expression felt threatened during a period of intense intellectual work. We addressed the anxiety she felt from being overwhelmed by an overload of concepts and theories. The conversation with Uranus in active imagination revealed new methods to creatively integrate all of the knowledge she was learning in her master's program.

Identifying Potentials through Archetypal Exploration

Both Carl Jung (1875–1961) and Roberto Assagioli (1888–1974), the founders of transpersonal psychology, were very engaged in the study and practice of astrology. For Jung (1968), a person's natal chart represents the fundamental qualities in their character and can therefore be regarded as equivalent to the individual psyche.

According to psychological research, our unconscious minds often prevent us from reaching our greatest potential, which can result in the Jonah complex – a fear of not living up to our full potential. This fear can stem from childhood experiences or societal expectations and can lead to self-sabotage or mediocrity. For instance, a person may have a deep-rooted fear of failure due to constant criticism from parents. This fear can lead to self-sabotage opportunities for success without realizing it.

To overcome these obstacles, we can examine how fears and resistances manifest in our birth charts. For example, a person with a strong Saturn placement may struggle with fear of taking risks due to past experiences of criticism or feeling inadequate. Facilitating information to clients on their astrological placements can help them understand and address their fears, enabling them to overcome self-sabotage tendencies and navigate their mindsets.

Clients are encouraged to investigate their latent potential story (see Appendix II) as a way of reshaping their narrative about themselves, others, and life. This process entails delving into the symbols and archetypes that emerged during coaching sessions to extract meaning and inspiration. The aim is to provide depth to the roots of the client's mythic conflict and illustrate flexible and intelligent responses to life events.

My client Rose, for example, revealed a long-held sense of undeserving via dream analysis (see Chapter 6). During guided meditation, we reviewed the dream and asked her Venus archetype for direction. Venus symbolizes creativity, joy, beauty, pleasures, connections, and doing what she enjoys. To express her creativity and cultivate her Venus archetype, she enrolled in a writing class. Rose wrote the poem "Looking Up" (see Chapter 6) as a creative exercise in rewriting her own narrative, which concludes with a plan to follow her birth stars. In her poem, she conversed poetically with the gods, just as the theurgists did. This new creative outlet allowed Rose to tap into her inner joy and beauty, fostering a deeper connection with herself through acknowledging her inner archetypes-gods. Through this process of self-discovery and expression, Rose began to shed the layers of undeservingness and embrace her worthiness to pursue her passions and desires.

When it came to professional choices, Rose engaged her Jupiter archetype in active imagination. Jupiter symbolizes our ability to express ourselves via large-scale projects. I guided her to somatic meditation, where she could interact with the archetype, speak to it, and receive its message. We did research on her Jupiter (power, expansion, and knowledge). After personalizing the archetype in herself, she was able to get the courage and self-assurance needed to challenge her earlier negative concept. In active imagination, Rose embodied the traits associated with her Jupiter and Venus (joy, doing the things we love). This practice empowered her to spread messages to people in the Middle East with her new breath workshops. Her metamorphosis was primarily characterized as a change of perspective, which gave her the confidence to attempt new things and chances that she never would have considered before.

The power of the archetypes lies in their capacity to act as mediating symbols; the analytical mind focuses on the symbols, relaxing the stress caused by a fixated attention on the problem. By engaging with archetypes, individuals gain new perspectives on the problem at hand. This shift in perspective allows for a more holistic understanding and opens up possibilities for creative solutions to emerge. I have often seen people relax and become more flexible and creative when they look at their issues through an archetypal lens.

When working with clients who express concerns about a lack of direction and structure in their lives, we may explore their natal chart, paying particular attention to the placement of Saturn. In astrology, Saturn symbolizes discipline, responsibility, and the ability to overcome limitations through a serious and practical approach. If Saturn's energy is not expressed constructively, it can lead to feelings of fear and frustration, often resulting in the creation of barriers to protect oneself from taking responsibility. For example, tense aspects between Saturn and the Sun or Moon may indicate a fear of expressing essential aspects of oneself.

However, Saturn also offers a solution to overcoming these fears by engaging in constructive, practical actions that focus on developing necessary skills. As coaches, we can assist clients by providing detailed explanations of the possibilities for manifesting their self-expression, taking into account the specific positions of the planets in their chart.

For a client who has a close connection between Saturn and the Moon, we can delve into the symbolism of Demeter in mythology and its connection to the Moon, exploring how this archetype can inform our understanding of nurturing and caring instincts. The Greek goddess Demeter symbolizes Earth and fertility, representing motherhood and life cycles. In astrology, Demeter is represented by the Moon, symbolizing our emotional nature and instinctual responses, reflecting our inner world and subconscious patterns. By exploring the connection between Saturn and the Moon in this client's chart, we can gain insights into their approach to nurturing others, their sense of responsibility, and their ability to set boundaries in relationships. By understanding the significance of the Moon (related to domestic and family life and emotional needs) and providing details about its sign and aspects, we can help the client create an archetypal image that represents a life sector where Saturn requires conscious work for balanced expression.

As clients come to comprehend that their Saturn astral positions are part of their journey to attain emotional maturity through resilience and conscious effort, they begin to break free from feelings of victimhood and grasp the role of frustration in their life plan.

A desired outcome of the sessions would be that clients recognize and merge positive qualities within their personalities, describing their signature presence and noting any changes from their past selves. Finally, they are encouraged to articulate these qualities through a creative medium such as a mandala, collage, vision board, sculpture, drawing, or writing a story or poem.

Findings in Consciousness

The nature of subjective experience, conscious intention, and free will presents some of the most elusive questions in science. Despite significant advancements in neuroscience, an understanding of consciousness and its full integration with science remains complex and speculative. Ervin Laszlo, a philosopher and systems theorist, explores this intersection between science and spirituality, offering a comprehensive approach to human experience by connecting scientific inquiry with wisdom traditions. In *Science and the Akashic Field: An Integral Theory of Everything* (2004), Laszlo discusses how the universe and all beings within it are interconnected via a quantum field he terms the "Akashic field," a form of divine or spiritual imprint that bridges material and immaterial realms.

Physicist Richard Conn Henry (2005) claims that the universe is fundamentally mental and spiritual, a reality constructed by the act of observation. The famous double-split experiment underscores this view, revealing that particles behave as either particles or waves based on whether they are observed. Observation thus appears to influence the fabric of reality itself, suggesting an intimate connection between consciousness and physical phenomena.

The perception angle of the observer, therefore, brings a specific observed fact into being. That which is within us is a powerful determinant of that which occurs around and to us. Our ideas, values, intentions, and decisions are probabilities that imply the existence of observation. Moreover, our internal states and choices not only impact our own experiences but also interact with the world, creating a reciprocal relationship between our inner and outer worlds.

Quantum theory itself hints at this interconnectedness. For Mensky (2010), the idea of a multiverse, or "many-worlds" interpretation, posits that a vast number of alternate realities exist simultaneously. Each universe reflects different potential histories and futures, with consciousness playing a crucial role in actualizing one reality over others (Bohr & Heisenberg, in McTaggart, 2007, p. 22). This aligns with Buddhist perspectives, which view consciousness as instrumental in creating a perceived singular reality, though multiple possibilities coexist in a quantum superposition of states.

Recent research reveals that consciousness is not merely a product of brain activity but rather a filtered experience tied to higher dimensions in the universe. In this framework, consciousness is thought to emerge from these dimensions, which give rise to spacetime itself. Complementing this view, some theorists argue that consciousness is not a simple binary – either on or off, conscious or unconscious – but instead spans a continuum of different states, each involving unique brain functions (Guay & Brown, 2024).

Together, these insights point toward a reality in which both science and spirituality contribute to a more expansive understanding of existence, one where consciousness actively participates in shaping the world we perceive.

Expanding on the idea that consciousness is about choosing between possibilities, the integration of astrological archetypes and dream symbols into therapy and coaching can offer an even more detailed picture of the psychic forces at play.

While archetypes, in Jungian terms, represent universal symbols embedded in the collective unconscious, astrological archetypes provide specific, nuanced insights into the individual's psyche and its dynamics.

In the realm of quantum discoveries and consciousness, our internal representations of the client take on a fascinating dimension. McTaggart (2007) suggests that positive representation and intention serve as focused attention, resonating with the client at the same frequency. This interconnectedness supports the idea that thoughts, intentions, and emotions can subtly yet profoundly influence others, even at a distance.

By understanding the positive manifestations of the client's archetypes, the coach can perceive the client as a whole individual, already holding the potential within themselves.

A therapist or coach, for instance, may support a client with low self-esteem by encouraging them to embody qualities of the Sun archetype, such as confidence and vitality. A detailed analysis of the client's Sun sign and house, along with its aspects to other planets, can provide insights into how they might cultivate this sense of vitality and self-assurance. Additionally, the therapist or coach might explore ways for the client to develop Jupiterian qualities, such as optimism and growth, to foster a more positive self-image. By understanding how the Moon archetype influences the client's emotional well-being, the therapist can offer information on how to nurture themselves in order to find inner happiness and fulfillment. Investigating the astrological archetype of Mars relates to drive, courage, and conflict, while Venus symbolizes love, harmony, and attraction.

Notes

1 Gnosticism, rooted in the Greek term "gnôsis" meaning "knowledge" or "insight," emerged as a philosophical and religious movement during the 1st and 2nd century CE. Its influences can be traced back to earlier sources such as the Corpus Hermeticum, Platonic philosophy, and the Hebrew Scriptures.
2 Assagioli's "ideal model" technique encourages clients to visualize their ideal self, using images to focus their energy and intention on personal transformation.
   Assagioli, R. (1991). *Transpersonal development*. Crucible.
3 Astrological psychology was initially developed by Swiss astrologers Bruno and Louise Huber while they were working with Assaglioli in Italy. It aims to combine the best of traditional astrological knowledge with modern psychology, especially psychosynthesis, and provides a useful tool for psychological and spiritual growth. Assagioli also collaborated on the book *Astrological Keys to Self-actualization and Self-realization*, published under the name of Clara A. Weiss.
4 The myth of Eros and Psyche is a tale of love, struggle, and transformation, originally found in Apuleius' *Metamorphoses*, written in the 2nd century CE. In the story, Psyche, a mortal woman of extraordinary beauty, captures the attention of Eros, the god of love. However, due to the jealousy of Eros' mother, Aphrodite, Psyche faces a series of nearly impossible tasks. With the help of divine forces and her own perseverance, she completes these trials, proving her worth and eventually uniting with Eros.
5 Campbell's work highlights the commonalities among diverse mythologies and their relevance to contemporary life. His approach centers on the idea of the hero's journey, a narrative pattern found in myths across cultures.
   Campbell, J. (1976). *The masks of God: Creative mythology*. Penguin Books.

6 Jung and French philosopher Henry Corbin significantly influenced archetypal psychologist James Hillman. Jung believed archetypal concepts exist in the collective unconscious, while Corbin believed they are cultural and anthropological and transcend empirical reality. For Jung, archetypes are phenomenal, while Corbin claims they are accessible to the imagination and initially appear as images.
   Hillman, J. (1985). *Archetypal psychology. A brief account.* Spring Publications.
7 *Diagnostic and statistical manual of mental disorders* (5th Ed., Text Revision). 2022 APA Publishing.

References

American Psychiatric Association. (2022). *Diagnostic and statistical manual of mental disorders* (5th ed., text rev.; DSM-5-TR). American Psychiatric Publishing.

Assagioli, R. (1965). *Psychosynthesis: A collection of basic writings.* The Viking Press.

Assagioli, R. (1966). *Jung and psychosynthesis.* Lecture at the Instituto di Psicosintesi.

Assagioli, R. (1991). *Transpersonal development.* Crucible.

Assagioli, R. (2007). *Transpersonal development: The dimension beyond psychosynthesis.* Forres, Smiling Wisdom.

Campbell, J. (1976). *The masks of God: Creative mythology.* Penguin Books.

Chodorow, J., & Jung, C. G. (2015). *Jung on active imagination.* Princeton University Press.

Dängeli, J. (Ed.) (2022). *The transpersonal coaching handbook* (3rd ed.).

Daniels, M. (2005). *Shadow, self, spirit: essays in transpersonal psychology.* Imprint Academic.

Daniels, M. (2013). Traditional roots, history, and evolution of the transpersonal perspective. In H. L. Friedman & G. Hartelius (Eds.), *The Wiley-Blackwell handbook of transpersonal psychology* (pp. 23–43). John Wiley & Sons, Ltd.

Eliade, M. (1963). *Myth and reality.* Harper & Row.

Friedman, H., & Hartelius, G. (2013). *The Wiley-Blackwell handbook of transpersonal psychology.* Wiley-Blackwell.

Greene, L. (2018). *Jung's understanding of astrology. Prophecy, magic, and the qualities of time.* Routledge.

Guay, C., & Brown, E. (2024, January 26). Consciousness is a continuum, and scientists are starting to measure it. *Scientific American.* https://www.scientificamerican.com

Hartmann, E. v. (1869). *Philosophy of the unconscious.* Kegan Paul, Trench, Trübner & Co.

Henry, R. (2005). The mental universe. *Nature,* 436(2), 9. https://doi.org/10.1038/436029a

Hillman, J. (1972). *The myth of analysis: Three essays in archetypal psychology.* Northwestern University Press.

Hillman, J. (1975). *Re-visioning psychology.* Harper Perennial.

Hillman, J., & Moore, T. (1989). *The essential James Hillman: A blue fire.* Harper Collins.

Johnson, R. (2009). *Inner work: Using dreams and active imagination for personal growth.* Harper One.

Jung, C. G. (1960a). The transcendent function (R. F. C. Hull, Trans.). In H. Read, M. Fordham, G. Adler, & W. McGuire (Eds.), *The collected works of C. G. Jung* (Vol. 8) Princeton University Press.

Jung, C. G. (1960b). The structure and dynamics of the psyche. In H. Read, M. Fordham, G. Adler, & W. McGuire (Eds.), *Collected works of C. G. Jung* (Vol. 8). Princeton University Press.

Jung, C. G. (1966). Two essays on analytical psychology. In H. Read, M. Fordham, G. Adler, & W. McGuire (Eds.), *Collected works* (Vol. 7.) Princeton University Press.

Jung, C. G. (1968). Archetypes and the collective unconscious. In H. Read, M. Fordham, G. Adler, & W. McGuire (Eds.), *The collected works of C. G. Jung* (R. F. C. Hull, Trans.) (2nd ed., Vol. 9). Princeton University Press.

Jung, C. G. (1969). *Psychology and alchemy* (2nd ed.). Routledge.

Jung, C. G. (1976). Psychological types. In *The collected works of C. G. Jung* (R. F. C. Hull, Trans.) (2nd ed., Vol. 6). Princeton University Press.

Keen, S. (1974). The golden mean of Roberto Assagioli. *Psychology Today*, 8, 97–107.

Laszlo, E. (2004). Science and the Akashic field: An integral theory of everything. Inner Traditions.

McTaggart, L. (2007). *The intention experiment.* Free Press.

Mensky, M. (2010). *Consciousness and quantum mechanics life in parallel worlds: Miracles of consciousness from quantum reality.* World Scientific Pub.

Nocelli, P. (2021). Know, love, transform yourself: Theory, techniques and new developments in Psychosynthesis. https://www.synthesiscenter.org/PDF/Firman-Disidentification.pdf

O'Brien, N., & O'Brien, J. (2021). *The professional practice of Jungian coaching: Corporate analytical psychology.* Taylor & Francis.

Parfitt, W. (2022). Astrological psychology and Roberto Assagioli. https://psychosynthesis-trust.org.uk/assagioli-and-astrology

Cooper, J. M., & Hutchinson, D. S. (Eds.). (1997). *Plato: Complete works.* Hackett Publishing.

Raff, J. (2000). *Jung and the alchemical imagination.* Nicolas Hays, Inc.

Segal, R. A. (ed.) (1992). *The Gnostic Jung.* Princeton University Press.

Shaw, G. (1985). *Theurgy: Rituals of unification in the neoplatonism of Iamblichus.* Traditio.

Shaw, G. (1995). *Theurgy and the soul.* The Neoplatonism of Iamblichus. Pennsylvania State University Press.

Shaw, G. (2016). *Archetypal psychology, dream work, and neoplatonism.* In H. T. Hakl (Ed.), *Octagon: The quest for wholeness* (Vol. 2, pp. 329–358). H. Frietsch Verlag.

Shaw, G. (2024). *Hellenic tantra: The theurgic platonism of Iamblichus Angelico press.* Kindle Edition.

Schelling, F. W. J. (1800). *System of transcendental idealism.* (P. Heath, Trans.). University of Virginia Press.

Tarnas, R. (2006). *Cosmos and psyche: Intimations of a new world view.* Penguin Publishing Group. Kindle edition.

von Franz, M. L. (1997). *Alchemy: An introduction to the symbolism and the psychology.* Inner City Books.

Whitman, E. (1970). *The influence of planets.* L.N. Fowler & Co Ltd.

Chapter 2

Archetypal Dynamics in Coaching Practice

The Archetypes

> The archetype—let us never forget this—*is a psychic organ present in all of us.* (Jung, CW 9i, para. 271)

The term "archetype" traces back to the Greek "arche" (primal) and "typos" (trace, seal, model), initially explored by Plato (428 BC). Freud viewed them as primal instincts and Jung (1960) viewed them as innate, cross-cultural patterns shaping the psyche. Hillman (1975) expanded on Jung's perspective, seeing archetypes as gods symbolizing occult aspects of the psyche.

In ancient myths, archetypes were personified as immortal gods and goddesses. Plato used the stories of Eros and Aphrodite to represent Love and Beauty, as well as the legend of Zeus to describe Power. These archetypes were also called Ideas, Forms, and Absolute Principles by the philosophers.

In his book *Archetypes and the Collective Unconscious*, Jung (1994, p. 39) states:

> There is not a single essential idea or conception that does not possess historical antecedents. They are all ultimately based on primitive archetypal forms, which became apparent at a time when consciousness did not yet think but perceived and thought was essentially revelation.

Jung calls the image "primordial" when it has an archaic character, i.e. when the image presents a striking concordance with mythological themes. "The primordial image or archetype is always collective, that is, common to entire peoples or epochs" (1994, p. 524). Archetypes, according to Jung (1968, para. 329), are universal expressions shaping human behaviors, rooted in ancient myths and philosophical concepts. Archetypal images are limited and reflect fundamental and typical human experiences. All these archetypes borrow from the individual culture's coloration and costumes, but they are basically the same universal archetypes, typical human ways of perceiving and reacting to life situations since primordial times.

DOI: 10.4324/9781003627258-3

These universal patterns, in the form of knowledge and images, accompany each individual from birth, providing a shared foundation rooted in ancestral experience of primordial images replicated in the myths of all cultures. My research participant Spring described the unified field of archetypes in the unconscious as a collective place to which she had access. Her elaboration of her experience concurs with Jung's archetypal theory of a collective universal unconscious that is present in all of us:

> ... so perhaps I'm just feeling into this archetype of freedom (Uranus); rather than just freedom belonging to me, it's more of a freedom that's available to us all. (pp. 96–98 in Carod, 2021)

Modern psychology, particularly Jung's theory of archetypes, is a contemporary expression of the same archetypal forces that have historically manifested in myths and collective symbols. It suggests that, despite its scientific framework, psychology functions as a modern myth that continues to shape our understanding of the human experience, linking the past and present through archetypal dynamics.

In his book *Jung to Live By*, Jungian psychoanalyst Eugene Pascal (1992) states that our ancestors genetically endure in us through local mythology, reflecting typical experiences of humans since primordial times.

Jung's approach to archetypal symbols emphasizes that the planetary "gods" are within the individual and can only be addressed on a psychological level through recognizing the psyche's mechanism of projection:

> In themselves, archetypal images are among the highest values of the human psyche; they have peopled the heavens of all races from time immemorial. To discard them as valueless would be a distinct loss. Our task is not, therefore, to deny the archetype, but to dissolve the projections, in order to restore their contents to the individual who has involuntarily lost them by projecting them outside himself. (Jung, CW 9i, para. 160)

In his work *Aion: Researches into the Phenomenology of the Self*, Carl Jung (1951, pp. 3–23) identifies four main components: the persona, the anima/animus, the shadow, and the Self. The persona reflects how we adapt and present ourselves in the world, using different social masks to protect the ego and repress unaccepted impulses and emotions. The anima represents the feminine image in the male mind, while the animus is the masculine image in the female mind. The shadow encompasses the repressed and dark aspects of the personality, such as instincts and desires unacceptable to society. Some of these (animus and anima) connect the ego to the unconscious, whereas others (persona) connect the ego to the outside world. They originate from the realm of shadow, which is beyond consciousness.

In Greek mythology, the anima is represented by nymphs, amazons, nereids, and other creatures, as well as by Persephone, Aphrodite, Artemis, and Athena in their more divine forms. However, as Hillman puts it (1972, p. 50), "the representations of the anima refer to a structure of consciousness relevant to the lives of both men and women."

> The archetypes transcend both men and women and their biological differences and social roles. Anima will always evoke it's Greek influences, which blend it with psyche and the experiences of it as an emotional, amorphous living presence of great value to the individual human.

Jung often spoke of the dynamic interplay of archetypes, suggesting that they work together like "the psychic organs of the pre-rational psyche" (CW 9i, para. 222), shaping our perceptions and behaviors in interconnected ways.

It is possible that Jung's clustering of astrological archetypes into Jungian archetypes was due to a lack of recognition for astrology at the time. It is shown in more detail in Chapter 5 that Jung's work with astrology was well known in the field of analysis but that some Jungian training groups and analysts found it unsettling because they considered astrology of a dubious nature.

Recognizing these archetypes is crucial, not only for understanding our psyche but also for integrating the unconscious – those concealed aspects that, when overlooked, can lead to challenges in personal development. By consciously engaging with these symbols, we can explore transformative pathways and cultivate greater wholeness.

For example, the myth of Persephone in Greek mythology, who is abducted to the underworld but eventually returns to the surface, symbolizes personal transformation and rebirth. By understanding this myth, individuals grappling with periods of depression or significant life changes can find solace and meaning, recognizing their struggles as part of a larger, transformative process. Similarly, the story of Hercules and his 12 labors can be seen as an archetypal journey of overcoming immense obstacles, inspiring individuals facing their own daunting challenges to persevere and grow stronger through their trials. Carl Jung's archetype of the Hero, prevalent in many cultures and mythologies, represents the journey of overcoming adversity and achieving greatness. By identifying with the Hero archetype, individuals can frame their own life challenges as part of a heroic quest, empowering them to tackle obstacles with courage and determination.

The study of the mythology and symbolism associated with the archetype facilitates both the acceptance of what is actually happening and the generation of creative responses. For instance, the archetype of the Wise Old Man or Woman embodies wisdom, guidance, and insight. Individuals seeking direction in their lives can look to this archetype to find inspiration and trust in the process of gaining knowledge through experience.

Engaging with questions such as "What is trying to emerge through this challenge?" or "What archetypal qualities might the client be seeking to bring to light?" fosters a deeper connection to the archetypes. For example, the myth of Orpheus and Eurydice, which explores the theme of love and loss, highlights the deep emotional struggles associated with losing a loved one and the lengths one might go to reclaim what has been lost. By relating to this myth, individuals can gain a deeper understanding of their own feelings of grief and the universal longing for reunion and closure.

Astrological archetypes offer a powerful framework for understanding the psychic dynamics that shape our lives. The planets Venus and the Moon, for example, are vehicles for the expression of the *anima,* representing the emotional and relational aspects of our psyche. These planets reflect the importance of recognizing and integrating feminine qualities to cultivate a sense of emotional balance.

The *animus* might be symbolized by the Sun and Mars, which embody assertiveness, strength, and purpose. Integrating these traits through a guided archetypal exploration can help individuals develop a stronger sense of confidence and direction.

In terms of the *shadow*, it could be symbolized by Pluto, the planet of transformation and the unconscious, as well as Uranus and Neptune. Pluto invites us to explore the darker, hidden aspects of our psyche, Uranus to embrace change and disruption, and Neptune to transcend illusions and connect with the spiritual aspects of life. Together, these transpersonal planets point to profound personal growth and transformation through the integration of unconscious material. The recognition of a facet of the personality through the corresponding archetype and its analysis in the client's astral map relieves the pressure that is experienced when we take full responsibility for the problem or challenge. This understanding allows individuals to see their issues as influenced by a collective entity/archetype, rather than as solely personal issues.

By engaging with these questions and finding meaning in our hidden shadows through the archetypes, we can foster a sense of connection and shared humanity, providing comfort and guidance on personal journeys.

The Origins of Coaching: Socratic Questioning

Socrates, a philosopher from 469 to 399 BCE, significantly influenced the conception of philosophy and is the dominant figure in Plato's philosophical dialogues. He was not a teacher but a guide, helping others recognize their truths and goodness, who embraced poverty and refused to take money for his work. Socrates frequently conversed with diverse individuals in public spaces, focusing on serious matters like courage, love, reverence, moderation, and the state of their souls. He was known for his irony and diligent learning, demonstrating his ability to tailor his questions to his audience. Socrates believed that through questioning and engaging in meaningful dialogue, individuals could uncover their own wisdom and values (Nails & Monoson, 2022).

Similar to Socrates' method of *maieutics*, which guides interlocutors toward self-discovery through questioning, the coach facilitates a process of exploration and introspection for the client. This approach seeks to uncover the client's personal truths and inner wisdom. Socrates' dialogues, as depicted in Plato's works like *Apology* and *Gorgias*, exemplify his emphasis on reflexivity, mutual respect, and human connection.

Socrates also introduced the concept of *boêtheia*,[1] meaning "protection and assistance," to foster a collaborative relationship with his interlocutors. In a similar way, the coach offers support and guidance, creating a safe space that encourages the client to explore their thoughts and emotions openly.

Archetypal coaching extends this principle by integrating archetypal exploration into Socratic questioning, offering foundational insights about the relevant archetype before initiating the inquiry. This preparatory step helps orient the client, deepening their reflection and enhancing the transformative potential of the dialogue. An archetypal approach further fosters self-reflection, facilitates strategic action, and promotes deeper insight into the psychological dynamics that shape an individual's perceptions, behaviors, and life patterns.

For instance, if a client is experiencing a Saturnian aspect characterized by restriction and limitation, the coach may ask targeted questions to help the client uncover where they feel restricted in their life and how they can overcome these limitations. Before questioning for self-reflection, the coach provides a thorough description of the myth related to the client's issue, offering diverse options for honoring the myth. This may include exploring the symbolism of Saturn as the god of time, discipline, and responsibility, as well as discussing various cultural interpretations and historical contexts associated with Saturn.

A specific question that could be posed to the client in this situation would be: "In what areas of your life do you feel the presence of Saturn's influence, and how do you perceive these limitations hindering your progress?" This question encourages the client to reflect on the specific challenges they are facing and to identify potential strategies for overcoming them.

Once the client has identified the areas of restriction, the coach can then guide them to explore the positive manifestations of Saturn's energy. A question addressing this aspect could be: "Considering Saturn's influence, where do you see opportunities for discipline, structure, and long-term planning in your life? How can you harness these qualities to achieve your goals effectively?" By addressing both the challenges and opportunities associated with Saturn's influence, clients can develop a comprehensive understanding of how to navigate their current circumstances and work toward personal growth and overcoming obstacles.

The Foundations of Modern Coaching

Coaching is about exploring human potential and possibility; it understands the past as context but primarily deals with a person's present, helping the client design and act toward a more desirable future. Clients must be in good health before consulting with a coach, as coaching focuses on mental development rather than mental health. Therapy focuses on both recovery and discovery, while coaching focuses solely on discovery.

While therapy often focuses on the past and presumes the client has a problem that needs solving, coaching looks to the future and assumes the client is whole, possessing the innate wisdom and tools to live a satisfying life. In coaching, the client is guided toward their potential and assisted in creating fulfilling solutions rather than receiving external advice.

Coaching is grounded in psychology, particularly in the humanistic approaches of Carl Rogers and Abraham Maslow, who emphasized the aspects of being human that promote health and happiness. The transpersonal psychology movement emerged in the late 1960s to include elements that empower humans to function at their best, focusing on mind, body, and spirit. It explored states of consciousness, transcendence, and what Eastern traditions and practices could teach Western theorists and practitioners.

Health-promoting practices prioritize identifying and leveraging an individual's strengths, resources, and potential. This approach, often termed "positive psychology" or "strengths-based coaching," encourages clients to build upon their inherent capabilities and virtues. By focusing on what is right and what can be improved, clients are empowered to see themselves as capable and resourceful, fostering a more positive self-image and greater self-efficacy.

Traditional coaching recognizes that a coach can help clients break free from unsatisfactory circumstances by helping them adopt new perceptions and beliefs, offering a framework for understanding their current path, and clarifying whether they wish to stay on it. This process illuminates options, enables clients to choose new directions, and supports them in persisting through change.

The popular GROW (Goal, Reality, Options, and Will) coaching model developed by Whitmore (2009) is a structured approach that moves the client through four stages of the coaching process:

Goal: What do you want?
Reality: Where are you now?
Options: What could you do? What are your skills?
Will: What will you do? Actions and behaviors that lead to the goals.

By focusing on specific goals, current realities, available options, and concrete actions, the GROW model aims to help individuals clarify their objectives and develop a clear path forward. However, the GROW coaching model may not be effective for individuals who thrive in more flexible and open-ended environments, as it may feel too rigid and constrictive for their preferred style of growth and development. Some individuals may find the emphasis on goal-setting to be limiting, as they may prefer to focus on exploration and self-discovery rather than specific outcomes.

People come to a coach because they want to change something in their lives. In most cases, the main obstacle to change is habit. However, when we dig deeper, we see that habits are not only behavioral patterns but also deeply tied to beliefs, thoughts, and emotions that have become ingrained over time, making them challenging to shift. An exploration of the archetypes associated with these thought and emotional patterns can complement traditional coaching practices by supporting emotional regulation (Lai & McDowall, 2014), enhancing self-awareness and personal responsibility (O'Connor & Lages, 2009), and facilitating goal progression (Whitmore, 2009).

The Psychodynamic Approach to Coaching

The goal of the psychodynamic approach is essentially to expand the client's capacity for emotional regulation – that is, to enable the client to revisit difficult emotional territory in a way that is contained, so that the need for defensive strategies is reduced, and thinking rather than reacting can take place. The potential of psychodynamic coaching is that it can help clients understand how they limit themselves and how to approach conflicts with more awareness and freedom (Lee, in Cox et al., 2010).

A psychodynamic approach recognizes that different parts of the mind can be in conflict with each other and uses self-awareness of bodily sensations and emotions as indicators of unconscious communication.

Both psychodynamic and transpersonal approaches emphasize the significance of a client's unconscious agenda in facilitating change. These approaches describe how defense mechanisms – such as repression, denial, and projection – operate as unconscious patterns of emotional regulation to avoid or minimize emotions that feel intolerable. Jung explored these mechanisms primarily in relation to the psyche's tendency to avoid facing uncomfortable truths and to integrate repressed aspects of the self.

In *Two Essays on Analytical Psychology* (1966, pp. 64–79), Jung discusses repression, suggesting that denial of darker or troubling aspects of the unconscious can lead to a split in the psyche, hindering growth. Jung explains that by denying parts of their inner experience, particularly "shadow" aspects, individuals limit their understanding of themselves, creating an incomplete self-perception. For Jung, psychic energies that struggle to find a path toward integration with consciousness and remain unacknowledged in our inner world manifest externally through projection.

In *The Archetypes and the Collective Unconscious* (1968, CW9, pp. 3–41), Jung examined how individuals project unconscious content onto archetypes, shaping their perceptions of others and themselves. In *Collected Works*, Volume 9, para. 80, Jung states that certain archetypes – such as the shadow, the anima, and the wise old man – can be directly experienced in a personified form. These archetypes often appear as active personalities in dreams and fantasies.

Projection occurs when we unconsciously attribute our own psychic content onto others or external situations. In projection, we live through these intense emotions in relationships to become conscious of them as vital facets of our psyche. Any person or object that reflects aspects of our unconscious energy, which needs integration for individuation, can serve as a "hook" for this projection.

The journey into the unconscious requires confronting the shadow, representing one's hidden nature; the anima or animus, the hidden opposite gender within each individual; and, beyond these, the archetypes. As archetypes enter consciousness, they shape the experiences of both typical and neurotic individuals; an excessively powerful archetype can overwhelm the psyche, potentially leading to psychosis. This dynamic is especially evident in relationships and can be illustrated through both dream symbols and astrological archetypes. Experiences such as fascination, jealousy, and addictive "love" can be illustrated by the archetype of Venus, while frustration often reflects the energy of Saturn.

Unconscious archetypes are addressed in two stages: first, they are brought into full awareness, and then they are integrated with the conscious mind through recognition and acceptance. Dream work and astrology are especially powerful here. Dreams can reveal aspects of our psyche that the inner self wants to bring to conscious awareness, while astrological archetypes helps us understand why we express particular archetypes in certain ways, shedding light on the mythological and psychological roots of specific behaviors or beliefs.

An Archetype is an image charged with an emotion by the client; it contains psychic energy and dynamism. This special feeling tone of the archetype can enable for a transformative experience within therapy or coaching.

The interplay between dream symbols and astrological archetypes can be explored and processed through active imagination, as discussed in the following chapters. The approach is totally participative and creative, merging oniric images and dormant archetypal qualities into a new self, like a new birth.

In coaching, an essential first step is to help clients uncover the values that drive their habitual patterns without judgment. For clients with unresolved childhood rejection, this may manifest as difficulties in forming healthy adult relationships, often linked to the Moon and Saturn archetypes. Fear of rejection can make setting boundaries challenging, leading to conflict. Coaches can guide clients in addressing these patterns by examining Saturn's position in the natal chart, which often reflects unmet emotional needs, fears, and a desire for security.

Exploring creative ways to meet the need for security and structure, we find that Saturn-Moon contacts encourage emotional self-sufficiency through inner exploration, recognition of repressed emotions, and healthy outlets for expressing them. By recognizing these patterns, coaches can help their clients work toward developing healthier coping mechanisms and communication skills.

However, people repress not only the unacceptable aspects of themselves but also their talents. For instance, someone with a strong Venus influence may suppress their artistic abilities out of fear of not being taken seriously. Another client with a prominent Mars influence may suppress their leadership skills due to societal expectations of aggression being negative. This perspective empowers the client, as it acknowledges their inherent potential and guides them toward finding solutions and achieving personal growth on their own terms.

Understanding the archetypal foundation allows us to be more flexible and take a non-judgmental view of our conflicts. By understanding these patterns, we can gain awareness of our emotional triggers and work toward finding constructive ways to express and transform them.

Transpersonal Work with Subpersonalities

In transpersonal work, the unconscious domain is differentiated into subpersonalities. We usually recognize the presence of a subpersonality when we find ourselves acting in ways we do not like or that go against our interests and are unable to change this by a conscious decision. Whether as with Freud we talk about the ego, id, and superego, or as with Jung about the complexes and the archetypes, or as with Assagioli about subpersonalities, we are in each case talking about the same thing, semi-permanent and semi-autonomous patterns of feelings, thoughts, perceptions, and behaviors in response to recurrent situations in life (Rowan, 1990, p. 8).

Each subpersonality may have its own thoughts, feelings, and desires. These parts can range from protective and nurturing aspects to wounded or traumatized aspects of the Self. Working with subpersonalities involves identifying, understanding, and engaging with these different parts to bring about healing and integration. This process typically involves dialogue and questioning techniques to explore the nature and purpose of each subpersonality and to develop a better understanding of how they contribute to the individual's overall functioning.

Therapists employ diverse questioning techniques to facilitate this exploration, supporting clients in understanding their subpersonalities and fostering greater internal cohesion and well-being. Some common approaches include internal dialogue, open-ended questions, reflective questioning, integration, and negotiation.

All of them encourage individuals to engage in an internal dialogue with different subpersonalities, allowing them to express their concerns, beliefs, and desires. Giving each part a voice provides insights into their motivations and needs. To work with subpersonalities, therapists may suggest clients imagine placing one side of the split onto one chair and the other side onto another, assuming these are two distinct individuals who can communicate. This personification of the split has proved to be an active and effective method of psychotherapy or counseling.

Open-ended questions are used to prompt individuals to explore and articulate the experiences and perspectives of their subpersonalities. This fosters a deeper understanding of each part and its role in the person's life. For example, the coach engages the client in a dialogue, asking about the thoughts and emotions experienced during work challenges. The individual responds, "I often feel anxious and doubt my abilities." The coach then inquires, "Can you identify which part of you is feeling anxious and doubtful in those situations?" The individual reflects, "I think it's my inner critic. It always shows up when I feel pressured at work." Continuing, the coach asks, "What role do you believe your inner critic plays in your life, and how does it affect you?" The individual shares, "I believe it's trying to protect me from making mistakes, but it ends up making me doubt myself even more." These responses suggest a connection with the Saturn archetype. To delve deeper, the coach will explore Saturn's position in the client's natal chart, uncovering valuable lessons related to effort and will development.

Once subpersonalities are identified and understood, archetypal coaching may involve facilitating dialogue and negotiation among these parts. Clients can identify predetermined patterns, understand their potential manifestations, and make choices that benefit them. By recognizing distinct parts of the self and using planetary archetypes, clients gain greater insights into their habits, values, and potential for change. The goal is to establish a harmonious relationship and integration among the various subpersonalities/archetypes, fostering greater internal cohesion and well-being (see Appendix I, Exercise "Integrating Archetypal Astrology into Subpersonality Work").

When we observe recurring patterns in our relationships, be it at work, with family, or friends, it often indicates the presence of unconscious archetypes influencing our behaviors. When our egos are dominated by an archetype, our behaviors turn automatic, and thus we become slaves to the archetypal impulses. This unconscious state often creates problems for both ourselves and those around us. For example, under the automatic influence of the moon, we can fall into what is commonly referred to as a "lunatic" person, that is, someone whose mood fluctuates according to the lunar phases. Mars can lead us to behave aggressively and impulsively, while the influence of Venus can result in a constant search for gratification and pleasure.

To break free from this repetitive cycle, we could apply Assagioli's technique of dis-identification (1974). This process can be deepened through the integration of astrological archetypes, which provide symbolic frameworks for understanding different psychological functions. In astrology, for instance, the Moon is associated with emotions and instinctive responses. Recognizing the Moon as an archetype and its dynamics within the natal chart can enhance one's understanding of emotional dynamics while reinforcing that these feelings, although significant, do not define the self. This creates space for a more balanced and conscious interaction with one's emotional life.

The exercise extends to desires as well, helping the individual reflect: "I have desires, but I am not my desires." Desires, like emotions, fluctuate and are influenced by both internal drives and external forces. They may pull a person in conflicting directions, but the act of dis-identification allows one to step back, observe these urges, and choose how to respond to them. Introducing the archetype of Mars, which governs desires and assertiveness, can further illuminate these impulses. Mars, as a symbol of action and drive, can represent the energy behind desires, but by recognizing its role as an archetype, individuals are reminded that their true self transcends these primal impulses.

Finally, in relation to thoughts and intellect, the reflection continues: "I have an intellect, but I am not my intellect." Thoughts, while vital for problem-solving and navigating the external world, are also subject to fluctuations and limitations. Dis-identification with the intellect encourages the recognition that the Self is not confined to rational processes. By associating the intellect with the astrological archetype of Mercury, which governs communication and cognition, one can become more aware of the mind's patterns without being consumed by them.

The technique of substitution, as described by Assagioli in *The Act of Will* (1974, p. 66), is a practical application of the skillful will and can be also enriched by incorporating astrological archetypes. This method involves replacing a persistent negative thought or image with a more constructive one. In astrology, the planets symbolize different psychological functions and qualities. By associating negative thoughts with their planetary origins, clients can recognize their higher potential and substitute the limiting expression with a more elevated one.

Take, for instance, Suzanne (referenced in Chapter 6). Her self-critical and incessant thinking, linked to the astrological archetype of Mercury (which governs communication and the mind), was transformed using the technique of substitution. Instead of allowing Mercury's negative manifestations – overthinking and criticism – to dominate, Suzanne's mercurial energy was redirected toward a higher expression: the capacity for insightful questioning. This shift was inspired by a dream and further developed through active imagination, resulting in deeper self-awareness and meaningful breakthroughs (see chapter 6). Assagioli explains that when we focus our attention on an unwanted thought, it paradoxically becomes stronger. By trying to "not think" about it, we increase its presence in our mind (1974, p. 66). The technique of substitution suggests that rather than struggling against the thought directly, we should choose another image or idea to concentrate on, which gradually weakens the grip of the unwanted thought. In Suzanne's case, she substituted her self-critical Mercury energy with Mercury's positive qualities, transforming her critical inner dialogue into a tool for insight and clarity.

In this way, we can apply substitution by identifying the planetary archetypes involved in a client's recurring negative patterns. Whether it is the impulsive force of Mars manifesting in aggression or the emotional tides of the Moon creating anxiety, understanding the higher manifestation of these archetypes allows for constructive redirection. By choosing to focus on a more positive expression, the client can channel their will toward personal growth and transformation, as Assagioli emphasized, with the skillful and strategic use of energy rather than direct opposition to the problem.

Besides using substitution within a planet's manifestation possibilities, we can also induce substitution between different planets, as Marsilio Ficino recommended (discussed in Chapter 5). Ficino, a Renaissance Florentine philosopher who revived Platonic philosophy in the Christian West, proposed counterbalancing the negative influence of one planetary archetype with the positive influence of another, thus offering a wider range of possibilities for transformation.

When Suzanne felt overwhelmed by constant overthinking, heavily influenced by Mercury's analytical energy, she consciously shifted her focus to Jupiter's expansive qualities. By embracing Jupiter's symbolism of wisdom and broader perspective, she transitioned from self-criticism to finding purpose and meaning in her thoughts.

Additionally, Suzanne drew on Neptune's archetype of universal love and compassion to transcend Mercury's intellectual chatter and connect with her heart. In an active imagination exercise, she visualized a heart, symbolizing her desire for deep connection. By focusing on Neptune's energy, she shifted from an analytical mindset to one filled with compassion and boundless love for herself and others. As Assagioli's psychological laws emphasize, images and ideas have the power to awaken corresponding emotions and feelings (1974, p. 50), and in Suzanne's case, Neptune's universal love evoked a soothing and nurturing energy that counteracted the frenetic influence of Mercury.

Active Imagination with Archetypes

The idea of working with our imagination through the encounter with divine images is rooted in the Theurgical Neoplatonism of Iamblichus (c. 245–c.325). Theurgic astrology used images and symbols to connect with the astral powers and receive direct knowledge from them. Theurgy considers symbols as means to free the human soul from the limitations of material consciousness and to begin to see itself as an image of God (Voss, 2000, p. 29).

As preparation for this encounter with the gods, Iamblichus suggested specific prayers and rituals that would allow one to reach higher states of consciousness. Gods reveal themselves to the soul through various symbols and tokens, including animals, plants, stones, images, letters, sounds, music, names, and shapes, showcasing their divine nature. This contact with the divine occurs only with an ecstatic exchange that transforms our imagination into an organ of the god while the soul – with empty mind – follows the visions and witnesses the divine reunions (Shaw, 2003, p. 11).

For Iamblichus, the soul, being immortal, becomes mortal and alienated not only from the gods but also from its own divinity. Iamblichus argued that the soul can only reconnect with the divine by mediating opposites, recognizing the "nothingness" (*oudeneia*) of its mortal identity, and engaging in theurgy – cosmogonic rituals that allow the soul to discover its fragmented self in the material world. Through these acts of recollection, the soul gradually transforms the suffering of embodiment into a cosmos, reconfiguring its subtle body *(ochēma)* as it reconnects with the divine through nature and ritual (Shaw, 2016, p. 333).

This process of recollection aligns with Roshani's account of her spiritual transformation after engaging with archetypes and dream symbols through active imagination. Roshani described her journey as one of reuniting her fragmented self, bringing together her scattered pieces:

> Oh, I think it's much bigger than understanding … I would have had these scattered pieces of understanding. But I think that through our sessions we put them together … like a Dali thing of me walking through the landscape with these scattered pieces … picking them up. (pp. 168–171, in Carod, 2021)

Jung attributed divine qualities to the collective unconscious, where symbols transcend opposites uniting psychic material in images. In Jungian thought, archetypes manifest to consciousness as images and symbols. Jung, who placed great significance on astrology, explored it not only intellectually but also through active imagination (Greene, 2018, p. 76). Jung defined "active imagination" as a participatory method for integrating the essence of archetypes:

> Since archetypes are, like all numinous contents, relatively autonomous, they cannot be integrated in a simply rational way, but require instead a dialectical method, i.e. a true discussion. (Jung, 1968, p. 47)

Jung describes these symbols as emerging from the interplay between the unconscious and the conscious mind, stating that "the interpretation of its meaning can start neither from the conscious alone nor from the unconscious alone, but only from their reciprocal relationship" (Jung, 1921, CW 6, para. 745).

The question is how can we today re-play this ancient neoplatonic tradition, respecting its historical context while adapting it to our modern understanding of spirituality and psychology? Reconciliation between conscious and unconscious forces does not occur spontaneously; we must actively seek it with intention, emotion, and alignment with unseen forces, a contemporary version of ancient Babylonian and Greek rituals. Archetypal coaching seeks to recover the original, sacred approach to working with imagination—receiving archetypal messages in an embodied way, much like the theurgists practiced—while adapting these principles to modern techniques such as active imagination and somatic meditation. By incorporating elements of Jungian psychology and contemporary techniques for accessing expanded states of consciousness, we can reimagine the ancient mysteries in a form that resonates with modern seekers of the divine—what Iamblichus referred to as "the gods" and Jung conceptualized as archetypes. In place of traditional prayers and rituals, practices such as active imagination, undertaken in a state of mindful awareness, offer a balanced interplay between conscious intention and receptive surrender to the mystery.

Both Jung and Iamblichus recognized the dangers of overthinking and abstract conceptualization, which can detach individuals from the natural flow of life. A third domain, the world of imagination, exists between the physical and spiritual realms, where dream pictures and archetypal symbols can function as an antenna to receive information.

If we wish to change our lives, it is essential to transform the unconscious images and the subpersonalities that shape them. By practicing active imagination, we are dialoguing with ourselves, consciously addressing the various subpersonalities, which we often do unconsciously. The mind participates in the events that take place on the imaginative level, which is neither conscious nor unconscious, and creates a life experience that combines the elements of both (Johnson, 2009).

In the practice of active imagination, clients are encouraged to acknowledge spontaneous images associated to archetypes and dream symbols and to give voice to what the image/archetype needs and what they appreciate about it. Active imagination enables individuals to reconnect with their chosen archetypes, activating inner symbols that guide them toward the divine. The symbolic act of addressing those dream symbols and archetypes that relate to the trigger provides the necessary space for the client to own their emotions without projecting or bypassing them.

Interacting with them in an expanded state of mind can allow significant insights to imprint on the client's subconscious mind. We allow these archetypal subpersonalities to manifest and reveal to us what they need to express, without careful analysis of what is occurring, so that the alchemical exchange flows without interruption.

The emphasis is not only on the attainment of high states of consciousness but also on developing an authentic relationship with the different subpersonalities, embracing both light and shadow. Astrological archetypes can be a powerful tool for enhancing the process of active imagination when combined with dream symbols. They function as universal patterns that speak to deep, collective forces within the psyche. By using them in dialogue with dream imagery, synergies are created that can reveal the unconscious patterns and dynamics brought by the client.

Spring (see Chapter 6) offers an example of how to develop an alternative story that resonates more with the client's values and needs through a dialogue between the archetypes and dream symbols. In a dream, Spring described being in a large room with a wise old man, where balls of clay were popping around her, and she sensed the need to leave to avoid being struck by them. We linked these clay balls to her natal Mars-Saturn conjunction – Mars symbolizing aggression and movement and Saturn representing the heaviness and gravity of the stones. We reflected on how this dynamic reflected her need for persistent effort, determination, and focus (Mars influenced by Saturn) to overcome obstacles, alongside her desire to access intuitive knowledge (Neptune). I suggested her to engage in active imagination, honoring both needs without prioritizing one over the other.

In active imagination, we invited Saturn (Chronos), an archetype related to the ability to set boundaries. During our work, Spring embodied each archetypal pattern with specific physical postures and facial expressions. She named Saturn the "wise man," and her insight was that he was taming her wilderness, protecting her from overexpressing. As she embodied Saturn, her hands faced upward, and she remarked that it felt like sensing energy before things happened, allowing her to protect herself. She described it as being "ever-present, detecting through my hands."

> As I stepped into this area in the dream, suddenly these balls of clay came and were like popping all over the place in all directions, so I had to move myself from this area... It seemed like it was restricted by this limiting force, which we connected with Saturn or this inner Saturn showing up... it seems like Saturn was there to kind of feel the environment, to feel what was happening. So, it wasn't necessarily a negative influence... in fact, it was maybe the inner protector. (Spring, pp. 35–81, in Carod, 2021)

The dialogue with Saturn (symbolizing how we can cope with difficulties and structure our work) in active imagination gave her tips about how to integrate her need for expressing with authenticity with her need for grounding and getting tasks done efficiently. She was inspired to listen to the advice of Saturn (representing order in the physical world) when her Mars energy (the need to act bluntly) is charging ahead at full speed. Spring gained embodied insights into Saturn's role as a protector and boundary-setter, helping her stay grounded and focus on her intellectual tasks. Rather than feeling overwhelmed, blocked, or frustrated, Saturn was guiding her toward sacred, mindful action, allowing her to balance Mars's impulsive energy with the discipline of Saturn.

Another illustration of the Jungian technique of active imagination, a dialogue between the archetypes of the Sun and the Moon, might explore the relationship between the client's conscious will and their unconscious reactions, linked to emotional needs. The Sun/Moon active imagination session that I guided for Roshani (see Chapter 6) brought up an internal struggle between her needs and wants, a pull in different directions – a highly logical mind and proactive personality versus an emotional side that had been blocked since childhood. During the active imagination exercise, Roshani identified and embraced her feelings of vulnerability.

Roshani's dreams highlighted the importance of acknowledging her feminine side, symbolized by her mother, daughter, and scenes where she felt powerless or had to wait. These images guided her toward greater self-compassion and inner balance. By embracing these symbols during active imagination, she began to nurture and accept this aspect of herself, leading to a calming effect on her childhood wound.

In active imagination with archetypes and dream symbols, the client has the possibility to create a symbol that unifies conflicting or dissociated aspects. Clients are encouraged to express these qualities creatively through mediums like mandalas, collages, vision boards, sculptures, drawings, stories, or poems that reflect their evolving selves (see Chapter 6).

As the client allows their dream symbols to interact with archetypal images, a form of inner alchemy can occur, and the client's psyche may naturally harmonize and integrate these archetypal energies, facilitating change at a foundational level.

Rewriting the Personal Myth

Self-knowledge through astrology fosters acceptance and fulfillment. Valuing our astrological archetypes and recognizing our potential help us feel more content with who we are and bring us closer to a greater sense of well-being. This self-acceptance deepens as we understand, through myth, why we sometimes act in certain ways and recognize the values that these behaviors aim to protect. It opens up more constructive ways to express these values. There's a heaviness that lifts when we mediate these archetypal energies, along with a relief that comes from knowing we can embody our archetypes in various ways that fulfill our values and support our goals.

What's particularly valuable about mythology is how stories featuring mythological gods illustrate the interplay and clashes among archetypal principles, guiding us toward resolving human conflicts. The client can look into the cosmic metaphoric mirror of myths for meaning and inspiration. In myths, we see different sides to things. For instance, Aphrodite stands for harmony, love, and pleasure and is linked to the planet Venus. However, in some stories where Aphrodite influences others – and in real life when women love abusive men – her impact can be harmful.

The study of the client's natal astrological map can reveal latent mythic forces. Each woman has different goddess traits inside her, reflecting various parts of her character and mind. By recognizing and connecting with these traits, women can learn about their strengths, struggles, and potential. Aphrodite, the Greek goddess of love, not only embodies love but also represents creativity and finding beauty in passions. Additionally, Aphrodite's lessons involve forming deep connections beyond physical attraction and showing love's caring side. By reflecting on the traits of their Venus archetype, people can become more self-aware in how they handle relationships, which can be a significant step toward breaking free from impulsive behaviors.

The main task of the archetypal coach is to assist clients in identifying and challenging their negative self-stories and guide them to reshape their own narratives. According to Jungian psychology, understanding myths can help us dealing with complex emotions like anger, anxiety, and depression. Therapists and coaches can further support this process by helping clients weave elements from significant myths into their self-concept, creating empowering and transformative personal mythologies.

For instance, a client facing a career setback could be encouraged to see themselves as a modern-day Prometheus, bringing innovation to their field despite challenges. In coaching, this journey aligns with the "hero's journey" framework, empowering clients to apply mythic principles to their current struggles. Like Prometheus, who brought fire and enlightenment to humanity despite adversity, clients can view themselves as agents of positive change in their own lives.

By exploring clients' personal myths and understanding how these stories shape their perceptions, coaches can foster deeper self-awareness. We may look into our client's personal myths and how they influence their perceptions of themselves and the world around them.

For example, when helping someone through a period of depression and withdrawal caused by divorce, job loss, or trauma, we can address the Sumerian myth of Inanna[2] and the Greco-Roman story of Persephone and Pluto.[3] Both stories involve going to the underworld, symbolizing letting go of the past and personal growth through transformation. Exploring the myth of Persephone can help clients understand that temporary depression is a natural response to loss, serving as a helpful companion during difficult times. When Persephone emerges from the underworld, she does so renewed, carrying spiritual treasures and a newfound confidence. Reflecting on this myth allows clients to find meaning in persistent painful emotions and to envision personal transformation.

In *The Goddess Within*, Jennifer and Roger Woolger (1989, p. 230) delve into Persephone's unique connection to the spirit world and her understanding of life and death mysteries. Unlike the Amazonian archetypes of Athena, Artemis, and Hera, the "Persephone woman" values privacy and inner projects. Though seemingly fragile, she has a profound ability to bring unconscious content into conscious awareness. By reflecting on Persephone's journey, clients can see their struggles as pathways to wisdom and strength, with the potential for personal renewal.

When a woman is overidentified with Persephone she will be very attracted to situations where she or others get hurt because of her powerless and passive attitude. It is crucial that she can rely on the support of the other goddesses to maintain balance and provide nourishment. It might help her to find Demeter's sense of connection to the earth and to the ground and to get good advice from Athena's calmness and determination. These qualities can offer her stability and guidance during times of emotional turmoil. Hera's nurturing presence can foster a sense of belonging and community, helping Persephone women navigate challenges with grace and resilience. Recognizing and embracing the wisdom and strength of these goddesses can help them discover their inner strength and purpose.

Exploring the relationship between quantum physics, perception, and narrative reveals how profoundly our beliefs shape reality. Quantum physics shows that human perception influences what we observe, suggesting that the stories we believe and tell can impact our reality more than we may realize.

In coaching, a client's natal chart and dream symbols provide a basis for exploring the archetypes that shape their behaviors and beliefs. For instance, a client with feelings of inadequacy might explore the myth of Saturn, their inner critic archetype, to cultivate self-compassion and acceptance (see Marguerite and Mary's example in Chapter 6). An archetypal coach can use the client's chart to help them reframe personal myths in alignment with their true values and desires. By examining Jupiter, the coach can identify areas of growth; through the Sun, avenues for self-expression; and through Venus, an understanding of what the client truly values. Jupiter's themes of adventure and growth align with heroic journeys, while Saturn represents discipline and responsibility, like wise mentors in myths.

Working with a myth allows clients to direct emotional energy toward it, providing a sense of release. Since myths are deeply woven into our patterns of thought and behavior, they are often resistant to change. However, by recognizing the diverse potentials of these myths, clients can craft new narratives that support their growth and well-being.

Rediscovering our archetypes requires little effort; these myths already reside in our subconscious, waiting to emerge. By delving into them, clients can find clues on how to adopt new ways of thinking, feeling, and acting. Negative emotions such as anxiety, depression, and fear, often linked to personality patterns, can also be traced to mythic figures. For instance, Aphrodite-Venus, the goddess of love, may manifest in women drawn to unhealthy relationships, turning her influence from a blessing to a curse. The challenge, then, is to redirect Aphrodite's energy toward building meaningful, nourishing connections that resonate with their values, identities, and aspirations.

Rose provides an example of how archetypal awareness can shape choices, leading to more fulfilling outcomes (see Chapter 6). Having endured an abusive relationship, Rose was committed to breaking free from this cycle. Together, we explored her Venusian archetype to find meanings and healthy ways to honor it, thereby strengthening her self-esteem.

Rose also benefited from exploring archetypes like Athena – the goddess of wisdom and strategy – who embodies self-assuredness and clarity. This connection was reflected in her Venus, positioned in the mental and communicative sign of

Gemini, within the air element. By integrating the constructive qualities of both Aphrodite and Athena, Rose was able to channel her creative energy into self-affirming pursuits.

Through her work with the Venus archetype, Rose uncovered a renewed ability to express creativity and joy, ultimately enrolling in a writing course that allowed her to engage deeply with activities she genuinely loves.

Expanding Reality Maps

Neurolinguistic programming (NLP) is a model of human behavior that focuses on identifying patterns that drive high performance. NLP stands for our thoughts, feelings, and behaviors within the nervous system (neuro), how language shapes our internal and external experiences (linguistic), and the capacity to change behavioral and emotional patterns to foster growth (programming).

In NLP, interpretations or "maps" of reality are shaped by unique filters – memories, values, beliefs, decision-making patterns, and sensory perceptions. These filters affect how we process experiences, distorting or generalizing information according to our personal perceptions (Dängeli, 2022). An extension of NLP, humanistic neurolinguistic programming (HNLP), focuses on "coaching the unconscious mind," deepening NLP principles to transform subconscious patterns that influence well-being and personal development.

Combining NLP or HNLP with archetypes allows clients to broaden their "map of reality," creating new opportunities for personal empowerment. The natal chart, with its archetypal symbols and configurations, can significantly enhance the NLP concept of "territory" by offering a unique map of psychological patterns and preferences. Archetypes present a rich spectrum of options for understanding and responding to life's challenges. They help increase clients' choices by offering a multidimensional "map" filled with various archetypal paths, which clients can use to reframe difficult situations.

For example, imagine a client whose natal chart highlights the Saturnian fear of failure. This fear may show up in dreams of obstacles when climbing a mountain or driving. When looking carefully at the client configuration of Saturn, we can help the them uncover the highest positive intention behind this fear: the intention to protect, providing a foundation for thoughtful planning, steady effort, and discipline. By honoring Saturn's intent, the client could adopt strategies like breaking down goals into manageable steps, creating a plan for progress, or setting realistic milestones, which helps them advance with less resistance.

In HNLP, the feeling associated with successfully reaching an external goal is termed the "End State Energy" (ESE) (Dängeli, 2022, p. 185). The ESE aligns with a person's core values, beliefs, and identities.

For instance, if the client mentioned above has a goal of developing assertiveness, their ESE may be tied to a sense of steady progress and control. By examining how Saturn is configured in their natal chart, we can foster reflection on how to channel this energy effectively. For example, if their Saturn is positioned in the practical earth sign of Capricorn, we might ask questions that encourage them to consider realistic, incremental achievements, which would enable them to build assertiveness in a structured and confident manner. One question could be "Can you describe some small, realistic steps that would help you move closer to your goals?" Additionally, we might ask, "What structures or routines could you put in place to support steady growth toward your assertiveness goals?" These questions are designed to guide the client in aligning their goals with Saturn's grounded energy and Capricorn's practical approach.

For another client the goal is to feel safe and connected in an intimate relationship. This client presents tense aspects between the Moon and Uranus, as well as the Moon and Saturn. This configuration creates an inner conflict between two opposing forces: Uranus represents a strong desire for freedom and independence, often pressing the individual to break free from past conditioning, while Saturn embodies a need for structure, tradition, and responsibility, compelling the individual to conform to family and societal expectations. When this client considers change, they may experience intense anxiety because they're torn between the excitement of liberation (Uranus) and the security of stability and approval (Saturn).

In coaching, investigating these opposing forces can help the client clarify the source of their anxiety around change. For example, they may feel that stepping into their individuality and pursuing freedom could betray their responsibilities or disappoint family members, creating inner tension. By working with these archetypes, the coach can guide the client to recognize how their current behavior might be an expression of Saturnian loyalty to tradition, while their urge to change stems from a deep Uranian impulse for self-liberation. Dreams may add further insights, perhaps presenting imagery like breaking out of an enclosure or escaping from constraints.

Exploring their Moon sign and its aspects within the natal chart can uncover conditions that support this sense of belonging. A client with the Moon in a fiery sign like Sagittarius or Aries might find emotional fulfillment through dynamic, adventurous connections. However, if Saturn (the archetype of stability and realism) also influences this Moon, the client may seek both excitement and security within these experiences.

To deepen this exploration, we can encourage the client to incubate a dream for added clarity. As part of this, we suggest starting a nightly ritual: each evening before bed, they write a brief "day residue" – a few thoughts on the day's events – to help analyze how their dreams may be compensating for conscious concerns.

In one dream, the client found herself driving a sporty car in a remote area, feeling the sun and wind on her face. She associated this with her current need for freedom and expanded this image further by examining how the planet Uranus, symbolizing liberation and change, appears in her natal chart. We might then ask, "Does this dream remind you of any current situation of your life? Does it bring up any new ideas, sensations, emotions, or insights?" Next, we could practice active imagination, inviting the associated archetypes into a dialogue to gain deeper insights.

By exploring these symbols, the client can find new ways to satisfy the need for both freedom and responsibility, perhaps by pursuing incremental change that respects Saturn's values while allowing Uranus to bring fresh perspectives and new choices. This archetypal exploration not only enriches the visualization of the ESE but also aligns with the client's unique potential. In this way, it becomes easier for the client to embrace the desired state, as they are rediscovering qualities that already exist within them.

Enhancing Coaching Techniques with Archetypal Insights

In the world of coaching, foundational techniques such as the GROW Model, visualization, reframing, Socratic questioning, and values identification provide essential tools for guiding clients. When combined with an archetypal perspective rooted in planetary influences, these techniques gain depth and resonance, allowing clients to connect with universal patterns that speak directly to their inner experiences.

For example, the GROW Model – guiding clients to define their Goal, explore their Reality, identify Options, and find the Way forward – can be enhanced by drawing on planetary archetypes. If a client's goal revolves around achieving discipline or structure, invoking Saturn's archetype as the *Wise Old Man* provides a guiding image of wisdom and resilience, while Saturn's role as the *Inner Critic* can highlight any self-imposed limitations they need to acknowledge and transform. By understanding their inner Saturn, clients gain a framework for steady, disciplined progress.

In his influential work *Coaching for Performance*, Whitmore (2009) highlights the importance of self-confidence and responsibility, key components of effective coaching (p. 18). He explains that coaching is about helping clients realize their potential by fostering both clarity and action. For Whitmore, we strengthen our self-confidence when we make decisions, when our actions are successful, and when we take full responsibility for both successes and failures. It is essential that the coach ensures that he/she has helped the person to reach optimal clarity and to commit to action, which involves anticipating obstacles.

Identifying values and strengths is crucial for aligning a client's goals with their core self. When approached with an archetypal perspective, planetary influences reveal the personal values and strengths that resonate on a deep, often unconscious level. Mars, for example, as the *Warrior* brings forth values like courage, loyalty, and assertiveness. Saturn's *Wise Old Man* emphasizes patience and integrity, while Jupiter as the *Teacher* or *Philosopher* encourages growth, wisdom, and adventure.

Questions can evoke specific archetypes, such as asking, "What wisdom might the *Wise Old Man (Saturn)* offer in this situation?" or "What would the Warrior in you bring forth in this moment?"

Visualization and guided imagery are powerful techniques on their own, helping clients mentally project themselves into future successes. Yet this practice becomes even more meaningful when aligned with archetypal symbols. When a client envisions embodying their inner Mars, they connect with the *Warrior* archetype, channeling courage, strength, and assertiveness. Alternatively, if the client's goal involves breaking old boundaries or fostering innovation, connecting with Uranus – the archetype of Prometheus or The Creator – can stimulate visionary thinking. For a client struggling at work who feels like an outsider, we might explore the myth of Prometheus alongside a study of Uranus in their natal chart, focusing on how it represents their unique approach and unconventional strengths.

This client recalled a dream where she found herself pushing aside a dusty, old wardrobe, discovering two powerful big tarot cards – the Sun and the Emperor. She sought help from teacher colleagues to clear the dust from these cards, but they refused, hiding them again behind the wardrobe. She wanted to voice her frustration to the school Director. The client associated these cards with her creativity and personal power, and we amplified the wardrobe image to reflect Saturn's frustrating influence, symbolizing how her creativity and potential might feel blocked by "heavy" external forces. Her impulse to complain to the Director reflects an inner desire to clear this blockage – perhaps a call from her higher self to reclaim her power.

If Uranus is prominently positioned, the client is likely to resonate deeply with Promethean themes, finding personal meaning and comfort in their distinct role. Examining Uranus's connections to other planets in the natal chart, especially strong aspects with the Moon or Sun, can reveal how these energies shape the client's self-perception and responses. By visualizing themselves as creators of new possibilities, they can draw on Uranian energy to transcend limitations and envision themselves beyond current circumstances.

Integrating archetypes into reframing and perspective shifts provides a powerful tool for turning challenges into growth opportunities. When a client feels confined by limitations, for example, accessing Jupiter's *Optimist* archetype invites a shift toward abundance and possibility, while calling on Mercury's *Messenger* archetype can help them see a situation from multiple perspectives, facilitating mental flexibility and adaptability.

Marguerite's story (see Chapter 6) illustrates how the challenging aspects of an archetype can be transformed to motivate a client toward their goal. Her natal chart features Mercury in a square aspect to Saturn—a traditionally difficult astrological configuration. Her fear of public speaking manifested vividly in her dreams, reflecting a classic Saturnian fear associated with Mercury – the planet symbolizing communication and learning. Saturn typically likes to build structure, be responsible, and organize, while Mercury rules communication, thinking processes, and learning. The trigger (fear of speaking in public) was then neutralized by the image offered by the Saturnian archetype, suggesting constant effort to become a professional coach and plant therapist.

> Saturn asked me to put in effort, to materialize…. A bit challenging because I have this fear of showing my truth. And it made me uncomfortable, but actually that was the solution to overcome my resistance and fears. Instead of focusing on my fears, I put effort into expressing my truth. (Marguerite, pp. 69– 73, in Carod, 2021)

Reframing through archetypes and dream symbols enables clients to not only think differently but also feel aligned with forces greater than themselves. This awareness of personal archetypes empowers clients to harness their strengths consciously and transform limiting patterns.

Archetypal Anchors

Besides reframing and perspective shifts, NLP also uses the concept of an "anchor." An anchor is a sight, sound, or feeling that is associated with a particular response or emotion in the past and triggers the same feeling in the present (O'Connor & Lages, 2009).

Exploring the archetypes in the client's natal chart unveils their inherent positive potential, enabling us to create meaningful and impactful anchors. These innate resources, present from birth, require a process of rediscovery, unveiling latent potential rather than imagining a disconnected reality. An essential role of the archetypal coach is to revive overlooked or concealed strengths embedded within the client's narrative, viewed through the lens of their archetypal configurations. For instance, we can pinpoint positive potentials in the client's birth chart directly related to their initial aspirations (how they wish to feel and be), establishing these potentials as guiding anchors.

In his book *Astrology's Higher Octaves* (2020, p. 25), Professor Greg Bogart affirms that "first and foremost, transformative readings emerge from dialogue, from posing questions." When coaches ask their clients open-ended questions, they can help them make connections between their answers and archetypal traits that will support their objectives and vision. After explaining the myth's basic symbolism, the therapist will ask the client open-ended questions such as "how do you express your moon" to encourage additional reflection and comprehension of their emotional reactions. By incorporating insights from Mars and Jupiter, we would gain an understanding of what ignites their energy and hope, while Venus reveals sources of happiness and joy in their lives.

If we wish to inquire about their goals for the future in an archetypally informed framework, we might inquire about their vision of success and link their answer to the archetypal positions of Jupiter, the Sun, and Saturn, adding details to illustrate their aspirations further.

This would provide additional insights into how to become brilliant (the Sun), grow and expand (Jupiter), and achieve tangible success in their chosen path (Saturn). For example, if someone's ambition is to become a successful entrepreneur, we may use Jupiter's placement in their natal chart to explain his willingness to take chances and embrace possibilities for growth and expansion in their business ventures. In addition, we look to the Sun's position to explain their leadership style, as well as Saturn's disciplined work ethic and strategic planning abilities, which contribute to long-term success and stability in the entrepreneurial enterprise.

In contrast to most therapies and coaching strategies, anchoring through an archetypal trait that inherently belongs to the client has a significant and powerful effect.

In a session with my research participant Rose, she expressed drawing upon the potential of her archetypes to materialize work projects, stating:

> I'm creative, I'm strong, I have a lot of wisdom... the main insight is that I have these abilities and I can do something with them. And I haven't been honoring them... so I haven't been expressing my true self, that's what I feel. (pp. 43–44)

My client Marguerite, whose Jupiter is prominently positioned in her natal chart, used Jupiter's energy as an anchor when dealing with communication insecurities. By focusing on Jupiter's symbolism of growth, expansion, and benevolence, Marguerite was able to build confidence in her communication skills which opened up career opportunities through groups of like-minded people. Anchoring in Jupiter's energy instilled in her a sense of optimism and a belief in her ability to express herself effectively.

Summer felt disconnected from her creative potential and expressed a desire to feel more fulfilled and expressive in her life. She shared a sense of frustration and unfulfillment, expressing a desire to reconnect with her creative side. Summer mentioned a passion for painting that she abandoned years ago due to career pressures and responsibilities. By analyzing her natal chart, I identified a strong placement of the Sun and Venus, two archetypes closely linked to creativity, self-expression, and beauty. While a well-placed Sun in the natal chart indicates strong potential for creativity and leadership, Venus symbolizes beauty, harmony, and artistic talents. A prominent Venus suggests a natural inclination toward the arts and aesthetics. The sign the Sun and Venus are placed and the contacts with other planets will inform us about the client's artistic inclinations.

In Summer's natal chart, Venus and the Sun in Cancer highlight her strong connection between creativity, emotions, and self-expression, emphasizing nurturing qualities. This alignment reveals her natural inclination toward emotionally resonant art, such as watercolor painting. Recognizing this, we set specific goals to reconnect her with her creative passions, like dedicating weekly time to dream-inspired artwork. By keeping a dream journal and translating these emotions into her art, she could harmonize her feelings and deepen her creative expression.

Let's take the example of a client who has a tense aspect between Mars (drive for action) and Saturn (representing fear and delays) and has faced persistent setbacks in achieving her goals. She experienced a business failure and struggled to complete her master's thesis. This aspect often represents a struggle between the drive for action (Mars) and internalized self-criticism or restriction (Saturn), which can lead to a sense of being "stuck" or blocked. Archetypally, this tension embodies the Warrior (Mars) and the Wise Elder or Taskmaster (Saturn). We first identify the client's negative state, linked to an archetype (e.g., Saturn as the *Inner Critic*), and then choose positive archetypal traits (e.g., Mars's courage, Saturn's discipline) to create a powerful resource anchor. We guide the client to mentally rehearse scenarios in which these new traits are applied, creating a strong link to future situations.

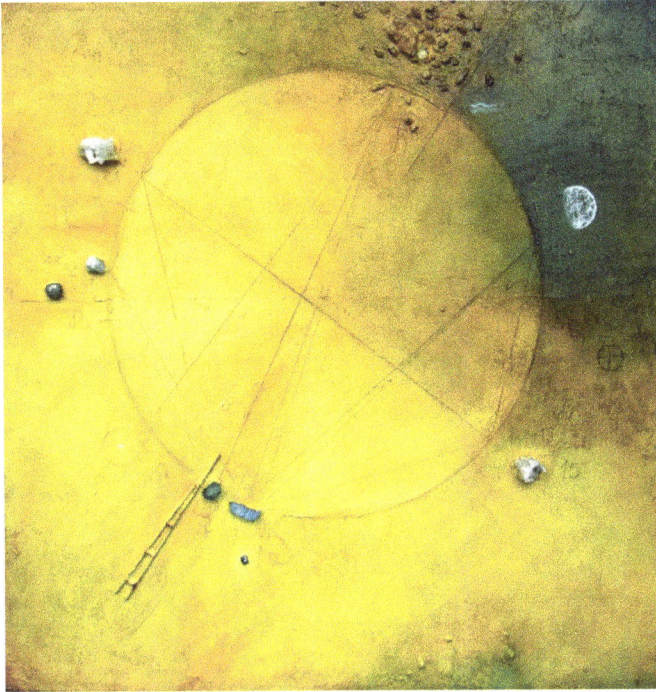

Figure 2.1 Astrological feng shui. Illustration by Joan Comella

Through guided visualization, the client aligns herself with the Warrior and Wise Elder archetypes, inspiring her to act with focused intention, release self-imposed limitations, and steadily pursue her goals.

(For a full breakdown of each stage in this method, please refer to Exercise D in Appendix I, which provides a detailed, step-by-step outline.) (Figure 2.1).

In this astrological chart, painter Joan Comella uses carefully chosen minerals to balance conflicting energies. These gems function as a form of astrological feng shui, bringing balance and harmony to the difficult aspects depicted in the astral chart. For example, Comella may place a piece of hematite to ground the fiery energy of Mars in Aries, while also incorporating a rose quartz to soften the intense passion of Venus in Scorpio.

The staircase, an element to access from one level to another, serves as a constant reminder that alchemy is attainable when we allow ourselves to be open to our higher consciousness.

Notes

1 By referring to his interlocutors as "friends," Socrates underscores his emphasis on empathy and affect. The Socratic approach prioritizes the interlocutor's character and the interpersonal dynamics of the dialogue (De Dominicis & Stelter, 2023, p. 27).

2 Inana, the Sumerian Queen of Heaven, descends to Earth under Ereshkigal's rule and undergoes seven gates in an initiation. At the final gate, she is stripped of her clothes, faces the sentence of seven judges, and is killed by Ereshkigal. Her lifeless body is displayed on a stake, resembling a crucifixion. Enki, the deity of waters and wisdom, rescues Inanna and restores her garments.

    With Enki's help, Inana reclaims her physical form and undergoes a transformative journey of resurrection and restoration. This process helps Inanna integrate her physical and spiritual selves, bringing balance and wholeness to her being.

    Barker Woolger, J. (1989). *The Goddess within: A guide to the eternal myths that shape women's lives*. Fawcett Columbine.

3 Persephone was known to the Greeks as the distant Queen of the Underworld, who kept an eye on the Souls of the Dead. She was also known as the maiden, or Kore, whom Hades kidnapped from her mother, Demeter, and transported to the underworld. Demeter's agonizing experience of losing her daughter gives birth to the seasons, as she mourns Kore's death during the winter. Persephone was eventually permitted to return to the world above for a portion of the year, bringing spring with her (Woolger, 1989, p. 257).

References

Assagioli, R. (1974). *The act of will*. Penguin Books Ltd.

Barker Woolger, J. (1989). *The Goddess within: A guide to the eternal myths that shape women's lives*. Fawcett Columbine.

Bogart, G. (2020). *Astrology's higher octaves. New dimensions of a healing art*. Ibis Press.

Carod, A. (2021). *The transformative experiences of coaching using archetypal imagery within a participatory framework: An organic inquiry* (Master's thesis, Alef Trust / Liverpool John Moores University).

Cox, E., Bachkirova, T., & Clutterbuck, D. (2010). *The complete handbook of coaching*. SAGE.

Dängeli, J. (Ed.) (2022). *The transpersonal coaching handbook* (3rd ed.).

De Dominicis S., & Stelter, R. (2023). A new purpose for Socratic questioning in coaching. *Philosophy of Coaching: An International Journal*, 8(1), 21–32. https://philosophyof-coaching.org/v8i1/03.pdf Greene, L. (2018). *Jung's understanding of astrology. Prophecy, magic, and the qualities of time*. Routledge.

Hillman, J. (1972). *The myth of analysis: Three essays in archetypal psychology*. Northwestern University Press.

Hillman, J. (1975). *Re-visioning psychology*. Harper Perennial.

Johnson, R. (2009). *Inner work: Using dreams and active imagination for personal growth*. Harper One.

Jung, C. G. (1921). *Psychological types*. Princeton University Press.

Jung, C. G. (1951). Aion: Researches into the phenomenology of the self. In R. F. C. Hull (Ed.), *Collected works* (Vol. 9). Princeton University Press.

Jung, C. G. (1960). The structure and dynamics of the psyche. In H. Read, M. Fordham, G. Adler, & W. McGuire (Eds.), *Collected works of C. G Jung* (Vol. 8). Princeton University Press.

Jung, C. G. (1966). Two essays on analytical psychology. In H. Read, M. Fordham, G. Adler, & W. McGuire (Eds.), *Collected works* (Vol. 7). Princeton University Press.

Jung, C. G. (1968). Archetypes and the collective unconscious. In H. Read, M. Fordham, G. Adler, & W. McGuire (Eds.), *The collected works of C. G. Jung* (R. F. C. Hull, Trans.) (2nd ed., Vol. 9). Princeton University Press.

Jung, C. G. (1994). *Tipos psicológicos.* Edhasa.

Lai, Y. L., & McDowall, A. (2014). A systematic review (SR) of coaching psychology: Focusing on the attributes of effective coaching psychologists. *International Coaching Psychology Review*, 9(2), 118–134.

Nails, D., & Monoson, S. (2022). Socrates. In E. N. Zalta (Ed.), *The Stanford Encyclopedia of Philosophy.*

O'Connor, J., & Lages, A. (2009). *How coaching works: The essential guide to the history and practice of effective coaching.* Bloomsbury Publishing.

Pascal, E. (1992). *Jung para la vida cotidiana.* Ediciones Obelisco.

Rowan, J. (1990). *Subpersonalities: The people inside us.* Routledge.

Shaw, G. (2003). *Containing ecstasy: The strategies of Iamblichean Theurgy* (Vol. 21). Dalhousie University, Dept. of Classics.

Shaw, G. (2016). *Archetypal psychology, dream work, and neoplatonism.* In H. T. Hakl (Ed.), *Octagon: The quest for wholeness* (Vol. 2, pp. 329–358). H. Frietsch Verlag.

Voss, A. (2000). The astrology of Marsilio Ficino: Divination or science? *Culture and Cosmos*, 4(2), 29–45.

Whitmore, J. (2009). *Coaching for performance: Growing human potential and purpose: The principles and practice of coaching and leadership.* Nicholas Brealey Publishing.

Chapter 3

Coaching in the Liminal Space

Transpersonal Coaching: A Holistic Approach to Life Coaching

Transpersonal coaching, as delineated by transpersonal coach Jevon Dängeli (2022, p. 18), is a specialized practice of coaching that takes a holistic and integrative approach to supporting client growth and potential transformation. Like transpersonal psychology, transpersonal coaching is based on an expansion of the sense of Self beyond (trans) the individual, connecting the psyche with the outer environment and the cosmos. This coaching approach navigates unconscious processes, fostering interconnected awareness by focusing on the alignment of one's inner and outer worlds. Although transpersonal coaching works best with people who have already done some spiritual work, it also suits those who are creative and open to new ideas.

Transpersonal coaching psychology is a framework that connects with the spiritual values of the clients, embedding this value into the transformative process and providing paths between the unconscious and the conscious mind (Law et al., 2010, p. 8).

Law et al. (2010, p. 5) suggested including an initial meditative state to the GROW model to increase self-awareness and a state of readiness. The authors remark that transpersonal coaches need to foster practices that support gaining greater control over the "I"-focused mind. According to Buddhist philosophy, the sense of "I" is a construct "recreated from moment to moment by the mind." Mindful practices can enable clients to have an outer perspective on this egoistic structure and facilitate access to information that is outside of it.

The concept that humans act based on their representation of the world aligns with both Buddhist philosophy and neurolinguistic programming (NLP). In Buddhism, the idea of dependent origination emphasizes the interconnectedness of experiences, attributing actions to perceptions and mental states. NLP explores the relationship between language, neurology, and learned behavior patterns, emphasizing that subjective experience is shaped by mental representations or "maps." Both traditions highlight the significance of these internal representations in

DOI: 10.4324/9781003627258-4

influencing actions and reactions, with the recognition that changing our internal representations can lead to shifts in behaviors and well-being.

Instead of following the recipe of goals and tasks, the transpersonal coach adopts the language of transformation and is more involved with potential and possibilities than finding fixed answers to problems (Rowan, in Cox et al., 2010, p. 152). Transpersonal coaches develop well-rounded strategies that support overall well-being, rather than just addressing isolated symptoms.

In this approach, the "liminal space" plays a crucial role, serving as a transitional medium where exploration, discovery, and healing occur. In *The Nature of Holding Space*, Dängeli and Geldenhüis (Dängeli, 2022, p. 127) explore the idea of liminal space and point out the components involved:

> Liminal relates to a transitional process or something that occupies a position at, or on both sides of, a boundary or threshold. It is the co-created medium in which coaching or therapy is performed that facilitates exploration, discovery and healing in a safe and responsive setting.

Coaching can occur in various transitional or transformative contexts, which aligns with the archetypal theme of crossing thresholds or entering new stages of personal development. This concept of liminal space as a medium for exploration and healing resonates deeply with practitioners who work in the realms of nature and spirituality. The interconnectedness of nature and spirituality further enhances this process, providing a sense of grounding and connection to something greater than oneself.

Mindfulness meditation, somatic awareness, contemplative practices, and guided imagery can facilitate a deeper connection to inner experiences and the unconscious mind. These practices promote relaxation, enhance self-awareness, and cultivate a sense of presence that allows individuals to experience what I term "archetypal synergies" – perceptions and revelations that arise from deep engagement with symbols and archetypes.

The body processes everything we encounter, with the mind continually receiving sensory data from multiple biological systems. Sensation and cognition are interrelated, as described in the early Buddhist scripture *The Four Foundations of Mindfulness* (Kerr, 2012). This holistic approach contrasts with the Western view, which often considers thoughts and sensations as independent from one another.

The integration of short somatic meditation exercises and active imagination in coaching sessions allows to enter this space, situated at the threshold of the unconscious. Working co-creatively in the liminal space can provide significant insights and inspired actions; my research participant Roshani expressed the liminal space as a process of thinning the wall between the conscious and the unconscious:

> I feel that somewhere the wall between my inner and my outer world became thin, and I could start crossing over.

This thinning of the wall between the inner and outer world can lead to a deep sense of connection and alignment with one's higher self, true self or Soul. As Roshani delved deeper into this liminal space, she found herself gaining a heightened sense of intuition and creativity.

In *Coaching for Transformation*, Lasley et al. (2015) define transformation as the process of moving from limitations to full creativity and full expression. According to the authors (p. 22), part of holding the transformational agenda is engaging with the mystery:

> If we stop at "The client has the answer" or "I know what this client is capable of," we miss the real power of coaching—engaging in places that neither the client nor coach can imagine.

The authors stress the significance of embracing the unknown and allowing for the unexpected to unfold during the coaching process. By resisting the temptation to rely solely on our preconceived notions of what's feasible, we open ourselves to new possibilities and deeper levels of growth and transformation. This readiness to delve into the mystery empowers both the coach and the client to unlock their full potential and achieve enduring change.

Lasley et al. propose a multistage alignment approach, which includes exploring needs, living in the present, envisioning the future, expanding one's perspective, and embracing one's shadow.

We can enhance Lasley's approach by integrating an archetypal lens, linking client values and beliefs to various perspectives through archetypal metaphors. For instance, in Marguerite's case (refer to Chapter 6), the dream of a tree with roots, symbolizing a profound connection with nature, resonated with her need for grounding and commitment to a place, translating values into tangible actions. This dream became central to her project of bringing sacred contact with nature to her community. During the second part of the session, delving into astrological archetypes revealed a desire for expression (Mercury) intertwined with underlying fears (Saturn). As a concrete step, she opted to seek permission for her project involving planting trees for healing and conducting ceremonies.

Some authors emphasize traits coaching shares with other professions. For example, English et al. (2019) use the term *coach-sultants* to describe coaches who offer personal experience or relevant expertise to fill a gap identified during the coaching conversation. The approach outlined here employs astrology and dream work as tools that penetrate the subconscious layers. The birth chart is a valuable tool for recognizing the unconscious, revealing the dynamic interaction between the personality traits represented by the planets. Essentially, the astrological chart provides information on how to express our archetypal configurations in the most constructive way.

Central to this coaching methodology is the interactive involvement with archetypes, akin to a painter using various materials to create diverse artworks. Unlike a simple intellectual analysis, this approach demands an expanded, integral global consciousness. In this heightened state of awareness, individuals can acquire profound insights and revelations through their engagement with archetypes and dream symbols.

Letting go of rigid, goal-oriented mindsets allows for a more authentic exploration of archetypes and their meanings. In traditional therapeutic settings, the emphasis often lies on achieving specific outcomes or resolving particular issues. While goals are important, an overly goal-oriented approach can limit the depth and breadth of self-exploration.

When clients are encouraged to adopt a mindset of curiosity and wonder, they become open to the unexpected and the unknown. This openness facilitates a deeper engagement with their unconscious mind, where archetypes and dream symbols reside. By exploring these symbols without the pressure of achieving a specific result, clients can uncover layers of meaning and insights that might otherwise remain hidden.

Participatory Cosmologies

Participatory cosmologies are based on two premises: an openness to the transpersonal realm and a dialogical participation with the cosmos or spirit, with the possibility of multiple spiritual paths (Ferrer, 2011, p. 2). A co-creative approach to working with archetypes implies an interaction between personal and transpersonal worlds rather than fixed structures waiting to be discovered. Openness to the transcendent dimension implies that higher energies can enhance or modify an initial impulse.

By engaging in a dialogical participation with the cosmos, individuals can tap into the transformative power of archetypes and co-create new possibilities for personal evolution. This perspective emphasizes the importance of openness, receptivity, and active engagement with the transpersonal realm in order to harness the full potential of archetypal energies. Individuals can receive messages in the form of insights, images, or sensations when they interact with archetypes and symbols in an expanded state of consciousness.

Hillman's imaginal psychology, centered on the exploration of images rather than their intellectual analysis or explanation, is highly suitable for coaching within a participatory framework. This approach fosters creativity, self-awareness, and transformation, making it a dynamic tool for a participatory coaching. However, it was Jung (1968, p. 47) who first suggested the idea of dialoguing with the archetypes:

> Since archetypes are, like all numinous contents, relatively autonomous, they cannot be integrated simply rationally, but require a dialectical method, i.e. a real discussion.

According to Richard Tarnas (2006), early human experience was embedded in the *anima mundi*—a world soul that fostered symbolic, participatory engagement with the cosmos through ritual and myth. In contrast, the modern mind is marked by a sharp division between subject and object, resulting in a profound sense of alienation as spiritual meaning is internalized and disconnected from the larger cosmos (pp. 16–17).This disconnection from the cosmos, while seen as an "achievement of human autonomy," has simultaneously led to a deep "experience of human alienation" (p. 25). No matter how close we come to other people, isolation from the order of the cosmos remains, and we are faced with the overwhelming task of constructing our own world. Spring illustrates this feeling in a reflective exercise after the coaching session:

> Living this modern life within the limitations of mainstream education and mainstream culture can create a lot of confusion as it attempts to separate us from the mystery that we are. By living this separation, I can feel like I am in an endless ocean swimming or drowning in ways of living that do not reflect my truest nature. (Carod, 2021, Appendix B)

In active imagination, we create an imaginative environment in which to interact with an archetype or symbol. However, it is the dynamic relationship with the symbols of their imagination in the held space (not only the analysis of the image) that provides an opportunity for transformation and healing.

By encouraging conversation between conscious and unconscious aspects, an unfolding of wider horizons or possibilities for action or meaning may occur. The importance of this method rests not with the coach's capacity for interpreting astrological archetypes and dream symbols but with the clients' growing awareness of the profound meaning contained within a dream image or archetype and how it relates to their present existential dilemmas.

> I could dialogue with Saturn and wonder, what he tries to tell me, to see it more of an ongoing mystery, rather than seeing something always being blocked and even perhaps getting into a victimized mindset, which is not empowering. (Spring, pp. 127–130, in Carod, 2021)

In Suzanne's initial coaching sessions, she identified self-criticism and overthinking as her primary challenges. These tendencies created an inner turmoil that demanded a compassionate and mindful approach to her restless mind. The process of addressing these challenges involved guiding Suzanne toward a deeper exploration of her inner world through active imagination.

During this journey, the archetypes of Mercury and Neptune emerged as significant influences. At first, Suzanne perceived Mercury's analytical nature as overly critical and Neptune's nebulousness as a source of confusion. However, by reframing these archetypes, Suzanne began to uncover their hidden gifts. Mercury, traditionally associated with intellect, communication, and quicksilver adaptability, was reimagined as a helpful guide for processing information and fostering analytical clarity. Neptune, often linked with intuition, dreams, and the dissolution of boundaries, revealed its potential to connect Suzanne to subtler, more spiritual realities.

A pivotal moment in this exploration came when Suzanne related a dream involving presents, which metaphorically signaled the hidden gifts within her struggles. Through this process, the qualities she once viewed as obstacles became tools for transformation. Mercury's sharpness enabled her to navigate complexities with precision, while Neptune's ethereal nature allowed her to embrace uncertainty as a pathway to deeper insight and connection.

In *Cosmos and Psyche*, Tarnas (2006, p. 96) explains that the principle of Neptune is especially associated with the flow of consciousness and the deep oceanic realms of the unconscious. It relates to all non-ordinary states of consciousness, including dreams, visions, images, and reflections. Neptune governs myth, religion, poetry, art, inspiration, and spiritual aspiration, encompassing experiences of the divine, the numinous, the ineffable, and the sacred. Its realm is more about meaning than matter and more symbolic than tangible. Neptune is linked to the soul, the transpersonal realm, the collective unconscious, the anima mundi, and the archetypal dimension of life, including the Platonic world of Ideas. More broadly, Neptune is seen as governing all modes of consciousness, shaping both external and internal experiences of reality by encompassing the archetypes and gods that inform those experiences.

The process of having a conversation with oneself can lead to surprising answers and allow for viewing situations from different perspectives, as Suzanne experienced during her transformative journey. Through this process, she learned to embrace all parts of herself, even those that had once seemed challenging or unclear.

> I think it's really interesting if you start having a conversation because the answers can really surprise us, and they really surprised me. And I could start seeing the situation from different perspectives. I felt that, everything has its place and that I can embrace all of it. (Suzanne, pp. 85–88, in Carod, 2021)

Working with the archetypes associated to her dream's symbols in active imagination served as a reminder that these archetypes embodied concealed facets of herself, previously overlooked and underappreciated. This process highlighted the dynamic interaction between dream symbols and archetypes, ultimately revealing that these archetypal aspects are gifts to be acknowledged and embraced in the journey of self-discovery.

Embodied Awareness

The typical human condition is one of not being fully present. Research suggests that modern humans spend nearly half of their waking hours (46.9%) in a state of mind-wandering, which is the opposite of embodied presence. In this state of mind, the interoceptive awareness network is suppressed, meaning we are not paying attention to what our bodies are experiencing (Heeter, in Carod, 2023, p. 70).

In *Hellenic Tantra: The Theurgic Platonism of Iamblichus*, Professor Gregory Shaw (2024, pp. 226–227) draws significant parallels between the neoplatonic philosopher Iamblichus and Carl Jung, particularly regarding their views on embodied psychosomatic experience. Shaw emphasizes that, for Iamblichus, the subtle body is not granted from above but is shaped through the chaotic, embodied experiences of the soul. This aligns with Jung's understanding of the chaos of psychosomatic experience, where both thinkers suggest that transformation comes not through escaping these embodied states but by integrating and ritualizing them. Iamblichus, like Jung, saw the impulses that entangle us as forces that can be interiorized, visualized, and transformed into a vehicle of spiritual liberation. Rather than seeking escape or perfection, both thinkers focus on the integration of these complex, embodied experiences into a path of self-transformation.

In both psychological and spiritual work, there is a need for grounding – to come down out of the thinking mind into the body. Including self-awareness through mindfulness and somatic awareness is a necessary step, shifting our focus from further ego development to cultivating an awareness of change. As Welwood (1984) notes, it can be so fascinating to delve into archetypes, dreams, and insights that we consider self-examination of the ultimate journey, with the risk that we become narcissistic, one who gets hooked on processing personal stuff. Welwood (2000, p. 120) suggests recovering the presence of being through opening directly to experience instead of problem resolution. This can lead to an increase in our capacity to let go of whatever arises in the mind and be present with our experience just as it is, promoting a vertical shift from personality to being (Welwood, 2000, p. 121).

Presence is defined as "the bare awareness of the receptive spaciousness of our mind" and "a state of receptive awareness of our open minds to whatever arises as it arises." It combines a temporal quality of focusing on the immediate now with an intention to experience that now directly. To be present and experience directly mean to minimize interpreting what occurs from within a framework of rigid mental constructs or ingrained emotional reactivity (Parker et al., in Carod, 2023, p. 71).

Embodied presence occurs when our mind integrates attention to embodied feelings with other bodily sensations to produce a heightened awareness of the moment and the sensory self. Through inner embodied awareness, I have witnessed a subtle change of consciousness, a *presence* arising in my clients and myself.

My client Elisabet Fábregas exemplifies how embodied presence can be channeled through symbolic and artistic activities, fueling her personal transformation. Her poetry acts as a powerful bridge between her internal and external worlds, channeling Venusian themes of love, sensuality, and emotional depth.

Her poem, titled "Shelter in the Fig Tree," reflects the depth of her Venusian archetype. It carries the theme of emotional nourishment and connection to nature, with vivid imagery that represents both vulnerability and strength. The repeated line, "I wrap myself among the rough leaves of the ripe fig," highlights the sense of seeking refuge and shelter, while the interaction with the fig itself – stripping it of its membrane and unpacking its pulp – symbolizes a deeper, sensuous engagement with life and self-discovery. In the final lines, where an animal seeks "torn parts in the gaps," there is a recognition of how sweetness, symbolic of life's beauty and joy, can emerge through gentle pressure and love. This closing speaks to the inherent tenderness and depth that her Venus in the sign of Pisces seeks, affirming her connection to the Venusian archetype through her embodied writing.

SHELTER IN THE FIG TREE
I wrap myself among the rough leaves of the ripe fig.
I gather the fallen twigs
I light a small fire.
I bring some fruits closer, they open slowly
I open my hand
I feed myself with the bright descent
of a cold milk that burns the skin.
I wrap myself among the rough leaves of the ripe fig,
I unpack the fruit in my mouth,
I strip its membrane, empty the pulp.
The seeds crouch under the body of the animal walking nearby,
it looks for the torn parts in the gaps,
knowing that sweetness always yields
and by loving it opens with a slight pressure.

In a reflective exercise, Elisabet shared her thoughts, noting that animals instinctively know when the fruit is ripe and that this reflects the calmness and deep nourishment the wild part of ourselves experiences in connection with nature. "When we fully enter into nature," she remarked, "that part of us matures, like the fruit, opening to love and universal knowledge."

Elisabet's reflection emphasized the poem's portrayal of presence through the senses and the importance of patience. She likened the natural instinct of animals, knowing when the fruit is ready, to the human ability to trust in the timing of life. The poem, she said, encapsulates the idea that sweetness and wisdom come when the time is right and that both nature and the self unfold naturally with patience and awareness.

Shifting Consciousness through Somatic Awareness

Our goal as coaches is to create an environment in which clients feel comfortable connecting with their unconscious parts, witnessing what arises in the held space, and offering a nourishing and warm presence. Next, we gently guide them toward beneficial steps inspired by their interactions with archetypes and dream symbols.

A desirable achievement for the coach is a shift in consciousness that puts them in grounded presence and stillness, focusing on what they feel inwardly as well as on what the client is saying.

When we incorporate somatic awareness into our coaching, we intentionally focus on our bodily sensations and reactions. This enables us to identify the emotions or physical responses that are triggered when we envision a particular activity with our clients. Before implementing a specific practice, we can practice empathic resonance through inner awareness to sense in our bodies if the activity resonates as coherent with our client in the here-and-now. Modern physics has provided us with the insight that all matter is in a constant state of vibration. Whether it is a chair in a library or a cell in the human body, everything vibrates. In light of this knowledge, the term "resonant body" can be interpreted to refer to the actual resonance that occurs within the body when it responds to the materials and stimuli of the environment (Walsh, in Carod, 2023).

The first foundation of mindfulness in Buddhism is focusing on the body and breath, which is an important step in learning to regulate emotions and moderate unpleasant or recurring thoughts. Simple mindfulness techniques can help to improve bodily awareness and flexibility in the brain's sensory-attentional system. This, in turn, allows for variances in the alpha rhythm, which contributes to better emotional and cognitive processing, including less negative thoughts.

To enhance clients' ability to shift consciousness, we can guide them through open awareness, a somatic-centered meditation developed by Dängeli (2022, p. 62), which cultivates a calm, receptive state that combines introspective, extrospective, and somatic awareness with a sense of interconnectedness and presence. Dängeli's approach fosters a state in which clients can access their body-mind system's wisdom, facilitating a safe exploration of triggers, unwanted behaviors, and potentials.

Open awareness meditations have proven invaluable not only for helping clients but also for deepening my own connection with them. This practice shifts my state from a purely analytical mindset to an embodied awareness, allowing me to attune to the client's unique story and experience. Inspired by Dängeli's method, I have found that incorporating archetypal work within this meditative state enhances the client's potential for transformation. By guiding clients into this "liminal space" – an expanded state where consciousness broadens – they can interact with archetypal energies and co-create insights into their personal narratives. In this shared experience of interconnected awareness, archetypes become powerful tools to help clients expand their focus and explore previously unexamined parts of themselves. This process, paired with somatic awareness, facilitates an alchemical transformation, enabling the client to consciously reflect on their experience with less reactivity and greater openness to the unconscious material that may emerge

Roshani's experience highlights the power of combining somatic awareness with active imagination, enabling her to uncover and integrate disconnected parts of herself. While being guided in somatic meditation, Roshani described the ephemeral touch of butterfly dust as initiating her healing process:

> For me it's about leaving an imprint, leaving a mark, however delicate, however ephemeral, and if you don't look closely it disappears. (Carod, 2021, Appendix G, p. 99)

In this expanded state, clients can move beyond "tunnel awareness," examining their situations with a broader perspective. Tunnel awareness can be understood as a narrowed focus of attention where one usually identifies only with the perceived danger while deleting whatever else is not necessary in our field of awareness (including positive thoughts and feelings) in order to survive an unpleasant or disturbing situation. Satisfying solutions might only be discovered when the individual succeeds in shifting their state of consciousness in a way that enables them to dis-identify from their limited self-concept (Danjeli, 2019, p. 19).

With gentle curiosity, we invite emotions to surface without pressure and support the process with exploratory questions, such as "What is important here?" and "If you had all of that, what would it give you?" This reflective, receptive space not only helps clients uncover their deeper needs but also allows the coach to illuminate potential blind spots. Through mindful boundary-setting, we stay centered and avoid being pulled into the client's unconscious issues, which may mirror our own. Examples of these issues were Rose's and Roshani's healing experiences with their inner child, Susanne's and Spring's concern that overthinking was blocking their connection with their soul and inspiration, and Marguerite's permanent feeling of needing more training and qualifications (see Chapter 6). Sharing this resonance and exposing a similar vulnerability provided authenticity to our relationship and built trust among the participants.

Coaching with Unconditional Presence

Good coaches possess presence; they are fully there for the client in a non-judgmental, open way, without imposing an agenda. As explains, this quality makes the coaching relationship both special and effective.

Welwood (1996, p. 122) emphasizes the ability to learn to be with our experience, which he calls "unconditional presence." Here, the focus is not so much on what we are experiencing as on how we are with it. Unconditional presence involves giving in to our experience while learning to ride the energy mindfully without becoming overwhelmed by it.

During the process of coaching with archetypes, we tune into the clients' personal stories, practicing what Welwood (1977, p. 3) named "diffuse attention." The conscious and unconscious are approached in a holistic manner, not as two separate parts of the psyche but rather as two different modes of knowledge.

By cultivating unconditional presence, we learn to embrace our inner world without judgment or avoidance. We become attuned to the nuances of our emotions and thoughts, and instead of attempting to suppress or control them, we practice being fully present with whatever arises. Participants interact with archetypes and images and perceive how they produce meaning endogenously through body sensations and kinaesthetic reactions.

Patience with any turbulence, confusion, or intense emotions arising from the unconscious allows space for transformation. We create the space necessary for growth and healing when we are patient with our symptoms.

Besides embodied awareness, empathic listening, and questioning, another key quality of transpersonal coaches is emotional self-awareness – noticing and processing not only the client's feelings and reactions but also one's own.

The mindful-awareness state facilitates the coach's recycling of overlooked or unconscious experiences and subtle feelings, beliefs, and values that determine the impact the coach will have on their client's development (Mindell, 2014). Guiding the client in a short, soma-centered open awareness has been a valuable tool for shifting my state from an analytical mind that reacts and judges to the wisdom of the entire body-mind system. Practicing self-awareness for a few minutes reinforces our ability to listen mindfully to the client's stories without rushing or manipulating them. Being mindful of my kinaesthetic responses before, during, and after the coaching sessions has allowed me to develop an intuitive ability that has added to my previous knowledge of coaching core competencies.

Once we achieve a state of unconditional presence, it is easy to connect with the essence of the client through empathic resonance. Practicing a mindful state with the client allows us to prepare the soil for empathic listening; by focusing on our kinaesthetic responses while listening, we can receive confirmation through inner resonance that we are getting the essence of their trigger. As the client describes their issue and current mental and emotional state, I try to focus on both the message and my embodied response. I noticed that when I allowed for some moments of silence between symbols (words and images) in the held space, the essence of the felt sense was captured, enabling clients and myself to participate in an embodied spirituality.

An example of this empathic resonance took place while I was listening to Mary in an expanded state of mind. As I guided her through open awareness, I felt within myself the very qualities she described. She dreamed of centeredness, a masculine archetype that provided her with clarity, serenity, and compassion. As she was describing these qualities in the active imagination exercise, she looked as if she were connecting to higher realms – uplifted, awakened, and luminous. I sensed that she was energized and light. She paused, and her words resonated within me at a sensory level, bringing a feeling of spaciousness and expansiveness to my head and chest area.

Embracing Intuitive Knowledge

Besides self-awareness and connection with a higher reality or state of mind, the primary tools of the transpersonal coach are intuition and imagery (Rowan in Cox et al., 2010, p. 151). O'Connor (2007, p. 111) defines intuition as the ability to have helpful ideas that come from unconscious processing of all the information that coaches have been picking up while they are listening.

Transpersonal development focuses on intuition as a relational, contextual way of knowing, involving contemplative practices and non-discursive experiences. Once a state of open receptivity is attained, it is possible to reach the part of reality one wishes to contact. This quieting of the mind may also be described as a lowering of the threshold of consciousness, which allows for awareness of normally unconscious processes (Assagioli, 1965). Like dreams, intuitive flashes are often mistakenly disregarded as illusory, imaginary, or irrelevant perceptions.

In exploring intuition, Jung and Assagioli provide valuable distinctions, identifying two main types: sensory-based or practical intuition and archetypal or spiritual intuition. Both thinkers view intuition as essential for accessing insights beyond the reach of rational thought, revealing latent potentials within the psyche.

Jung (1976) classified intuition as one of the four primary psychological functions, along with thinking, feeling, and sensation, and emphasized its role in connecting the individual to both immediate perceptions and deeper, universal truths. He identified two types of intuition: sensory-based (or concrete) intuition, which offers insights into concrete situations through a "gut feeling," and archetypal (or abstract) intuition, which connects individuals to the collective unconscious and accesses universal symbols and insights. Jung viewed archetypal intuition as a bridge to the "archetypes," deep-seated patterns that shape human experience and provide access to transpersonal wisdom. This type of intuition supports self-discovery and individuation, as it guides individuals toward a sense of unity with broader human experience and wisdom.

Jung also differentiates intuition from sensation, feeling, and intellectual reasoning, seeing it as an unconscious perceptual process that produces a holistic understanding without conscious analysis. Derived from the Latin *intueri*, meaning "to look at or into," Jung saw intuition as an instinctive, "whole" perception – whether of an object, experience, or relationship – that presents itself fully formed, without evident logical steps (Jung, 1976, para. 770). Like sensation, intuition is an "irrational" function that operates without logical inference. Jung noted that intuitive knowledge holds an intrinsic sense of certainty and conviction, akin to the certainty found in physical sensation. However, the "certainty" of intuition is rooted in an unconscious psychic alertness, an instinctual awareness.

In his work *Psychological Types* (1976, para. 771), Jung elaborates on the distinction between concrete and abstract intuition. Concrete intuition, he explains, directly responds to sensory data, orienting individuals to possibilities in the physical world, whereas abstract intuition requires direction or will, engaging more fully with symbolic or conceptual realms, as in dream interpretation or archetypal analysis. This abstract type draws from a transpersonal realm, resonating with what Jung called the "collective unconscious," which holds the archetypal images and wisdom that help to guide personal and collective human experience.

While Jung viewed intuition as a passive, unconscious mode of thinking that accesses images, ideas, and possibilities, Assagioli stressed its active, directed use, particularly in its spiritual form, for accessing the higher wisdom of the Self. In *Transpersonal Development*, Assagioli delineates the difference between the concrete analytical mind and the higher level of philosophical reason, or nous. He explores the expansive realm of imagination, spanning lower and higher variations, as well as the realms of intuition and will. Additionally, Assagioli refers to indescribable domains as "worlds of transcendence" (1991, p. 92).

Many people find that accessing intuition is challenging due to the relentless activity of their thoughts, often tied to anxiety and negative emotions. In coaching sessions, we help clients calm their racing thoughts and tap into their intuition by incorporating brief, guided somatic meditations. Quieting the mind and guiding clients through these short embodied practices expand their capacity to access intuitive insights. Reaching a state of stillness and grounding allow intuition to emerge through dreams, active imagery, and meditation – expressed as kinaesthetic responses, like feelings and bodily sensations.

Researchers recognize two main categories of meditation practices: focused attention and open monitoring. Focused attention meditation directs the mind toward a single mantra or object, encouraging full immersion in the present. Open monitoring meditation, by contrast, involves observing the unfolding content of one's experience with calm awareness. An example of this type of meditation is Dängeli's open awareness meditation (2022), which combines introspective, extrospective, and somatic awareness with a sense of interconnectedness and presence. Clients often report embodied responses to these meditations, describing sensations like "an inner happiness," "a good feeling in my gut," and "a feeling of lightness in my chest."

To further cultivate intuition, we blend meditative states with active imagination exercises, enabling clients to tap into creative and symbolic realms. Using dream imagery and planetary symbols, clients enter a transformative space where intuition and imagery can function as powerful agents of change.

References

Assagioli, R. (1965). *Psychosynthesis: A collection of basic writings.* The Viking Press.

Assagioli, R. (1991). *Transpersonal development.* Crucible.

Carod, A. (2021). *The transformative experiences of coaching using archetypal imagery within a participatory framework: An organic inquiry* (Master's thesis, Alef Trust / Liverpool John Moores University).

Carod, A. (2023). Exploring the influence of somatic awareness and embodied practices on transformative learning and wellbeing in higher education students and teachers. *Journal of Transpersonal Research,* 15(1), 69–77.

Cox, E., Bachkirova, T., & Clutterbuck, D. (2010). *The complete handbook of coaching.* SAGE.

Danjeli, J. (Ed.) (2019) *The open awareness handbook.*

Dängeli, J. (Ed.) (2022). *The transpersonal coaching handbook* (3rd ed.).

English, S., Sabatine J.M., & Brownell, P. (2019). *Professional coaching: Principles and practice.* Springer publishing company.

Ferrer, J. (2011). Participatory spirituality and transpersonal theory: A ten-year retrospective. *The Journal of Transpersonal Psychology,* 43(1), 1–31.

Jung, C. G. (1968). Archetypes and the collective unconscious. In H. Read, M. Fordham, G. Adler, & W. McGuire (Eds.), *The collected works of C. G. Jung* (R. F. C. Hull, Trans.) (2nd ed., Vol. 9). Princeton University Press.

Jung, C. G. (1976). Psychological types. In H. Read, M. Fordham, G. Adler, & W. McGuire (Eds.), *The collected works of C. G. Jung* (R. F. C. Hull, Trans.) (2nd ed., Vol. 6). Princeton University Press.

Kerr, C. (2012). *Mindfulness starts with the body: A view from the brain [YouTube Video] TED College Hill.* TEDx Talks. https://www.youtube.com/watch?v=AGnGRgyLwMs

Lasley, M., Kellogg, V., Michaels, R., & Brown, S. Y. (2015). *Coaching for transformation: Pathways to ignite personal & social change.* Discover Press.

Law, H., Lancaster, B. L., & DiGiovanni, N. (2010). A wider role for coaching psychology — Applying transpersonal coaching psychology. *Coaching Psychologist, 6*(1), 24–32.

Mindell, A. (2014). *Working on yourself alone.* Lao-Tse Press.

Shaw, G. (2024). *Hellenic tantra: The theurgic platonism of Iamblichus Angelico press.* Kindle Edition.

Tarnas, R. (2006). *Cosmos and psyche: Intimations of a new world view.* Penguin Publishing Group. Kindle Edition.

Welwood, J. (1977). Meditation and the unconscious, a new perspective. *The Journal of Transpersonal Psychology, 9*(1), 1–26.

Welwood, J. (1984). Principles of inner work: Psychological and spiritual. *The Journal of Transpersonal Psychology, 16*(1), 63–73.

Welwood, J. (1996). Reflection and presence. The dialectic of self-knowledge. *Journal of Transpersonal Psychology, 28*(2), 107–128.

Welwood, J. (2000). *Toward a psychology of awakening: Buddhism, psychotherapy, and the path of personal and spiritual transformation.* Shambhala Publications.

Chapter 4

Coaching with Dream Symbols

Dreams as Divine Messages in Ancient Traditions

Different cultures and religious traditions have interpreted dreams as messages from the divine with similar notions regarding dreams and their interpretation. Ancient civilizations like the Egyptians, Greeks, and Mesopotamians considered dreams to be sacred, often seeking dream interpretations for decision-making, healing, or understanding divine will. The Egyptians and Mesopotamians believed in "message dreams" in which a deity or person in anthropomorphic form delivered an "understandable" message (Hughes, 2000, p. 8).

They categorized dreams between those that required interpretation and those that did not. In Christianity and Islam, dreams are often viewed as revelations from God or Allah, while in Hindu and Buddhist traditions, dreams may offer spiritual insights into one's path toward enlightenment (Bulkeley, 2008).

The Sumerians believed in the symbolism of dreams; dreams were encrypted, and the dreamer had to convey the dream to a knowledgeable person who was assigned to interpret them. Mesopotamians would also try to understand or answer concerns about dreams through incubation, which is the practice of sleeping in a temple chamber in order to obtain oracular or healing dreams. For example, Nabonidus of Babylon had a dream in which the deity Marduk instructed him to build a temple for Sin, the Moon god. When a woman named Mahituaskhit was unable to bear a child to her husband and incubated a dream, Sin revealed to her the measures she needed to do to conceive a child (Hughes, 2000, p. 10).

Central to Greek mythology and religious practices, dreams were viewed as a bridge between the human and divine realms, carrying sacred significance for both personal and communal matters. This belief is evident in works like Homer's *Iliad* and *The Odyssey*, where prophetic dreams play a key role (Lewis, 1996). In *The Odyssey*, for instance, Penelope dreams of an eagle killing 20 geese, which then reveals itself as Odysseus. This vision, sent by Athena, was understood as a divine message signaling her husband's imminent return and the end of the suitors' presence in her home. These kind of stories exemplify the Greek view of dreams as prophetic windows into future events, sometimes providing clarity and reassurance during difficult times. Such dreams were central to Greek divination,

DOI: 10.4324/9781003627258-5

often interpreted as revealing the will of the gods or offering guidance on personal matters. Specific deities, including Athena, Zeus, and Hermes, were associated with sending dreams that could alter the destinies of the dreamers.

The belief that dreams were a medium through which the gods communicated vital messages to humans influenced Greek religious practices such as incubation. Individuals would sleep in sacred temples, particularly those dedicated to Asclepius, the god of medicine, with the hope of receiving healing or prophetic dreams. According to the legend, Asklepios, a priest and healer, wandered the countryside offering cures through sacred mantras, music, dance, herbs, and dreams. Although his services were free, a gift or sacrifice was customary in exchange for healing. It was said that Asklepios became so attuned to the life force that he could even recall the dead from the underworld. This greatly troubled Hades, who felt slighted by a mere mortal interfering with the souls under his domain. Hades persuaded his brother Zeus to strike down Asklepios, but Apollo, another powerful god, intervened, pleading for mercy. As a result, Asklepios was allowed to ascend to the stars, joining the ranks of the gods as the patron of healing and medicine. For centuries thereafter people visited the healing temples of Asklepios, where they fasted, took ritual baths, meditated, prayed, and then retreated to the abaton, the innermost sanctuary (Johnson & Ruhl, 2007).

Dreams requiring interpretation were typically not analyzed by the dreamer alone; instead, *oneirocritai*, or professional dream interpreters, were often consulted. Respected members of society, these interpreters helped individuals and communities understand dreams as symbolic messages from the gods. Skilled in identifying archetypal symbols and mythological patterns, the *oneirocritai* linked dream imagery to religious, mythological, and psychological meanings.

After sleeping in the abaton, or sanctuary, dreamers would recount their visions to the *oneirocritai*, who would interpret them to reveal guidance for healing or transformation. Rituals like fasting, bathing, and meditation prepared the dreamer to receive these sacred messages, often involving symbolic imagery like animals or mythic characters that signaled physical, psychological, or spiritual shifts needed for healing. The *oneirocritai* used a blend of symbolic knowledge, local customs, and intuition to provide accurate interpretations. They also referenced established texts like Artemidorus's *Oneirocritica*, a 3rd-century manual cataloging common dream symbols, as a framework to guide their analysis.[1]

Similarly, the Romans adopted these beliefs, seeing dreams as powerful indicators of divine favor or displeasure. The role of dreams extended into political and military spheres, where leaders would use dream interpretation to make important decisions.

Theurgy and the Transformative Role of Symbols

In his article "Archetypal Psychology, Dream work, and Neoplatonism," Professor Gregory Shaw (2016) describes the work of Iamblichus, a philosopher of late antiquity influenced by Neoplatonism, who was deeply interested in dreams, theurgy, and divination as pathways to the divine. Iamblichus emphasized the necessity of cosmogonic rituals to overcome the soul's self-alienation, which occurs when the immortal soul descends into the mortal body. This process of reuniting the divine with the human is essential to preserving the theurgical vision, where the divine and natural worlds are deeply interconnected.

Before Christian dualism and before materialist science, the supernatural was not something distant but was inherent in the natural world. The gods were everywhere: in plants, rocks, animals, and temples and within us. The later Platonists sought to ensure that this integration of the supernatural with the natural, and the divine with the human, remained alive (Shaw, 2024, p. 38). Unlike other Platonists, Iamblichus viewed the material world as divine and essential for the soul's evolution. Through the rhythmic mediation of opposites like sameness and difference or rest and motion, the soul participates in the One, the ineffable principle that underlies all existence. He regarded dreams not merely as psychological phenomena but as direct communications from the gods and higher spiritual entities. Iamblichus believed that the soul could transcend the material world and connect with the divine during sleep, making dreams a crucial spiritual tool.

In his work *De Mysteriis* (in Shaw, 2016), Iamblichus (245 CE) explains how dreams serve as a medium through which humans can receive divine instructions. He expanded on earlier Platonic and Aristotelian views of dreams by incorporating elements of theurgy – rituals designed to invoke the presence of the gods. Theurgy, an integral aspect of Neoplatonism, combined cosmology, ethics, and rituals to reconnect the soul with its divine origins, facilitating spiritual evolution.

For Iamblichus, dreams were more than passive experiences; they were integral to spiritual practice, as the dream state allowed the soul to communicate with the divine without the distractions of the material world. Dreams, especially when induced through theurgy, could reveal deep truths and instructions for personal and communal well-being.

Dream interpretation, in Iamblichus' view, required an understanding of the symbolic language used by the gods. This symbolism was not straightforward, and as with the *oneirocritai*, interpreting the messages from the divine required a nuanced and spiritually attuned mind. In a key passage from *De Mysteriis* related to dreams and their interpretation, Iamblichus distinguishes between different types of dreams and their sources:

> For these visions that are sent from the gods in dreams are not merely of a prophetic character, but impart also a healing and saving power, so that they not only foreshadow what is to come, but prepare the soul, through the divine good that fills them, to receive the future rightly and be saved from its afflictions. (De Mysteriis, III.2)

Iamblichus viewed divine dreams not only as predictive but also as sources of healing and spiritual empowerment, filled with divine energy that enables the soul to foresee events, align with divine will, and overcome life's challenges.

By participating in theurgic rituals, the soul transforms the chaos and suffering of earthly life into a harmonious order. These rituals are not intended as escapes from the material world but as means to reunite the fragmented soul with its divine origins.

According to Iamblichus, theurgy does not involve manipulating divine forces; instead, it entails opening oneself to divine energies, allowing the gods to act through the soul. This view aligns with Jung's concept of active imagination and Hillman's imaginal psychology, where a greater intelligence communicates with us through symbolic or sensory experiences. Both approaches stress a passive receptivity to symbols and opposites rather than a forced interpretation, fostering a reconnection with divine forces within and around us, which purifies and liberates the soul.

In theurgic practice, different souls engage in varied rituals according to their needs and capacities. Iamblichus emphasizes the importance of preparing the soul as a proper "receptacle" (*hupodochē*) capable of receiving the divine presence; hence, a careful assessment of the soul's state is essential before performing any ritual (Iamblichus, in Shaw, 2016, pp. 334–335).

The gods reveal themselves to the soul through *sunthēmata* ("tokens") or symbols, manifesting in various forms – such as animals, plants, stones, sounds, and geometric shapes – which each embody the divine in action. These symbols simultaneously reveal and conceal the divine essence, acting upon the soul without conscious interpretation. Theurgy, thus, is a passive process in which the symbols themselves work on the soul, providing guidance and transformation without the need for intellectual analysis (Shaw, 2016, p. 335).

This approach to symbols in theurgy mirrors Hillman's imaginal psychology, where images are not manipulated or forced into intellectual frameworks. Like Iamblichus' theurgic symbols, Hillman encourages letting images speak to us directly, allowing the symbols to work on the psyche without the interference of conscious reasoning. In both systems, the emphasis is on opening up to the transformative power of the symbols, which act as bridges between the mortal soul and the divine.

He further explains that dream interpreters (akin to the *oneirocritai*) must possess a high level of spiritual understanding to properly interpret the symbols and messages sent by the gods. Iamblichus affirmed that theurgic or *god-sent* dreams do not come when we are unconscious but when we are between waking and sleeping, that is, in a hypnagogic state. This in-between awareness is conscious but not active, and it perceives but does not analyze or exert its will (Shaw, 2003, p. 62).

According to Iamblichus, "all theurgy must begin with the material gods, who govern growth, decay, and the struggles of embodied life, because attempting to connect directly with immaterial gods without this grounding severs the soul from all divine influence" (Shaw, 2016, p. 4). In the same way that Iamblichus emphasizes the importance of starting theurgy by embodying the gods through rituals, archetypal coaching seeks to communicate with the gods, or archetypes, by promoting access to the liminal space, where the conscious and unconscious realms intersect. Archetypal work mirrors this process by first engaging with tangible, earthly symbols and experiences, creating a vessel through which the archetypal energies and dream symbols can be contained and integrated.

Modern Dream Work Perspectives

Freud and Jung pioneered the study of dreams in modern Western psychology. In 1899, Sigmund Freud's *The Interpretation of Dreams* revolutionized psychotherapy by establishing dreams as meaningful psychological structures. His work laid the foundation for using dreams in therapy and introduced a model for understanding unconscious processes. Freud posited that dreams are shaped by day residues and influenced by day-to-day experiences, which reflect the unconscious mind's attempt to process daily events and shape the content of dreams.

Freud developed the "free association" technique, where the dreamer, in a relaxed state, recounts their thoughts and associations, helping uncover the hidden meaning of dreams. His focus was largely on sexual symbolism and childhood experiences, which he believed were central to psychoanalytic theory.

In *The Symbolic Life* (1976), Jung explains the compensatory function of dreams, which guides individuals on their path to individuation. Jung highlights the importance of the unconscious, noting that because consciousness is easily distracted by external influences, it can veer into behaviors misaligned with one's true individuality. He emphasizes the necessity for therapists to develop a thorough understanding of dreams and the varied expressions of the unconscious.

In *Man and His Symbols* (1968, p. 50), Jung explains that dreams serve a fundamental role in maintaining our psychological balance by compensating for imbalances in our conscious attitudes. Dreams, Jung suggests, help restore mental equilibrium by providing compensatory content to balance one-sidedness in the waking mind (CW 18, par. 471). This compensating function is especially significant when dreams contain archetypal images from the collective unconscious – the part of the psyche that holds humanity's shared psychological heritage.

In the process of individuation, dreams help us adjust to society by revealing how we identify with our social mask, or "persona," and confront the darker, less acknowledged parts of our personality, referred to as the "shadow." This process can be unsettling, as the unconscious holds powerful and sometimes troubling energies. When repressed, these elements can permeate the psyche in disruptive ways, potentially leading to neurosis. Dreams, therefore, play a crucial role in restoring psychological balance by allowing these repressed elements to surface and be reintegrated into the conscious mind.

They also bring awareness to the natural qualities of the opposite gender within us, known as the "anima" (soul) in men and the "animus" (spirit) in women. When these aspects are brought into harmony, dreams often symbolize the integration of the whole personality, representing a state of completeness and unity, sometimes referred to as the "Self." Thus, dreams are not just a window into the unconscious but an essential tool for personal growth and self-realization.

In *Man and His Symbols* (1968, p. 64), Jung discusses the inherently ambiguous nature of dreams, noting that a dream loses its character as a dream if it starts to form clear, definitive thoughts. This ambiguity is due to dreams occupying what he describes as the "fringe of consciousness," similar to the faint glow of stars during a solar eclipse. Jung explains that dreams often bypass the specific details that the conscious mind considers essential, which makes them elusive and indirect. This subtlety is why working with dreams through active imagination – a hypnagogic, expanded state of awareness – is particularly effective. In this state, the mind is receptive to the symbolic and indirect messages of dreams, allowing deeper insights to emerge without crossing fully into conscious thoughts.

Although Jung held dreams in high regard, he considered active imagination to be an even more effective path to the unconscious. In the practice of active imagination, like in the theurgic hypnagogic state, the conscious mind participates on the imaginative level, which is neither conscious nor unconscious, and provides an experience that exists at the threshold between consciousness and the unconscious. Active imagination facilitates a dialogue between the conscious and unconscious mind, enabling the dreamer to interact with dream symbols and uncover deeper insights. When we spontaneously associate a dream to a particular experience, the surprise of this meaningful association wakes the mind up to a fresh insight, leaving a mark on our attention and emotions.

Jung described the "initial dream" as a type of dream that appears at the onset of an analysis. Through his extensive experience with patients, he observed that these dreams are frequently strikingly lucid and well-defined, providing valuable insights that aid the analyst in both diagnosing the primary issue and anticipating potential outcomes. This initial dream often serves as a foundational tool, helping to guide the therapeutic process by revealing underlying themes or conflicts early in the analysis (CW 16, para. 296).

For example, my client Rose, who had been struggling with the trauma of childhood abuse by her stepfather, shared a dream she had at the age of nine. In the dream, she wandered her street unable to find her home. Upon reflection, she recognized that this dream symbolized her sense of disconnection from her body, a dissociative defense mechanism developed during the abuse. Now, Rose is on a journey of learning to love herself and rebuild trust in others.

Jungians contextualize images by linking them to mythological material and distinguishing between personal dreams – which express elements of the personal unconscious – and archetypal, visionary, or big dreams, expressing elements of the collective unconscious (a part of the psyche that retains the psychological inheritance). For Jung (1960), visionary dreams serve as bridges to the transpersonal dimension, allowing us to access our inner wholeness.

Tibetan dream yoga makes a distinction between ordinary (samsaric) dreams and "dreams of clarity" (Wangyal, 1998). This division is akin to Jung's distinction between "little" and "big" or archetypal dreams. According to Tibetan dream yoga, dreams of clarity (big dreams) occasionally may be experienced by anyone but become more and more prevalent, providing guidance as one advances on a spiritual path.

From the perspective of Hillman's archetypal psychology, a post-Jungian framework, any dream holds the potential to be a big dream. For Hillman (1979),

the metaphorical value of the image is inherent in it, as it is a precise configuration of the psyche, and instead of aiming at a final interpretation of the dream,
one should reflect on it, letting the images speak to us and treating the dream with
respect without trying to transform it into something we want or prefer. Hillman
suggests surrendering to the message sent by the psyche, perceiving how the images produce meaning endogenously, related to body sensations and kinaesthetic
reactions.

Hillman's approach marks a significant departure from the classical Jungian
view of dreams. In traditional Jungian theory, dreams are typically interpreted as
compensatory messages from the unconscious, intended to correct imbalances in
the conscious attitude. They are often seen as offering insight or guidance to help
individuals navigate waking life more effectively. While Hillman (1975) does not
entirely reject this, he reframes the function of dreams: rather than offering direct advice or prescriptions, dreams illuminate the dreamer's current psychic state.
They reveal internal conflicts, desires, fears, and unresolved issues—providing
orientation by showing the dreamer "where they are" in the inner landscape. In
this sense, Hillman's stance complements Jung's, as shining light on a particular
psychic area already initiates a shift in perspective.

This reorientation aligns with Hillman's broader framework of imaginal psychology, a post-Jungian model that extends beyond archetypal typologies to embrace
the full spectrum of images encountered in dreams, fantasies, and imagination.
Emphasizing metaphor, symbol, and poetics over literalism, imaginal psychology
adopts a rhetorical, expressive mode of inquiry. Its therapeutic aim is not to cure or
fix, but to restore the soul's access to multiple layers of reality.

In *The Dream and the Underworld* (1979), Hillman articulates this vision of
dream work more fully. He argues that dreams do not exist to serve the ego's goals
for self-improvement or psychological integration. Instead, they are expressions of
the underworld—a mythic dimension of psyche that resists reductive interpretation. Hillman cautions against decoding dreams with the aim of extracting practical
benefits, proposing instead that they be experienced as autonomous realities. By
engaging with dreams as symbolic expressions of the soul's mythopoetic depths,
he redirects the purpose of dream work toward soul-making. In doing so, Hillman
emphasizes the transformative power of dreams when they are treated not as tools,
but as portals to archetypal meaning and the mythic layers of the self.

The Symbolic Function of Dreams

Jung (1990, para. 431) considers "dreams are the commonest and universally accessible source for the investigation of man's symbolizing faculty, apart from the
contents of psychoses, neuroses, myths, and the products of the various arts."

Jung drew heavily from Neoplatonic theories, especially regarding the nature
of symbols. He embraced the idea of symbols as visible expressions of unseen
realities, a concept rooted in the Stoic-Platonic idea of *sumpatheia* (sympathy).
This notion suggests that all parts of the cosmos are interconnected and mutually

dependent through chains of correspondences that operate on various levels of reality (Greene, 2018, p. 80).

While Freud (1899) treated dream symbolism very literally, claiming that dreams reflect our unconscious wishes, Jung (1968) asserted that dreams are not simply manifestations of repressed contents but symbols by which the unconscious tries to bring meaning and wholeness to our lives. These dream symbols, according to Jung, are meaningful in and of themselves, rather than being arbitrary or veiled representations of underlying desires. They are the unconscious mind's attempt to connect with us, providing insights that might bring balance, meaning, and a sense of wholeness into our lives. Jung emphasized that dreams do not follow the same logical process as conscious thought, making them seem like "absolute nonsense," which often leads people to dismiss them (CW 7, paras. 176, 289).

In his book *Dreams* (1974, para. 546), Jung says:

> If the conscious attitude to the life situation is in large degree one-sided, then the dream takes the opposite side. If the conscious has a position fairly near the middle, then the dream is satisfied with variations.

A symbol connects seemingly distinct qualities, ideas, or experiences that may seem contradictory to conscious thought. Dreams use symbols that appear in the unconscious to unite our fragmented energies into a cohesive whole. Jung stated repeatedly that dreams and symbols are "not invented but happen to us":

> One cannot invent symbols; wherever they occur, they have not been devised by conscious intention and wilful selection, because, if such a procedure had been used, they would have been nothing but signs and abbreviations of conscious thoughts. (CW 18, para. 432)

Jung (1968, p. 98) suggests that certain dreams use symbols to connect our conscious mind with the "original mind," a primitive layer of the psyche that once formed the entirety of human personality. Over time, as consciousness evolved, it separated from this primal energy, which then became embedded in the unconscious. For Jung, some dreams act as a bridge to this deep, unconscious mind, bringing forward symbols that represent these ancient, instinctual aspects.

Jung recommended that therapists search for archetypal motifs when analytical dream interpretation ceases to elicit new insights (1966, CW 7, pp. 80–89). He argued that for psychologists to interpret dreams and other expressions of the unconscious accurately, they must be well-versed not only in the realm of dreams but also in mythology in its broadest scope (1968, p. 67). This knowledge of mythological symbols and themes forms a foundation for understanding the archetypal imagery that often surfaces in dreams, enabling a more nuanced and comprehensive analysis of the unconscious mind's expressions.

Jung dedicated significant effort to analyzing dreams, identifying their archetypes and symbols, and amplifying these images by linking them to myths and legends while connecting them to the dreamer's daily experiences. He recognized mythological motifs as essential elements of the collective unconscious, frequently appearing in what he called "big dreams." These motifs reflect humanity's shared myths, legends, and fairy tales, which contain universal symbols and archetypes – innate patterns that shape behaviors and perceptions (CW 17, para. 209).

Common archetypes found in such dreams include figures like the mother, father, child (*puer*), wise elder (*senex*), and the trickster. Each archetype embodies fundamental human roles and dynamics, linking the individual to a broader, universal experience of the psyche.

In *Symbols and the Interpretation of Dreams* (1990, para. 464), Jung explains that dreams naturally use symbolic, pictorial language, which can seem obscure simply because of our difficulty in grasping its emotionally charged imagery. He advises analysts to "learn as much as you can about symbolism and forget it all when analyzing a dream." This practice helps avoid over-reliance on preconceived notions and keeps the focus on the dreamer's unique experience.

Ethics in Dream Interpretation: Jung versus Hillman

Jung highlights the complexities of interpreting another person's dreams, cautioning against projecting one's own thoughts onto the dreamer. He warns that such projection can distort understanding by presuming the dreamer's thoughts mirror those of the interpreter. Emphasizing humility in dream interpretation, Jung admits he deliberately avoids assuming complete comprehension of any dream. This approach minimizes the influence of the analyst's associations, creating space for the dreamer's uncertainties and insights to surface (1990, para. 483).

In *Symbols and the Interpretation of Dreams* (1990, para. 464), Jung describes dream analysis as a dialectical process rather than a rigid technique. He argued that reducing it to a mere technique risks disregarding the dreamer's individuality, potentially transforming therapy into a power struggle. Jung abandoned hypnotic treatment for this reason, advocating instead for healing that emerges organically from the patient's personality rather than being shaped by the imposition of the analyst's suggestions (para. 492).

While Jung emphasizes honoring the dreamer's autonomy (1990, paras. 483, 492), Hillman (1998) highlights that dream images are themselves autonomous and should be allowed to "speak for themselves", treating them as autonomous and allowing them to guide exploration. Hillman (1979) encourages dreamers to approach their dreams with openness, curiosity, and respect, rather than attempting to rationalize or impose conscious interpretations. He emphasizes treating dreams delicately and avoiding overly analytical approaches, reflecting his belief that seeking guidance from a dream requires attunement to the nuanced and often enigmatic nature of the dream world.

Archetypal Psychology holds that the true iconoclast is the image itself, which explodes its allegorical meanings, releasing startling new insights. For Hillman, every image contains an invisible connection that constitutes its Soul. Hillman and

Moore (1998, p. 25) elaborate, "If, as Jung says, image is psychic, then why not go on to say images are souls, and our job with them is to meet them on that soul level." This engagement requires no specialized knowledge, though familiarity with symbols can culturally enrich the process. He poetically states that words and their arrangement – syntax – are "soul mines" (Hillman & Moore, 1998, p. 26). This perspective encourages an experiential participatory relationship with the image, inviting the dreamer to explore its depth without imposing conscious interpretations.

Hillman (1998, p. 26) suggests that all images can have an archetypal quality, which emerges through a precise and attentive portrayal of the image itself. This process involves sticking to the image, hearing it metaphorically, and discovering the inherent necessity and richness within it. By exploring the analogies and metaphors inherent in the image, its archetypal nature becomes more apparent, revealing deeper meanings that might not be immediately obvious.

A compelling example of this concept is found in Mary's dream (see Chapter 6). Mary, a teacher of mindfulness and a mother of two, often found herself overwhelmed by fear, particularly in her relationships with her husband and children. Despite years of self-reflection, she struggled to distance herself from the fear. Through our work together, we explored how her dreams could support her emotional regulation and personal growth.

In one pivotal dream, Mary encountered an 18th-century masculine figure, embodying centeredness, clarity, serenity, and compassion, who was being threatened by an angry mob intent on lynching him. This dream became a crucial symbol for Mary, representing the integration of conflicting aspects of her personality. The centered man served as an archetypal image of harmony, enabling her to transcend internal conflicts with acceptance and compassion. By focusing on the image and its rich metaphors, Mary was able to move closer to understanding and integrating these parts of herself, illustrating Hillman's point that the archetypal quality of an image can emerge through a deep, metaphorical engagement.

After leading a group meditation one night, Mary experienced a sinking feeling of fear and rejection. The following morning, during her own meditation, she became aware of this discomfort and tuned into the associated body sensations, emotions, and thoughts. She then embodied the centered man from her dream and observed the discomfort from this calm, compassionate position, allowing herself to rest in stillness while holding space for the reactivity. As she wrote in her journal:

> I embodied the centered man and was curious to view the discomfort from this position, just resting in the stillness whilst allowing the reactivity, offering a loving presence. (journal entry, 17th March)

This dream offered Mary a new way of being – one that allowed her to accept all parts of herself: the helplessness she felt in the face of inner conflict, the conflict itself, the fear it held, and the centered part of her that could embrace it all in compassionate love.

In active imagination, Mary explored the dream further and transmitted her ability to hold polarities in balance, without favoring one side over the other. The centered man in her dream helped her realize that she often became stuck in moments of reactivity instead of simply observing them.

Dreams as Creative Expressions of the Unconscious

In *Collected Works* (18, para. 449), Jung reflects on the enigmatic nature of dreams, highlighting their potential as a wellspring of creativity. He explains that while conscious thoughts can sink into the unconscious, new content can also emerge from it. This includes not only recollections but also genuinely original ideas and creative insights that have never entered conscious awareness. Jung likens these emergent thoughts to a lotus growing from the depths, emphasizing their significance within the subliminal psyche. He notes that dreams often incorporate such new, unconscious material, not merely memories, making them a vital source of innovative and previously unknown ideas.

Dreams break habitual thought patterns, offering creative solutions and alternative perspectives to seemingly intractable emotional problems; moreover, this capacity for fresh thinking, self-regulation, and problem-solving makes dreams a powerful tool in therapy and coaching. Like art, dreams invite us to interpret and reflect, providing a unique language through which the unconscious communicates. Professor Vedfelt (2016) suggests that our dreaming brain is connected to unconscious intelligence networks, including creative default networks, mindfulness meditation networks, empathy networks, and mind-reading networks.

The most prominent or emotionally charged image in a dream often holds the key to its meaning. Jung (1974) called this the dream's "nuclear element" and suggested it could point to the central issue the unconscious is addressing. He encouraged his patients to paint the images that arose from their imaginal work, and there are numerous case studies in the *Collected Works* that present evidence of how efficacious this creative effort could be in aiding the process of psychological integration (Greene, 2018, p. 79).

James Hillman argued that dreams should be approached as poetic and artistic experiences, rich in symbolic language that reveals the soul's desires and conflicts. Building on Jung's psychological framework, Hillman (1998, p. 22) emphasizes the centrality of fantasy images in psychic life. He describes these images as self-originating, spontaneous, and organized in archetypal patterns, functioning as both the raw material and refined expressions of the psyche. Hillman views fantasy images as the primary medium for understanding the soul, asserting that all feelings and observations initially manifest through these images.

Rather than anchoring psychology in physiology, language, social structures, or behavioral analysis, Hillman's approach elevates imagination as a core function of the psyche, presenting it as the primary means of accessing and understanding the soul's inner workings. This perspective emphasizes the poetic and dynamic essence of psychological life, aligning it with archetypal and creative processes. Interestingly, Hillman's theoretical assumptions share significant parallels with the theurgical Neoplatonism of Iamblichus (c. 245–c. 325). Robert Bosnak, a Dutch psychologist and student of Hillman, developed a dream work ritual practice of encountering imaginal entities, which also bears striking similarities to the theurgical rites advocated by Iamblichus (Shaw, 2016). This alignment highlights the deep, transformative power of engaging with dream symbols as part of a broader spiritual and imaginative process.

Robert A. Johnson (2009), a Jungian analyst and author, presents a creative and structured approach to dream work in *Inner Work: Using Dreams and Active Imagination for Personal Growth.* Johnson's method for dream analysis begins with the process of associations, where the dreamer explores the symbolic elements of their dream by noting spontaneous thoughts, feelings, and associations with each image (p. 56). As a result, this step encourages an openness to the unconscious, allowing unexpected connections to surface without the constraints of logic. Through this creative engagement, the dreamer begins to unlock the deeper meanings embedded in their dreams.

Building upon this, Johnson emphasizes Jung's Archetypal Amplification, a method where personal dream symbols are linked to universal archetypes, such as mythological figures or cultural motifs. By connecting dream imagery to collective human stories, the dreamer enriches their understanding of the unconscious forces shaping their life. Further, Johnson highlights the importance of interpreting dreams through rituals, where the dreamer takes conscious action to embody the dream's message. Whether through drawing, writing, or performing symbolic acts, these rituals help ground the dream's insights and integrate them into daily life (p. 101). Ultimately, this final step reflects Jung's idea of individuation – the process of becoming whole through active engagement with the unconscious. Thus, by using creativity and symbolic acts, the dreamer fosters personal transformation and deepens their connection to their inner self.

In my own journey, different dreams and symbols have marked stages of growth and self-awareness. In one dream, I stood by a lake with my high school boyfriend, unaware of the tiger approaching from behind. The lake, symbolizing the unconscious, and the tiger, representing untamed instinct, reflected my early unawareness of deeper psychic forces. In contrast, a later dream showed me as a woman holding a stick, guiding a young lion – an image that symbolized my conscious engagement with these instinctual and creative energies. Over time, I later discovered that Athena, the Greek goddess of wisdom and strategy, is often depicted holding a spear or staff. Consequently, this archetypal connection amplified the dream's meaning, linking my personal experience to a broader mythological narrative of wisdom, guidance, and inner strength. Through linking the symbol of the stick to Athena, I was able to amplify the dream's meaning further, marking a significant step in integrating my instinctive unconscious parts with conscious awareness through dream work.

Figure 4.1 Split sunset lake scene. Illustration by the author

The Role of Dreams in Self-Regulation and Emotional Balance

Dreams often reflect our deepest fears, desires, and unresolved conflicts. They help integrate emotional patterns, promote emotional development, and balance psychological energy and self-regulation.

Jung (1990, para. 474) highlights the nuanced impact of dreams on our psyche, emphasizing their subliminal influence. Dreams often operate below the level of conscious understanding, subtly shaping our mood for better or worse – even when they cannot be fully recalled. When a dream is particularly vivid and emotionally striking or recurs frequently, interpretation and conscious engagement become valuable.

Scientific research has shown that dreams, even when not consciously recalled, play a vital role in consolidating learning, stimulating creativity, and contributing to emotional balance. Neuroscientist Antonio Damasio, as cited by Vedfelt (2016, p. 46), suggests that dreams are an integral part of the ongoing self-regulation of our personality, helping us navigate challenges in everyday life.

Professor Ole Vedfelt, a Jungian analyst, offers a comprehensive framework for understanding how dreams contribute to self-regulation and emotional balance. According to Vedfelt (2016), consciousness alternates between introverted and extroverted states in a pulse-like rhythm. In introverted states – such as self-reflection, creativity, relaxation therapy, imagination, meditation, and dreaming – we are freed from the demands of daily life, creating the mental space needed to process information (p. 47). This allows for self-organizing activities that help re-establish balance between our internal needs and external pressures. Dreams lift us above the trivialities of everyday life, enabling us to process both consciously and unconsciously received information while comparing it to the deeper, over-arching patterns shaping our lives. This framework complements Jung's theory of dreams as a compensatory mechanism, balancing parts of the psyche that may be underdeveloped or unconscious in waking life.

Dreams use symbols and metaphors to communicate complex emotional experiences, providing a rich source for deeper insights. For instance, when a symbol like a snake appears repeatedly in dreams, it can evoke strong emotional reactions, such as fear or anxiety. However, by reinterpreting the symbol through the lens of archetypal psychology, clients can transform their relationship with these symbols and, by extension, with their own unconscious mind. The snake is a powerful archetype that carries rich symbolic meanings across various cultures and mythologies. Like the planetary archetype Pluto, it is often associated with transformation, healing, and renewal due to its ability to shed its skin. Pluto, the god of the underworld in Roman mythology, represents profound transformation, death, and rebirth. Similarly, the snake's shedding of its skin is a metaphor for letting go of the old and embracing renewal. This shift in perception can alleviate fear and open up new pathways for healing and self-discovery. The relationship between Pluto and the symbol of the snake emphasizes deep, sometimes difficult transformations. Pluto's energy can bring to light what has been hidden, just as engaging with the snake archetype can reveal underlying issues and potentials within the psyche.

The images in Figure 4.2 symbolize how my own creative dream work also served as a tool for emotional self-awareness. The dream image of myself in

Figure 4.2 Climbing bookshelves. Illustration by the author

Figure 4.2, climbing up a bookshelf, trying to reach the ceiling, reflected a stage of my research where I felt overwhelmed by the vast amount of literature in which I was immersed. When my research tasks became overwhelming, I stepped back from the written words, letting the dream images speak to me and dialoguing with them. This ritual calmed me and inspired me to get my research moving again. The cave suggested my incursion into the unconscious while the moon reflected in a mirror symbolized how my participants' stories showed me my own unconscious issues as part of a divine order that brought me the themes I was meant to deal with at that moment. During my active imagination exercise with the dream symbols, the deer told me that the missing horn represented old emotional patterns that my participants had evoked and that were no longer needed by me.

This revelation allowed me to see how my own personal growth and healing journey were intricately intertwined with the work I was doing with my research participants. It was a powerful reminder that our inner worlds are constantly reflected in the outer world and that by delving deep into the unconscious, we can uncover hidden truths and patterns that can lead to profound transformation.

Archetypes, Complexes, and Dreams: Navigating the Autonomous Psyche

Dreams offer a direct line to the unconscious, helping to untangle the emotional knots caused by complexes – those hidden, unresolved emotional patterns that influence our behaviors and thoughts. Jung's concept of complexes in dreams refers to our basic difficulties and conflicts, which can cause recurring problems in our lives.

Jung's understanding of archetypes reveals them as autonomous elements of the unconscious, capable of manifesting through complexes and influencing us independently of our conscious will (Jung, 1984, pp. 182–183). He described these archetypal forces as resistant to conscious control, often behaving like external entities – akin to gods or daemons – that can overwhelm emotions or seem to impose alien intentions. This autonomy of archetypes accounts for feelings of possession by powerful, inexplicable emotions.

Complexes, in Jungian psychology, are clusters of psychic energy organized around archetypes, functioning as semi-independent entities when unconscious. They are energized by specific archetypes or their interactions, shaping behaviors, thought patterns, and emotional responses (CW 8, para. 201). Jung emphasized that these complexes disrupt memory, interfere with willpower, and act according to their own internal logic (CW 8, para. 253). Mother and father complexes, rooted in early attachment experiences, are foundational, while others – such as power or inferiority complexes – often stem from childhood dynamics or unresolved traumas (Bogart, 2009).

Dreams provide a window into the unconscious, often revealing the workings of archetypes and complexes. In *Dreamwork and Self-Healing*, Bogart (2009, p. 118) illustrates how dreams can reflect unresolved complexes, manifesting in recurring themes like anger, self-doubt, or relational conflicts. Complexes become problematic when they compel us to react irreflexively, rooted in past conditioning, rather than responding mindfully to the present.

For Jung, the key to overcoming a complex lies in living it out fully (CW 9i, para. 184). This transformative engagement involves consciously experiencing the emotional energy tied to a complex, recognizing its archetypal core, and integrating its influence into our psyche in a balanced way.

Rather than resisting these unconscious forces, Jung advocated for a welcoming attitude. By becoming aware of archetypes and complexes, especially through dreams, we gain the opportunity to engage with their messages constructively. This process of dialogue and integration fosters psychological wholeness, transforming disruptive energies into sources of growth and creativity. As Jung suggested, by honoring and understanding the archetypal energies rather than suppressing them, we enable their potential to guide our psychological evolution harmoniously.

Somatic Awareness in Dream work

Eugene Gendlin, an American psychologist and dream worker, pioneered the integration of body awareness into dream analysis. His method, called "focusing," emphasizes tuning into the body's subtle physical sensations, or felt sense, that accompany emotional experiences. Instead of relying solely on intellectual or theoretical interpretations, Gendlin believed that these bodily responses could offer deeper insights into the meaning of dreams (Gendlin, 1986). His approach encourages a more experiential and intuitive way of engaging with dreams, helping individuals connect with their embodied experiences and uncover personal meanings that might not surface through traditional cognitive analysis.

Some recent approaches to dream work include the cultivation of somatic awareness. Instead of asking what the dream meant by trying to analyze the symbols, we allow the mind to be receptive, bringing awareness to our physical senses and trusting the process.

Embodied imagination is a creative form of working with dreams pioneered by Jungian psychoanalyst Robert Bosnak (2007). It is rooted in the key principles of Carl Jung's analytical psychology (1974), James Hillman's archetypal psychology (1975), and Henry Corbin's broadened understanding of the imagination (1964). Though grounded in these historical frameworks, it presents a distinct conceptual and practical approach to working with the imagination and the unconscious. Bosnak's approach to dream work introduces a unique and creative way of engaging with dream symbols by emphasizing their embodiment and fostering a dynamic relationship with them. He encourages clients to immerse themselves in the dream's landscape and interact with its characters and elements as though they were part of waking reality. Through this process, individuals can evoke the emotional and sensory dimensions of the dream, deepening their connection to its meaning and significance. Bosnak's method also incorporates elements of active imagination, enabling clients to dialogue with dream figures and symbols, often leading to transformative insights and resolutions.

Similarly, Professor Stephen Aizenstat, founder of Dream Tending at Pacifica Graduate Institute, offers a complementary approach to dream work. In *Dream Tending* (2011), he focuses on animating dream images, allowing them to come alive and engage with the dreamer as living entities. Aizenstat encourages the use of all senses in these interactions, treating dream figures as dynamic presences. He also employs techniques like association and amplification to link dreams to personal and archetypal themes, his emphasis on animation distinguishes his method.

Roshani, one of my research participants, beautifully demonstrated the healing potential of dreams through a somatic approach. In her dream, three butterflies represented three significant moments from her childhood. During a session where I guided her to engage with the butterflies using active imagination, she vividly felt them caressing her face, fluttering on her skin, and leaving their colors behind. Reflecting on the experience, she shared, "It was like connecting to certain details of my childhood that I had almost forgotten."

Inspired by this encounter, Roshani painted an image of the three butterflies alongside three children (see Chapter 6), creating a unified symbol of her healing journey across different life stages.

Later, she crafted a three-dimensional butterfly as a tangible reminder of the transformative and healing touch of her dream imagery. This symbolic artwork became a source of emotional healing, integrating and nurturing her inner child across these various life stages.

Fostering somatic awareness while approaching dreams non-interpretively allows insights and meanings to flow naturally. When the barriers between clients and myself dissolve through a higher level of self-awareness, knowledge shifts from a

Figure 4.3 A three-dimensional butterfly crafted from yellow silk paper. Picture taken by Roshani

rational mode of knowing-about to an intuitive mode of knowing-by-direct-experience (Clark, 1973). This intuitive understanding often emerges through somatic awareness, manifesting as kinaesthetic responses such as feelings and sensations.

Mary (see Chapter 6) offers an example of this. She associated some of her dream images to qualities that she needed to integrate; self-confidence, for example, was represented by a cockerel, "that kind of chest opening." Ingrained sensory memories were described as: "I felt uplifted, I felt like awakened and lifted," "… Yeah, and I felt a lot lighter," "And I felt more luminous as well."

Somatic awareness allowed the participants and me to fully embrace the present moment, opening ourselves to intuitive insights and connecting our bodies to the wisdom emerging from the space between breaths.

The Transcendent Qualities of Dream Symbols

Besides supporting the reflection and integration of unconscious material, dreams also play a crucial role in fostering psychospiritual development (Kuiken, 2014). Research indicates that perceiving dreams as sacred enhances their potential to inspire meaningful, positive change in one's life (Phillips & Pargament, 2002). Ziemer (2014) suggests that dreams enable a fusion between the dreamer and the transcendent qualities symbolized within the dream, elevating consciousness and allowing individuals to integrate the transformative, even "magical," dimensions of dreams into their waking lives. This view aligns with my own research (Carod, 2021), which underscores how consciously engaging with the symbolic depth of dreams can support both personal and spiritual growth. Mary identified with a dream image that she named "the centered man" (Figure 6.4), a big man who stood peacefully while being attacked by a furious crowd. Being in contact with this image in active imagination made her feel very peaceful and calm. Reminding herself of this archetype while living through stressful events provided her with clarity, serenity, and compassion. The centered man in the dream reflects the Jungian archetype of the animus, which frequently appears in dreams as a figure of the opposite gender to the dreamer. This particular dream could be classified as a "big dream" due to the numinous quality of the archetype – represented by the centered man – standing apart from the ordinary patterns of everyday life. Such dreams often carry profound psychological significance and suggest transformative potential. When Mary reflected upon this dream, she experienced "lucid surrender," what Ziemer (2014) describes as an integration of feeling, thinking, and knowing that leads to an "awareness of being," a fully integrated state of inner alignment with the higher realms of consciousness.

I began my dream practice using Jung's technique of association (Jung, 1960). I recorded the memories evoked by the dream, along with interpretations and related mythological images to amplify its meaning. Following this, I practiced active imagination by dialoguing with dream symbols, archetypes, and the associated images, eventually capturing the results through drawing. In time, I closely adopted archetypal psychologist James Hillman's approach (1975) of not wanting to transform a dream image into a strictly defined meaning but rather allowing a rich reflection on it.

I continued to practice this creative method regularly, combining images from different dreams and allowing them to speak to me. Rather than analyzing or elaborating on the images in detail, I chose to let the dreams work on my psyche, focusing on their somatic effects. I surrendered to their messages, observing how the images generated meaning from within, often intertwined with bodily sensations and kinaesthetic reactions. This non-interpretive approach fosters the natural emergence of insights, facilitating a state of flow and a sense of inner calm.

In my dream, "The Blue Elephant" (see Figure 4.10), I dove into pristine blue waters, and at the bottom, I found a beautiful indigo blue elephant. Just by seeing it, I experienced a sense of peace and awe that stayed with me throughout the day. The sight filled me with a profound sense of respect and fascination for its powerful healing energy.

In another of my dreams, I found myself witnessing a mesmerizing scene – a turtle embracing the world. The sight filled me with a profound sense of respect and fascination for its powerful healing energy. I reflected on the symbolism of turtles in different cultures, such as their connection to Vishnu in Hinduism, the sustainer and preserver of the universe (Figure 4.4).

The presence of Vishnu in the form of a turtle symbolizes stability, patience, and profound wisdom, attributes that were certainly evident in the dream image of the turtle. In addition, I considered its sacred significance to Native Americans, representing connection to the Earth and compassion for all beings. This dream awakened me to a deeper understanding of my connection to the Earth and healing, leaving a lasting impact on me and reminding me of the importance of incorporating the qualities symbolized by the turtle into my daily life.

These two dreams could be described as transcendent because of their magical atmosphere and the sensation of spreading warmth. The contact with the numinous (not only the content of the image) was in itself healing (Bogart, 2009; Hillman,

Figure 4.4 The turtle embracing the world. Illustration by the author

Figure 4.5 Resting in the back of the bus. Illustration by the author

1975; Jung, 1960). This direct experience can be noticed through somatic awareness by tuning into subtle physical sensations.

Embodying the dream through active imagination and somatic meditation – focusing on symbols, breath, and body signals – enables clients to fully experience its transformative power. This approach facilitates deeper integration of the dream's healing message on a physical and emotional level.

The dream image in Figure 4.5, which shows me sitting with eyes closed at the back of a bus, symbolizes the initial research phase of preparation, where there is an intention of setting ego aside. This image prompted me to turn inward and inspired trust in my subconscious mind to guide the process of inquiry.

The dream image depicted in Figure 4.6 also explored the themes of letting go, turning inward, and finding rest. The hot water bath evoked an inner kinaesthetic experience, symbolizing a deep connection to my inner self. The water pipeline extending from outside the window suggested that by surrendering to these kinaesthetic sensations, I could access the symbolic waters of the collective unconscious.

In both dreams, I am resting with eyes closed, not facing reality in the physical realm; I am in a process of gestation between worlds.

At that moment, the dream imagery encouraged me to lower the threshold of my consciousness, allowing me to observe the powerful forces at work within the unconscious.

Connecting Dream Symbols with Astrological Archetypes

Like archetypal symbols, dreams speak to us in the language of the soul, a blending of emotion and symbolic meaning. While astrological patterns symbolize both the conscious and unconscious possibilities of our psyche, the dream brings light to a specific unconscious area that the inner self wants to explore at that moment (Johnson, 2009; Jung, 1960; Moore, 2014).

Figure 4.6 Relaxing in the waters of the subconscious. Illustration by the author

In dream work, coaches must avoid superimposing interpretations on clients' dreams, as this approach can hinder the client's personal exploration and understanding. Instead, coaches should encourage clients to engage in open-ended conversations with their dream symbols. By allowing clients to explore dream symbols and archetypes on their own terms, they can gain a fuller awareness of the depth inherent in their dream images and their connection to present existential concerns.

If the client can recall a recent dream, we will pay attention to what the subconscious mind is now wanting to explore. We start working with it, sensing the meaning more in our bodies than in our minds, empathizing with characters in the dream who seem at first to be the antagonists until a fresh and surprising idea appears (Moore, 2014). Next, through archetypal amplification, metaphors, myths, and archetypes can be used as tools to amplify dreams through different channels of creative expression. Archetypal amplification, a technique from Jungian psychology, involves analyzing dream or fantasy symbols by linking them to universal archetypes found in myths, folklore, and cultural imagery. This method deepens the understanding of personal experiences by connecting individual symbols to collective themes, revealing their psychological significance.

According to Bogart (2009, p. 7), the only correct interpretation of a dream is one that meets the dreamer's assent, which comes from the person's embodied "gut sense." We explore associations until they reveal their emotional core and psychological significance. When a powerful feeling emerges, we can assume that we've reached the essential core of the dream.

We then proceed to practice active imagination, dialoguing with the dream symbols and the archetypes and images associated with these symbols. What I find

Figure 4.7 Connecting dreams with astrological symbols. Illustration by the author

especially interesting is to use dreams as a magnifying glass to focus on specific archetypes and to identify links between dream symbols and planetary symbols. The image below shows how the dream themes that Marguerite brought reflect both planetary symbolism and the insights that arose from these connections.

When I began working with Marguerite (see Chapter 6), she was fully immersed in her Moon archetype. Deeply connected to her feminine side, she embraced her past memories and wounds while allowing herself the space to process her emotions. The dreams that Marguerite brought were associated with the Moon, the Sun, and Saturn. We found that the dream in which she was resting in the cave, not showing up, resonated with the Moon archetype; she described it as a phase in which she felt like the Earth when it is resting before giving its fruits again. In a later session, we connected her dream of giving birth to a baby without assistance to the Sun archetype, which symbolizes self-empowerment and the drive to create. This archetype reflected her impulse to initiate a new project for the community. As the central star of our solar system and a transcultural symbol, the Sun represents inner strength and vitality, embodying the life-giving energy that fuels creativity and purpose.

Marguerite associated her dream in which she felt "uncomfortable in the city, wearing fancy clothes, hanging out with old friends…" with the fact that she was now letting go of the old self (the consultant in business, the city girl). We associated this to the previous manifestation of her Saturn archetype, symbolizing old structures from which she was now distancing. This planetary archetype corresponds with the Jungian persona archetype, which is the social mask we present to the outside world.

Though Rose found joy in supporting others, she harbored an underlying belief that she didn't deserve love, care, or appreciation. Her dreams began delivering messages emphasizing the importance of self-care and assertiveness. One dream, in particular, about a root vegetable that was old, highlighted her pattern of self-neglect, encouraging her to reflect on her worthiness and her right to embrace life's pleasures. This realization found expression in real life when she treated herself to a beautiful sourdough bread, sparking a meaningful conversation with a woman from India who shared similar interests.

During a guided meditation, we revisited this dream and invoked her Venus archetype, associated with creativity, joy, beauty, relationships, and pleasure. Through this process, Rose recognized the need to express her creativity and enrolled in a writing course to nurture her Venusian archetype. As part of a creative exercise to rewrite her personal narrative, she composed the poem "Looking Up" (see Chapter 6), which concludes with her resolve to follow her birth stars.

Dreams contain symbols that play a significant role in our internal self-regulation processes. In the cases of Rose, Marguerite, Roshani, Spring, and Summer, we saw how these dream symbols became powerful tools for emotional healing and personal growth. For instance, Dreamer's old food, Marguerite's centered man, Roshani's butterflies, Spring's clay balls, and Summer's mask became focal points in their psychological energy landscapes, attracting energy and sparking processes that persisted in time.

Creating a Unifying Symbol through Synergy

The word "symbol" derives from the Latin *symbŏlum*, which in turn comes from the Greek *symbolon*. Etymologically, *symbolon* is formed from *syn* (meaning "together" or "union") and *ballein* (meaning "to throw" or "cast"). This term originates from the Greek practice of breaking a piece of ceramic in two, where one half was given to a sender and the other to a receiver. When the two pieces fit together perfectly, it signified that the messenger was legitimate and carried an authentic message. Thus, the etymology of "symbol" reflects the idea of things being "thrown together," highlighting the union of multiple elements in a symbolic representation. Synergy, originating from the Greek words *syn* ("together") and *ergon* ("work"), literally translates to "working together" or "cooperation." In the context of the psyche, it refers to the harmonization achieved by integrating its fragmented parts. This process is facilitated through active engagement with symbols that hold significance for the psyche.

The transcendent function of the unconscious, which Jung linked to the capacity for creating symbols, enables consciousness to move beyond internal conflicts and achieve a state of balance, peace, and unity. Jung's theory of the transcendent function asserts that the psyche has the capacity to reconcile opposing traits by creating unifying symbols:

The individual symbol has a duality: one aspect accessible to reason and another inaccessible. Its symbolic nature stimulates both sensation and intuition by being sensorially configured. The activity of the unconscious reveals a content that is balanced by opposites, forming an intermediate base where these opposites can be united. (1994, p. 560)

For Jung, symbols serve as gateways; they encapsulate and enable the transition into a liminal zone, allowing movement from one dimension of reality to another. These symbols effectively express the bipolarity of the archetypes and/or dream images involved (Jung, 1968, para. 553). They serve as gateways to flashes of intuition and moments of revelation (Jung, 1960, p. 92).

Jungian analyst Robert A. Johnson and Ruhl (2007), building on Jung's theory of the transcendent function, emphasized the unifying power of symbols in human life. For Johnson, symbols, which appear in religion, art, poetry, music, and culture, are key to healing the divisions within ego consciousness. Although modern life has distanced us from symbolic meaning, Johnson and Ruhl (2007) contends that the potential for symbolic sensibility remains within reach. By noticing and engaging with symbols that naturally arise in daily life and incorporating simple, personalized rituals, individuals can reconnect with the transformative power of symbols, unlocking their capacity for deep psychological healing.

Since the word "symbol" originates from the idea of "throwing together" different parts, we can create a unifying symbol through the process of active imagination, where archetypes and dream symbols interact.

Based on the big picture that the archetypes and dream symbols are offering, clients can create a visual symbolic image of the qualities that are emerging, expressing their new self. This artistic creation will serve as an anchor to focus attention and embody the desired state. The stories in Chapter 6 illustrate the transformative power of the unifying symbols. Marilyn's centered freedom, Mary's centeredness, Marguerite's heart hologram, Baijanti's heart, and Roshani's butterflies worked as unifying symbols of their psyche.

> In a dream, Spring encountered a wise old man in a room filled with popping clay balls and felt compelled to leave to avoid being struck. Later, her son's birthday gift—a bowl filled with stones—evoked vivid memories of the earlier dream. Here is the little bowl that my oldest son made. And when it was my birthday, he wrapped it up and put some special stones in it. Stones are very stable and can represent Saturn's stillness, and in the bowl itself, it's like more stability, like calming down, slowing down. (Spring, pp. 151–153, in Carod, 2021)

I encouraged her to engage in a creative work incorporating the archetypal qualities of her personality into a unifying symbol – an anchor to focus attention and embody her desired state or vision. Spring's artwork was prospective and anticipatory, revealing what was beginning to emerge within her. For the representation of her inner Saturn (structure in the physical world), she decided to build a container with clay and burned some sage as a symbol of her potential transformation.

Figure 4.8 Centered freedom. Illustration by Spring

She described her experience as "journeying into Saturn" and named the integration of her opposed needs – freedom and efficiency – "centered freedom." The visual image of this integration served as a powerful anchor, inspiring Spring to approach her tasks with greater focus and balance. It enabled her to harness her creativity while staying disciplined in her intellectual pursuits.

After her creative experience, she said:

> … I feel like the clay was representing the holder, the container of life, and the fire was representing the potential transformation. (pp. 127–130, in Carod, 2021)

Marguerite's journey of integrating archetypes (see Chapter 6), especially through the symbolism of her dream of the Merkabah, led to a powerful unifying symbol that encapsulates the archetypes she had been working with throughout her sessions. The Merkabah, a sacred geometrical symbol representing spiritual ascension, emerged in her dream as a central image, symbolizing transformation and divine connection. By engaging in drawing symbolic representations, she synthesized the archetypal energies of Jupiter (the teacher), Chiron (the wounded healer), and Mercury (the messenger).

Her drawing expressed a dynamic relationship between these archetypes:

The fire of Jupiter (the mentor, the teacher) transmutes my fears (Saturn) while the Merkabah occupies the heart space. Chiron (the wounded healer) uses her wound to guide others and Mercury (the messenger) uses his voice to share with the world.

Dreams played a central role in this process, as Marguerite integrated archetypal energies into her meditative practices and dream incubation. The archetypal synthesis became more than symbolic – it empowered her to align with her personal goals as a coach. Through somatic meditation and creative expression, she

Figure 4.9 Merkabah and archetypes. Illustration by Marguerite

fully embraced the archetypes of the Sun (self-expression, confidence) and Jupiter (expansion), using them as visual anchors of her future potential.

Her evolving perception of Chiron, transforming from a passive centaur to one in action, reflected her personal growth. Meanwhile, Jupiter's benevolent energy encouraged her to trust in her coaching opportunities, and Saturn guided her in establishing healthy boundaries in her relationships.

Guiding clients to engage with their personal symbols places them at the center of their healing journey, empowering them to actively participate in their growth and transformation. By embracing the role of creators, they can move beyond a victim mindset and take charge of their own narrative.

Insights and Synchronicities

The principle of correspondence between the inner and outer worlds, known in quantum physics as the "observer effect," is also recognized in Jungian psychology. Observing the connection between psychological states and external events led Jung to formulate the principle of synchronicity, which he defined as an "acausal connecting principle" or "meaningful coincidence" where something beyond mere chance is at play. Jung described the relationship between mind and matter as "the simultaneous occurrence of a certain psychic state with one or more external events which appear as meaningful parallels to the momentary subjective state – and in certain cases, vice versa" (Jung, 1952, para. 850). Jung (1990, para. 480) also describes such experiences in *Symbols and the Interpretation of Dreams*:

> Symbols are natural products that do not occur only in dreams. They can appear in any number of psychic manifestations: there are symbolic thoughts and feelings, symbolic acts and situations, and it often looks as if not only the unconscious but even inanimate objects were concurring in the arrangement of symbolic patterns.

Recognizing the transformative potential of these "meaningful coincidences," Jung considered them "empirical evidence of a *psychoid unconscious* – an underlying ordering principle in the *unus mundus*, or unified reality, that reflects a transcendental teleological meaning" (Jung, 1952, para. 942). These synchronistic events often initiate a healing process by integrating inner and outer realities, giving individuals a new sense of orientation in a world that seems to embody deeper purposes and meanings beyond human subjectivity (Tarnas, 2006, p. 50).

Sometimes an event or something someone says will bring a recent dream to mind. However, the dream frequently comes into awareness silently and rapidly on its own. When a dream meets with reality, one must remain aware in order to find connections and get insights.

Working with dreams and archetypes fosters the emergence of insights and synchronicities. Signals that persist, such as images (including archetypal images) from dreams or visions, may be received as synchronistic manifestations. An essential characteristic of synchronistic events is an emotional or psychic charge that makes them meaningful, producing a numinous effect on the person experiencing them. Insights arrive suddenly and vividly and bring a great deal of knowledge in a brief period with a sense of permanence (Miller & de C'Baca, 2001, p. 19). Mary and Spring expressed a sense of immediate recognition, as if they somehow already knew it to be true:

> … and that what came up was something that needs to come up because of the interconnected intelligence of life, and this is what needs to be heard in that moment. (Mary, pp. 123–124, in Carod, 2021)
> … suddenly that idea came in a field of information, through my body, and perhaps I was open to this subjective field or transpersonal field, and something else was guiding me. (Spring, pp. 110–112, in Carod, 2021)

Once participants opened up to archetypes in general, once they started acknowledging them, they received more and more insights about their issues, and synchronicities turned up to show them even more. Some of the active imagination sessions were followed by meaningful synchronistic events. While watching a film with her daughter, Mary experienced a spontaneous synchronicity. The association between a recent dream image (black and white tiles) and the ying-yang symbol provided her with a spontaneous insight:

> My daughter came into the room showing me the symbols of the ying and the yang. Then, a couple of days later, I created a montage of a dream, and actually this morning, I realized there was something missing, and it was the black and white tiles and the connection between the ying and the yang, the working of the ying and the yang together in harmony. (Mary, pp. 38–30, in Carod, 2021)

The ying-yang symbol suggested her to embrace all the parts of her personality, the positive as well as the parts that felt fearful.

It is remarkable that synchronicities increased once my research participants created a symbolic representation of their archetypes and dream images. Both Mary's ying-yang symbol and Spring's bowl filled with stones appeared in their lives after they had actively engaged with archetypes in a participatory co-creative process during their active imagination sessions.

Jung highlights the importance of analyzing a series of dreams rather than interpreting isolated ones, emphasizing how such an approach reveals the ongoing dynamics of the unconscious. In *Collected Works*, Vol. 18, para. 162, he states:

> You can speculate anything about an isolated dream; but if you compare a series of, say, twenty or a hundred dreams, then you can see interesting things. You see the process that is going on in the unconscious from night to night, and the continuity of the unconscious psyche extending through day and night.

Jung underscores the value of dream series in uncovering patterns, recurring themes, and gradual psychological shifts, offering a more holistic view of the psyche's processes. By identifying changes and developments across multiple dreams, one can better understand the continuity and evolution of unconscious material.

During 2020, I started creative work with dream series. I dreamed about many symbols related to actors, birds, singers, dancers, and people who were expressing themselves. While looking at the images that I painted, I felt a new method of action was calling for me to become more extroverted and to express my creativity. As in my other dream collage using Pandora's box, the journey is represented by a variety of images: traveling by bus, car, and rail, as well as routes and pilgrimages that cross mountains and rivers. These images raised awareness of how I progressed through life. Looking at it from a spiritual perspective, a journey is never just a trip across distance; it's an expression of the deep longing for revelation and transformation that drives the very act of traveling. Therefore, the voyage here is a symbol of a period of studying, inquiring, seeking, and intensely living via new and meaningful experiences.

The little bird in the upper left corner in a jar full of liquid is meant to be released. The bird is immersed in water, in a moment of reflection and transformation. The bird symbol has been associated with concepts, spiritual messages, and imagination. A series of dreams about birds began with this one, and I came to associate the bird's desire for freedom with my own soul's yearning for expression.

In the lower left corner, I'm doing yoga on the roof of the building while half of it is on fire. I wasn't worried since I understood the fire was helpful for me as a purifying force and symbol of transformation. Next to this I'm writing on a blackboard. Teaching and library dreams were common themes that reflected my daily activity. A bath in the swimming pool depicted in the center of the painting serves as a metaphorical cleansing of the mind and body, preparing for the next phase.

I drew the Temperance as an archetype that coordinates all these symbols. The figure of Temperance is absorbed in the act of pouring water from one cup to another. To temper means to create balance or a desirable state by blending or adding.

Figure 4.10 The temperance. Illustration by the author

The liquid within the cups springs from an inexhaustible source, symbolically representing the flow from the higher unconscious to the lower mind. This act reflects the slow but harmonious process of balancing mundane concerns with the higher realms. There is grace, wisdom, and a sense of inner connection in the act, which conveys a strong presence.

As I reflected on this, I experienced a synchronistic event: I went to the kitchen for a drink of water and, without thinking, found myself pouring water from one full glass into an empty one. In this instance, like Temperance, I felt drawn to reconcile two worlds or opposites and find a way to blend them harmoniously.

To work effectively with synchronicities, a metaphorical understanding of events is essential.

Through engaging in art inspired by dream and planetary symbols, I stepped into a transformative force field that culminated in this synchronistic experience.

Note

1 Artemidorus, a 3rd century AD soothsayer from Ephesus, authored *Oneirocritica* ("Interpretation of Dreams"), a significant work offering insights into ancient beliefs, superstitions, and religious rites. The first three books of *Oneirocritica* provide an extensive overview of dreams and divination for a general audience, while the last two were intended for his son, an aspiring dream interpreter. Book four shifts focus from general dream content to interpretative techniques, emphasizing the need to understand

the dreamer's background – occupation, health interpretative techniques, – to accurately interpret dreams. Book five presents a collection of 95 additional dreams for practice. Artemidorus highlights his empirical approach, stating that his findings are based on extensive experiences, fulfilled dreams, and consultations with interpreters across Greece, Italy, and Asia Minor.

Artemidorus. (1992). Artemidorus Daldianus. In *The New Encyclopædia Britannica* (15th edn., Vol. 1, p. 599). Encyclopædia Britannica Inc.

References

Aizenstat, S. (2011). *Dream tending: Awakening to the healing power of dreams.* Spring Journal, Inc.

Bogart, G. (2009). *Dreamwork and self healing.* Routledge.

Bosnak, R. (2007). *Embodiment. Creative imagination in medicine, art and travel.* Routledge.

Bulkeley, K. (2008). *Dreaming in the world's religions: A comparative history.* New York University Press.

Carod, A. (2021). *The transformative experiences of coaching using archetypal imagery within a participatory framework: An organic inquiry.* John Moores University.

Corbin, H. (1964). Mundus imaginalis or the imaginary and the imaginal. *Spring: Journal of Archetype and Culture,* 1964, 1–19.

Clark, F. V. (1973). Exploring intuition: Prospects and possibilities. *The Journal of Transpersonal Psychology,* 2, 156–170.

Freud, S. (1899/1913). *The interpretation of dreams.* James Strachey Ed.

Gendlin, E. T. (1986). *Let your body interpret your dreams.* Chiron Publications.

Greene, L. (2018). *Jung's understanding of astrology. Prophecy, magic, and the qualities of time.* Routledge.

Hillman, J. (1975). *Re-visioning psychology.* Harper Perennial.

Hillman, J. (1979). *The dream and the underworld.* Harper & Row.

Hillman, J., & Moore, T. (1998). *The essential James Hillman: A blue fire.* Routledge.

Hughes, J. D. (2000). Dream interpretation in ancient civilizations. *Dreaming,* 10, 7–18.

Johnson, R. (2009). *Inner work: Using dreams and active imagination for personal growth.* Harper One.

Johnson, R. A., & Ruhl, J. M. (2007). *Living your unlived life: Coping with unrealized dreams and fulfilling your purpose in the second half of life.* Tarcher Perigee.

Jung, C. G. (1952). Synchronicity: An acausal connecting principle. (R. F. C. Hull, Trans.). In H. Read, M. Fordham, G. Adler, & W. McGuire (Eds.), *Collected works* (Vol. 8). Princeton University Press.

Jung, C. G. (1960). The transcendent function (R. F. C. Hull, Trans.). In H. Read, M. Fordham, G. Adler, & W. McGuire (Eds.), *The collected works of C. G. Jung* (Vol. 8). Princeton University Press.

Jung, C. G. (1966). Two essays on analytical psychology. In H. Read, M. Fordham, G. Adler, & W. McGuire (Eds.), *Collected works* (Vol. 7). Princeton University Press.

Jung, C. G. (1968). *Man and his symbols.* Anchor Press.

Jung, C. G. (1974). *Dreams* (R. F. C. Hull, Trans). Princeton University Press.

Jung, C. G. (1976). The symbolic life. In H. Read, M. Fordham, G. Adler, & W. McGuire (Eds.), *Collected works* (Vol. 18). Princeton University Press.

Jung, C. G. (1984). *Seminar on dream analysis: Notes of the seminar given in 1928–1930.* (W. McGuire, Ed.). Princeton University Press.

Jung, C. G. (1990). *Symbols and the interpretation of dreams*. Princeton University Press.

Jung, C. G. (1994). *Tipos psicológicos*. Edhasa.

Kuiken, D. (2014). Impactful dreams, sublime feeling, and reflective awareness [Paper presentation]. Conference of the International Association for the Study of Dreams, Berkeley, California.

Lewis, N. (1996). *The interpretation of dreams & portents in antiquity*. Bolchazy-Carducci Publishers.

Miller, W. R., & de C'Baca, J. (2001). *Quantum change. When epiphanies and sudden insights transform ordinary lives*. The Guildford Press.

Moore, T. (2014). *A religion of one's own* (2nd ed.) Penguin Publishing Group.

Phillips, R. E., & Pargament, K. I. (2002). The sanctification of dreams: Prevalence and implications. *Dreaming, 12*(3), 141–153.

Shaw, G. (2003). *Containing ecstasy: The strategies of Iamblichean theurgy* (Vol. 21). Dalhousie University, Dept. of Classics.

Shaw, G. (2016). Archetypal psychology, dream work, and neoplatonism. In H. T. Hakl (Ed.), *Octagon: The quest for wholeness* (Vol. 2, pp. 329–358). H. Frietsch Verlag.

Shaw, G. (2024). *Hellenic tantra: The theurgic platonism of Iamblichus*. Angelico Press. Kindle Edition.

Tarnas, R. (2006). *Cosmos and psyche: Intimations of a new world view*. Penguin Publishing Group. Kindle Edition.

Vedfelt, O. (2016). *A guide to the world of dreams: An integrative approach to dream work*. Taylor & Francis. Kindle Edition.

Wangyal, T. (1998). *The Tibetan Yogas of dream and sleep*. Snow Lion.

Ziemer, M. (2014). Lucid surrender and Jung's alchemical coniunctio. In R. Hurd & K. Bulkeley (Eds.), *Lucid dreaming: New perspectives on consciousness in sleep* (Vol. 1, pp. 145–166). Praeger.

Chapter 5

Astrological Archetypes in Coaching Practice

Astrology's Transcultural Legacy: Seeking Guidance from the Stars

The fundamental premise of astrology is that the cosmos is designed by a higher intelligence and operates according to an intricate order. The Greek etymology of astrology, originating from "astro" meaning stars and "logos" meaning words or conversation, underscores its profound focus on divine communication. The stars speak to us through their geometric configuration and their symbolic meaning.

Thus, astrology teaches us that the stars communicate this beautiful order existing in the universe, guiding us toward a deeper understanding of ourselves and of our interconnectedness with the cosmos.

Fascinatingly, astrology is practiced in the majority of cultures, albeit at varying degrees of complexity and evolution. It is interesting to note that all civilizations originally started from the assumption that everything in the universe is interconnected and manifests itself in a mathematical or geometrical sequence determined at different times with differentiated qualities. Astrology's influence on human affairs transcended cultural boundaries, shaping early scientific and philosophical thought in several ancient civilizations. In Mesopotamia, astrology laid the groundwork for scientific development, integrating celestial observation with earthly events. Ancient China saw emperors rely on court astrologers to guide decisions by interpreting celestial movements, while in India, Jyotish (Vedic astrology) has been practiced for centuries to foresee events and inform choices. Across these cultures, a shared belief in the cosmos' interconnectedness emphasized the importance of living in harmony with the natural world.

The heavenly bodies were bestowed with divine character; stars and planets conveyed messages as well as warnings ("namburbi" in Babylon, "omen" in Latin) on behalf of gods and goddesses or God that could be avoided. Professor Angela Voss (2000, p. 33) explains that divinatory practices in early societies were less about predicting the future and more about seeking guidance from unseen powers in human endeavors. The process, rooted in ritual, was known in Greek as *katarche* (later evolving into the Latin terms *auspice* and *augury*). Success in these practices relied on the proper alignment between humans and divine forces. Voss emphasizes

DOI: 10.4324/9781003627258-6

that destiny was seen as negotiable, with outcomes shaped by human choices and the ability to interpret omens intuitively. Significance was not derived from rigid theories or techniques but from recognizing signs in relation to current concerns.

Professor Richard Tarnas (2006, p. 63) notes that astrology flourished during some of the most intellectually and culturally creative periods in Western history, such as classical Greek and Roman antiquity, the Hellenistic era, the High Middle Ages, the Italian Renaissance, and the Elizabethan age. The same pattern can be observed in periods of scientific and cultural prominence in the Islamic world and India. Astrology maintained a close relationship with astronomy throughout the evolution of Western cosmology, including during the Copernican Revolution. Tarnas highlights the high intellectual caliber of those who supported astrology, including key figures like Plato, Aristotle, Kepler, and Jung.

Modern astrology has evolved from being solely a predictive tool to serving as a vehicle of self-reflection and personal development. Many individuals now turn to astrology to gain insights into their relationships, careers, and daily lives, seeking meaning and connection in an uncertain world.

By exploring astrology, we can tap into the universal energy that flows through everything and gain insights into our own unique path and purpose in the grand scheme of the cosmos. Ultimately, astrology allows us to see that we are not just isolated beings but rather integral pieces of the intricate puzzle that makes up the universe. The connection to a higher intelligence provides us with a compass that guides us to follow our stars, as we navigate the sometimes turbulent waters of the human experience.

The Roots of Western Astrology: From Sumeria to Egypt and Greece

Both Egyptian and Babylonian civilizations played crucial roles in the origins of Western astrology, each contributing distinct emphases and developments to the field. However, despite their rich astrological histories, astrology has often encountered disdain from historians, resulting in the neglect of many Sumerian and Egyptian astrological tablets.

In ancient Babylon, around 3000 BC, the development of writing, commerce, and a complex religious system laid the groundwork for astrological practices. The classical sky map with 48 Greek constellations originated from Mesopotamia between 3200 and 500 BC and a Mediterranean-based tradition around 2800 BC, which used constellations for navigation (Rogers, 1998).

Star lists were used to classify groups of fixed stars relevant to the celestial omen series *Enūma Anu Enlil*. The constellations evolved in phases between 3200 BC and 500 BC, with the 12 zodiacal signs and their associated animals being the most crucial part of the divine set.[1] Babylonians attributed divine significance to every element in the universe, as seen in the *Enuma Anu Enlil* series, indicating that gods designed constellations and established heavenly signs. The *Enuma Anu Enlil*, a comprehensive Babylonian astrological work, comprises 70 tablets and interprets 6,500–7,000 omens related to celestial and atmospheric phenomena, particularly relevant to the king and the state (Baigent, 1995, p. 73). The Venus tablet of the *Enuma Anu Enlil* from the first dynasty of Babylon (1900–1600 BC) shows that astrology had become a systematic discipline of significance to the king and the state.

The Mesopotamian worldview saw earth and heavens as complementary, with mankind being partially divine, created from the gods' divine flesh and blood (Baigent, 1995). The *Enuma Elish*,[2] a poem of seven tablets, contains the Sumerian account of the creation of the earth and mankind, providing a foundational text for understanding their worldview and the role of divine order. This ancient epic tells the story of Marduk, the chief god of Babylon, who defeats the elder goddess Tiamat, restores order to chaos, and becomes the Lord of the Gods of Heaven and Earth. The Babylonians believed in Marduk's rule as the ultimate authority, providing guidance and protection in all aspects of their lives. His sacred animals and association with Jupiter further solidified his importance, shaping their beliefs and values.

The creation stories of Canaanite, Greek, Egyptian, and Phoenician civilizations are also similar to the *Enuma Elish*. These myths frequently depict a battle between chaos and order, with a powerful deity emerging victorious to establish the world as we know it.

Babylonian and Greek astrology shared elements, including mythology, the zodiac, and constellations' associations with planets. Marduk, identified with Greek Zeus and Roman Jupiter, rose to lead the Mesopotamian pantheon, elevated by Babylonian king Hammurabi (1792–1750 BCE).

The Chaldeans, a group of ancient Babylonian philosophers, were guardians of the sacred science, combining astrological knowledge, divination, religion, and magic. Neoplatonic Iamblichus, in his work *On the Egyptian Mysteries*, described the means of union with God and elevated the Chaldean Oracles to supreme authority.

Astrology developed progressively during the second millennium BC, culminating in the standard canon found in the 7th century BC library at Nineveh. In each city, a team of astrologers worked for the king, preserving mythology and other texts such as omens, astrology, divination, the Gilgamesh epic, esoteric writings, ritual texts, medical recipes, dream books, and astronomical books (Parpola, in Baigent, 1995).

Babylonians viewed celestial and terrestrial omens as signs or warnings, indicating the gods' determination of fate.[3] However, these predicted events could be averted through magical rituals or *namburbi*, challenging the notion of inevitability (Van der Waerden, 1974).

They believed in a pantheon of gods who controlled various aspects of life, with the sky god Anu being the most powerful. Their religious rituals often involved offerings and sacrifices to appease these gods, ensuring a bountiful harvest or successful military campaign. Their advanced knowledge of astronomy and astrology allowed them to predict future events and make decisions. This fascination with the heavens influenced their religious beliefs, with ziggurat temples built as connections between Earth and the divine realm above. These buildings had a distinctive stepped pyramidal design, and only priests and highly respected individuals could enter the temple at the top, believed to be the gods' residence.

On the other side, ancient Egyptian astrology emphasized the symbolism of the Sun, often associated with royalty and the belief in resurrection after death. Particularly notable is the fourth Old Kingdom dynasty, during which the construction of the Pyramids of Giza occurred around 2613–2589 BCE. This period also saw the first surviving evidence of interest in planetary movements among the Egyptians (Campion, 2012, p. 84).

Furthermore, the Egyptians' interest in astronomy led to the development of a calendar based on the celestial motions of stars and planets. This calendrical system not only facilitated accurate predictions of agricultural cycles but also demonstrated the Egyptians' keen observation of celestial phenomena and their integration into daily life.

Egypt's esoteric and occult traditions have deeply influenced philosophical thought, drawing inspiration from a rich tapestry of ancient civilizations spanning India, Persia, Chaldea, China, Japan, Assyria, ancient Greece, and Rome. Egyptian religion is best described as cosmotheism, with many gods playing roles in the cosmic order.

The two most significant gods in Egyptian mythology were Osiris, lord of the underworld and god of the dead, and Ra, the Sun god. Osiris symbolized death, resurrection, and the Nile flood cycle. He was murdered by his brother Seth, but his wife Isis resurrected him, allowing them to conceive a son, Horus. Isis was also a divine mourner and maternal carer for the dead in the underworld. She was one of the last ancient Egyptian gods to be worshiped, often associated with the Greek goddess Aphrodite.

During the first millennium BCE, Egyptians' devotion to religion thrived, as noted by Herodotus. Religious rituals focused on the cosmos, including the spinning of stars, the daily movement of the sun, the monthly changes of the moon, and the shifts of seasons. Key themes emerging from Egyptian cosmology include the existence of an immortal soul, divine planets, and an unchanging order of heavenly bodies.

The concept of *maat* (order) was fundamental in Egyptian thought. The king's role was to set *maat* in place of *isfet* (disorder). *Maat* embraced notions of reciprocity, justice, truth, and moderation. *It* was personified as a goddess and the creator's daughter and received a cult of her own. The pharaoh was tasked with ensuring *maat* by maintaining order and harmony in society through fair and just rule. This system allowed for the flourishing of arts, sciences, and overall well-being of the people.

Similarly, in Greek society, astrology played a crucial role in decision-making and understanding the will of the gods. The Greek ideas of truth, justice, and equilibrium are closely related to the Egyptian concept of *maat* which guided their lives and beliefs. Both civilizations believed that by following the guidance of the stars, they could maintain balance and order in their societies. For example, when a solar eclipse occurred in ancient Egypt, it was seen as a warning that *maat* was being threatened and immediate action needed to be taken to restore balance.

The ancient Egyptians believed that astrology primarily influenced the mortal body, leaving the soul independent. In their cosmology, the soul underwent trials in the afterlife, judged by Osiris, where its deeds were weighed against Maat's feather of truth. Successful souls were purified in the eighth sphere and reunited with the divine source.

Egyptian astrology significantly influenced Greek and Roman systems, associating celestial bodies with specific deities. Saturn corresponded to Khnum, the creator god shaping humans on a potter's wheel. Jupiter paralleled Amun, symbolizing control and power, while Mars aligned with Montu, representing war and aggression. Ra, the Sun god, embodied vitality and illumination, Venus was linked to Hathor, goddess of love and fertility, and Mercury was connected to Thoth, the god of wisdom and magic. Khonsu, associated with the Moon, symbolized transformation and rejuvenation.

These myths found their way into Hermetic traditions, blending Egyptian deities with esoteric teachings. Hermetism, rooted in the figure of Hermes Trismegistus, revered as the father of astrology and alchemy, expanded on themes like causation, transmutation, and polarity. The teachings emphasized the symbolic significance of planets across disciplines such as philosophy, alchemy, and astrology, reflecting the enduring influence of Egyptian cosmological thought.[4]

In Babylon, the earliest horoscopic chart that has survived to this day is dated to the year 410 BCE and pertains to an individual. Introduced in Greece from Babylon and Syria in the 4th century BCE, the worship of planetary deities laid the groundwork for astrology, which could be practiced in various forms – naturalistic or religious, scholarly or simple, elite or popular (Campion, 2012, p. 156). In the year 280 BC, the Babylonian priest Berossos established an astrology school on the island of Kos in Greece. This school was instrumental in the dissemination of the zodiac throughout the Hellenistic world.

When Alexander the Great conquered Alexandria in 332 CE, Greek dominance and Hellenistic culture merged Greek Babylonian and Egyptian cosmology, forming the basis for contemporary Western astrology. In the 2nd century BCE, ancient practices and philosophies were intertwined, including Babylonian astrology, Egyptian calendars, Hermeticism, Pythagorean sacred mathematics, and Stoics and Platonist teachings.

The Platonic Academy in Athens faced closure in 529 AD under the orders of Emperor Justinian, leading the last philosophers, persecuted by Christians, to move East to the court of the Persian King Cosroes I in the city of Ctesiphon.

After the attack of the Catholic Church against all forms of paganism, and in the face of the overwhelming power of monotheism and the rational philosophy of the Greeks, the possibility that we are connected to gods was no longer tolerated (Shaw, 2008).

The Ordered Cosmos in Greek ThoughtThe belief in astrology's fundamental premise of causality, according to which planetary movements directly influence earthly events, has persisted for the past 2,000 years. This concept has its origins in ancient Greek beliefs of a finite universe, in which the planets occupy a hierarchical position below the creator. In Greek cosmology, the god Uranus, representing the heavens and stars, lies over Gaia, the Earth, every night. His children, the Titans and other beings, displease Uranus, who banishes them to the womb of Gaia, symbolizing the rejection of parts of ourselves that we do not accept. Gaia persuades her son Cronus to castrate Uranus. After the castration, Uranus's genitals fall into the sea, giving birth to Venus, the goddess of love. This event symbolizes the restoration of balance or the rectification of justice, suggesting that facing and transforming problematic aspects can lead to harmony and love. The classical period, spanning from the 8th century BCE until the early 6th century CE, marked a pivotal era in the development of astrology. This period saw the emergence of astrology as a means to understand one's place in the universe and seek guidance in decision-making.

In Greek, the term "kosmos" signifies an order of great beauty, a concept highly esteemed by Platonic and Stoic Greek philosophers, who perceived magnificent order and beauty in the universe. They believed that this order was evidence of a divine creator or intelligence guiding the cosmos. To them, the cosmos was not just a random collection of matter, but a harmonious and purposeful whole. Greek philosophers saw the idea of the cosmos as the gods' sharing of power, explaining how the heavens and natural powers are organized logically and giving each one a role and a limit.

Most authors suggest that the term "kosmos" achieved the meaning used today thanks to the Pythagoreans. The biographer Diogenes Laërtius (180 CE) states that Pythagoras was the first to call the sky kosmos, which refers to the universal order that governs and permeates all aspects of existence. Nevertheless, the idea of kosmos was mentioned earlier by Anaximander[5] and Anaximenes.[6]

Pythagoras, a renowned figure in ancient Greek philosophy, lived from approximately 570 to 490 BCE. Evidence suggests Pythagoras was a mathematician and cosmologist, as referred to by Herodotus as a wise man and by Heraclitus as a man pursuing inquiry. Isocrates attributes mathematical work or rational cosmology to Pythagoras, who brought "other philosophy" to Greece from Egypt, focusing on temple rituals. Properpticus says that Pythagoras affirmed that human beings were born to contemplate the heavens and described himself as an observer of nature (Zhmud, 2012, pp. 56, 259–260).

With few educational options in his hometown of Samos, Pythagoras set out on a voyage of intellectual discovery. He sought answers to fundamental questions about existence and the cosmos. Traveling across Greece, he eventually found himself in Asia Minor, where he studied Zoroastrianism before settling in Egypt.[7] Immersed in esoteric Zoroastrian mysteries, Pythagoras formulated the famous Pythagorean doctrine of the musical harmony of the universe. In Egypt, he immersed himself in the teachings of the Egyptian priests in the cosmopolitan city of Memphis until the Persian invasion in 525 BCE led to his capture and relocation to Babylon (Clayton & Price, 2002).

Heraclitus (550–480 BC),[8] like Pythagoras, viewed the soul as the fundamental principle, considering it a spark of the stars' intrinsic essence. Heraclitus saw the soul as embodying harmony through the synthesis of opposites. Pythagoras, meanwhile, divided the soul into three parts: intellect (in the brain), passion (in the heart), and reason (immortal and uniquely human). He defined soul harmony as the balance and moderation of these three dimensions, enabling the soul to reach its highest potential and connect with the divine.

Pythagoras believed that enhancing intelligence through learning and reason, restraining desire through self-discipline, and balancing these aspects would result in a fulfilled soul, capable of experiencing a profound connection to the divine and true enlightenment. The Pythagorean school required strict adherence to a code of conduct that included abstaining from meat, refraining from speaking ill of others, and maintaining a disciplined lifestyle. Only those who could demonstrate virtuous behaviors were allowed access to the philosophical teachings of Pythagoras and his followers.

By adhering to these principles, Pythagoras himself attained great wisdom and insight, inspiring his followers to value balance and moderation in all aspects of life. His teachings have influenced many philosophers and spiritual leaders, highlighting the importance of cultivating intellect, controlling emotions, and finding inner harmony to unlock the soul's true potential.

Pythagoras was the first to introduce the concept of the natal chart divided into 12 houses as we know it today. The Pythagoreans derived their ideas about numbers and measurement from the Egyptian priests. In Plato's Elench. 4.28, Hippolytus says that according to the Pythagoreans, the Sun, the greatest geometer and mathematician, "is set in the whole cosmos like the soul in bodies," and "the Sun makes the cosmos numerical and geometrical, dividing it into twelve parts" (Afonasin & Afonasina, 2019).

The Pythagoreans passed down a collection of unique sayings attributed to the Master. These offer intriguing mythological explanations for questions like "What are the Pleiades? The Muses' Lyre. What are oceans? The tears of Cronos." These were referred to as symbols, and they served as forms of identification. It was easy for anyone in possession of these symbols to recognize other members of the group. Pythagoras also had a privileged relationship with Apollo, the god of the arts, the light of the sun, and beauty, and incorporated the authority of Delphic Apollo in his teachings (Kahn, 2001).

It is known to us that a number of Greek Philosophers (Pythagoras, Democritus, Plato, and others) set journeys to the East in quest of knowledge. Pythagoras was familiar with the teachings of a number of Indian, Persian, Babylonian, and Egyptian mature scholars of the time. The Greeks borrowed the Egyptian idea of souls ascending to the stars, which later became a key component of Hellenistic astrology and ultimately encouraged Christian belief in a celestial paradise (Campion, 2012).

In the 6th century BC, the Pythagoreans integrated science and spirituality, viewing contemplation and alignment with cosmic order as keys to liberation from the cycle of reincarnation and achieving immortality. In Pythagoreanism, the doctrine of metempsychosis, that is, the transformation of the human soul into another form, is one of the most striking examples of the Hindu worldview.

According to Clement of Alexandria, Pythagoras learned from Sonchis, a prominent Egyptian prophet, and exchanged ideas with Chaldeans, Magi, and Brahmans (Afonasin et al., 2012). Pythagoras's exposure to these varied traditions deeply influenced his philosophical outlook, leading him to adopt beliefs in reincarnation and the transmigration of souls, concepts often associated with Indian spirituality but which Pythagoras integrated into his own philosophical framework.

The Platonic Archetypal Cosmos

The Platonic archetypal cosmos finds its roots in the Greek mythological pantheon, the rituals of mystery religions, and the Pythagorean vision of a unified, numinous order. This divine reality transcends human reason and is best conveyed through myth, metaphor, and symbolism. The Pythagorean tradition highlighted a mathematically ordered and numinous universe, reflecting archetypal principles and divine intelligence. From this perspective, understanding the cosmos is intrinsically tied to self-knowledge (Tarnas, 2011, pp. 65–69).

Plato (470–399 BCE) and Aristotle (384–322 BCE), two prominent figures of this period, shared the belief in an ordered cosmos where humans are intricately connected to the stars and planets both physically and spiritually. His Myth of Er in *The Republic* emphasized the interplay of fate, free will, and cosmic order, depicting the universe as governed by the "spindle of necessity," with stars and planets influencing the soul's journey.

Plato introduced the concept of "kosmos" as a world order, focusing on humans and their internal experiences. This shift toward relationship bonds and friendship emphasizes the importance of communal spirit in creating an ordered world, interconnecting humans with gods (Zelinová, 2021).

This viewpoint was later adopted by Pythagoreans and Neoplatonists. Plato's Poimandres[9] narrative emphasizes the importance of self-awareness and spiritual growth in order to break free from the cycle of reincarnation and ascend to a higher plane of existence. It offers a unique perspective on the nature of the soul and the path to ultimate liberation.

According to the Poimandres narrative, God created man in his own image, as well as a creator deity (the demiurge), who created seven administrators (the planets) ruled by Fate. Man is both immortal, above the heavenly authority, and mortal, and so a slave inside the system, because he has some of the characteristics of each of the seven planets. At death, the soul of the individual who acknowledges their immortal, intellectual, and divine essence ascends, progressively giving up undesirable attributes through each planet (for example, arrogance to the Sun, aggression to Mars, etc.).

Plato depicted the cosmos as a rational and living being, with the soul playing an integral, participatory role. In *Timaeus*, he likened the universe to a living organism, reflecting humanity as a microcosm of its structure. Celestial bodies such as the Sun, Moon, and planets are portrayed as divine entities, embodying heavenly qualities and connecting to the eternal nature of the soul.

Timaeus outlines a cosmogony that distinguishes the mutable physical world from the immutable, eternal realm. Plato attributes the universe's creation to the demiurge, a divine craftsman who, guided by fairness and goodness, shapes the cosmos based on an eternal model. This process gives rise to the world soul, imbuing the universe with intelligence and initiating its rational, eternal existence. In this framework, the visible gods – the world, planets, and stars – play pivotal roles in humanity's creation and in governing moral existence.

In *Phaidros*, he depicted the soul's journey as a chariot procession of 12 principal gods, symbolizing its connection to divine forces influencing human behavior (Van der Waerden, 1974). Furthermore, Plato believed that each soul is tied to a specific star, returning to its celestial origins upon death, rediscovering eternal values like beauty, justice, and goodness.

Plato's *Epinomis* linked the planets to Greek deities (later Romanized as Mercury, Venus, Mars, Jupiter, and Saturn), underscoring their symbolic roles in human affairs. Plato's allegories of Eros and Aphrodite highlighted love and beauty, while Zeus symbolized power and its impact. His cosmology also emphasized that the soul forgets its original knowledge when entering the material world and regains it through a virtuous life (*Phaedo*, 87d–88b).

Platonism, deeply rooted in the teachings of Plato and later expanded by Neoplatonic philosophers like Plotinus, is centered on the theory of Forms or Ideas. This theory distinguishes between two realms: the material world perceived by the senses, characterized by change and impermanence, and the eternal realm of Forms, which represents true, unchanging reality. Forms encompass archetypes, properties, patterns, and relationships, influencing later metaphysical and psychological concepts.

Neoplatonic thinkers, such as Plotinus,[10] Iamblichus, and Proclus, expanded upon Plato's ideas, introducing a metaphysical system based on emanation. This system posits a hierarchical structure descending from the One (ultimate reality), through Intellect and Soul, to the material world. As entities move further from the One, they become more fragmented, embodying imperfection and multiplicity. Plotinus, in his *Enneads*, described this process as cyclical, emphasizing the soul's potential to ascend back to the divine unity.

The Mystery Religions

Hellenistic mystery religions represented an essential aspect of spiritual practice in the ancient world. These religions coexisted with the state cult and philosophical traditions like Neoplatonism, offering transformative, esoteric rituals aimed at spiritual enlightenment. Unlike public worship, mysteries relied on initiation and secrecy, as the Greek term *myein* ("to close") suggests, symbolizing silence and introspection.

Plato, through Socratic dialogues such as in *Phaedrus*, emphasized that participation in the mysteries led to perfection, hinting at their role in spiritual awakening. Aristotle highlighted their transformative nature, explaining that initiates did not gain knowledge but underwent a profound change of state (Shaw, 2016).

Greek mystery schools often employed Socratic questioning to lead initiates to deeper self-understanding and awareness of their cosmic connections. This method encouraged students to explore their inner worlds and recognize the macrocosm within the microcosm. Astrology provided a framework for these explorations, with the positions and movements of celestial bodies serving as guides for personal and spiritual growth (Kingsley, 1995).

Aristotle reminds us (as cited in Shaw, 2016) that the mysteries are not about acquiring knowledge but about experiencing transformation. Describing the Eleusinian mysteries, Aristotle noted that initiates "do not learn anything, but experience something by being put into a changed state of mind."

According to Plato, Iamblichus, Proclus, and other Alexandrian philosophers, the initiates of the elite experienced extraordinary and ecstatic visions within the temple.[11] Plato himself was seen not just as a philosopher but as a *mystagogue* – a leader into sacred mysteries. His teachings were considered a form of initiation, revealing the divine mysteries to those ready to receive them.

The Greek mysteries, deeply entwined with myths and legends, are associated with deities such as Dionysius (god of fruitfulness), Demeter (goddess of grain), and Orpheus (god of arts and sunlight). Herodotus attributed the origins of these mysteries to Orpheus, son of Apollo, whose seven-stringed lyre symbolized the seven levels of initiation. The Orphic mysteries were designed to help individuals transcend their base instincts and awaken their divine nature. These rituals emphasized living a disciplined and ethical life, incorporating practices like asceticism and vegetarianism to foster spiritual growth and alignment with the divine.

As initiates progressed through the rituals, they transitioned from passive observers to active participants. They gradually realized that the captivating story of Persephone and her journey to Hades was unfolding deep within them. This transformative journey from observer to participant underscored the profound nature of the mysteries and the individual's evolving role within them.

A segment of the ancient Greek astrological community was taught the mystery tradition, with many of the ancient doctrines possibly kept secret, and some astrological schools remaining private or underground.[12] Certain texts were not widely available to every astrologer but instead were passed along in mystery schools from teacher to student for generations. Firmicus Maternus, a 4th-century Sicilian astrologer, treated astrology as a mystery religion, with Pythagoras, Plato, and Porphyry as like-minded keepers of mysteries.[13]

These strict requirements for the dissemination of sacred knowledge highlight the belief in the importance of purity of heart and mind in the pursuit of divine wisdom. Maternus emphasizes the need for those seeking this knowledge to be of impeccable character, free from any moral blemishes that could taint their understanding of the teachings. This insistence on moral purity as a prerequisite for spiritual enlightenment reflects the belief in the interconnectedness of ethics and metaphysics in the ancient philosophical tradition.

Greco-Roman mystical initiation systems included great ancient figures like Plato, Pythagoras, Plutarch, Cicero, Iamblichus, and Porphyry, as well as Christian fathers like Clement of Alexandria and Origen. Porphyry believed that through a life of virtue and wisdom, individuals could align themselves with their guardian daimon and mitigate the influence of fate. He emphasized the importance of free will in shaping one's destiny, even within the framework of astrology.

As per Helena P. Blavatsky (in Barker, 1925), the Mysteries were a series of theatrical performances of the myths. During these performances, priests and neophytes would portray the mysteries of cosmogony and nature, bringing to life various gods and goddesses and reenacting scenes from their lives as symbolic representations.

The Eleusinian Mysteries, among the most celebrated, were associated with Demeter and Persephone, whose myth encapsulates cycles of life, death, and rebirth. These mysteries were heavily influenced by the rites of Isis in Egypt, reflecting the interconnectedness of ancient religious practices.

The ceremonies, lasting nine days, were divided into three stages: *telete* (perfection), *muesis* (ordeal or learning), and *epopteia* (divine illumination). Initiates fasted and underwent purification, progressing from observers to active participants. Their rituals dramatized cosmic myths and included sacred reenactments, such as Persephone's descent into the underworld and return, which symbolized the soul's journey and redemption (Taylor, 1891). Breaking the secrecy of these rites was punishable by death, underscoring their sacred significance.

Astrology and Ritual in Theurgical Practice

Between the late 2nd and early 3rd century CE, the term "theurgy" emerged within Platonist circles, heavily influenced by the *Chaldean Oracles*. Theurgy referred to ritual techniques designed to communicate with and participate in the divine. Iamblichus' *theurgia* ("divine action") involved rituals that aligned the practitioner's soul with the divine order. He argued that symbols in astrology helped the human soul transcend its earthly confines and recognize its connection to the divine (Voss, 2000). In this context, astrology took on a theurgical dimension, using symbols and images to engage with celestial deities and gain direct knowledge from them. Divine illumination was achieved not through reason alone but through active participation in sacred rites that aligned the soul with cosmic intelligences. The philosophers of the School of Athens considered the Oracles the culmination of studies but advised students to approach them only after careful research on Aristotle and Plato's works (Viglas, 2013).

Iamblichus (c. 245–c. 325 CE) integrated Greek traditions with elements from other cultures, establishing a spiritual astrology that emphasized the divine nature of matter. Babylon, or Chaldea, became synonymous with astrological divination practiced by the Chaldean magi. The Chaldeans, regarded as the founders of astrology, considered stars to be living deities. Their rituals were seen as magical-religious acts that connected humanity to these divine beings.

Iamblichus believed that theurgy allowed humans to act from their immortal soul, or *nous*. He viewed the stars as divine and emphasized theurgy as a means of transcending material limitations.

Gregory Shaw, in *Theurgy and the Soul: The Neoplatonism of Iamblichus* (1995), explains how Iamblichus synthesized Platonic and Pythagorean metaphysics with the Chaldean Oracles, thereby elevating oracular practices within the Neoplatonic tradition. By integrating philosophical contemplation with theurgic rituals, Iamblichus reframed Platonism as part of an oracular tradition that valued trance states and direct engagement with the divine. These rituals were not merely symbolic but served a transformative purpose: they prepared the soul to become a purified and receptive vessel, capable of receiving the messages of the planetary gods. Gods were seen as omnipresent in nature, with rituals serving as pathways to divine union (Shaw, 2016, 2024). These rituals included specific prayers, offerings like perfumes, animals, and plants, and symbolic acts designed to harmonize with celestial gods, not for personal gain but for spiritual transcendence (*The Mysteries* 8.7).

One notable theurgic practice was the "animation" of statues of gods through ritual invocations, symbolizing the manifestation of divine energies in the material world. The ultimate goal of theurgy was unity with the *daimon*, the soul's guiding deity, which served as an intermediary between humans and gods. Daimons were believed to influence the soul's choices, often tied to planetary influences.

Iamblichus described two methods for discovering one's personal *daimon*: through rituals or planetary calculations. These practices aimed to prepare the soul for union with the divine by fostering ethical purification and awakening the imagination (Redondo, 2015). The imagination acted as a mediator between the sensory world and the divine, facilitating insight and spiritual growth. Prayer, hymn-singing, and offerings were traditional methods of connecting with the divine, with modern parallels found in imaginative spiritual practices.

In *On the Mysteries* (8.6), Iamblichus highlighted the dual nature of the soul. One aspect connected to the divine creator and another tied to the material world. By engaging in theurgy, individuals could transcend the sensible world, uniting with higher realms of existence.

> For man, as these writings say, has two souls. And one, indeed, is derived from the first intelligible, and participates of the power of the Demiurgus; but the other is imparted from the circulation of the celestial bodies, to which the soul that sees God returns.

Theurgy was not mere superstition but a synthesis of philosophy and ritual. In *On the Mysteries* (8.6), Iamblichus emphasized that planetary gods, collectively known as *Fate* (*heimarmenē*), influenced both material life and the soul's liberation (Shaw, 2024).

Hence that of which you are dubious is not true, "that all things are bound with the indissoluble bonds of Necessity," which we call Fate. For the soul has a proper principle of circumduction to the intelligible, and of a separation from generated natures; and also of a contact with real being, and that which is divine. While Fate initially bound the soul, recognizing and aligning with these noetic symbols allowed for spiritual freedom.

Unlike dualistic worldviews, Neoplatonism treated the natural world and human body as direct expressions of the divine. This nondual tradition, embodied in theurgical practices, sought to integrate divine symbols into human experience. Gods were embodied through human forms, and aesthetic and sensory experiences were pathways to divine union (Shaw, 2024, pp. 36–37). This perspective upheld the physical world as sacred, an idea central to Neoplatonic thought.

Both Iamblichus and Hillman stress the need to surrender intellectual control when encountering archetypal or divine realities. In this context, an archetypal approach that combines active imagination with dream symbols and archetypes in an expanded state of consciousness emphasizes embodied awareness and somatic engagement. This mirrors Iamblichus' notion of preparing "appropriate receptacles" to receive divine influences. In coaching or therapy, we can help individuals engage these symbols meaningfully by encouraging deep reflection and cultivating receptivity through somatic awareness and meditative practice—thus honoring the sacredness of body and symbol as gateways to the divine.

Astrology: A Path to Virtue and Free Will

Plato expressed skepticism toward judicial astrology, which sought to determine free will and intruded on the soul's domain. Meanwhile, the Stoics adopted a nuanced view, proposing that while external circumstances might be predetermined, individuals could influence their lives through virtuous conduct. These virtues implied a process of catharsis or purification of the soul, cultivated through self-control, courage (understood as fearlessness in the face of death), magnanimity (detachment from material possessions), and wisdom. For the Platonists, Eros was not merely a physical impulse but an inner fire that seizes the soul and draws it toward divine beauty—a transformative force that elevates desire from physical attraction to a higher, spiritual longing for the transcendent. By cultivating self-discipline and aligning with the natural order, Stoics believed one could transcend fate's pressures, achieve inner peace, and navigate life with resilience. This philosophy emphasized the coexistence of ethical responsibility and deterministic cosmic laws. Stoic thought highlighted that virtue was a divine gift, whereas vice stemmed from external conditions tied to the soul's entrapment in matter.

Stoic philosophers integrated astrology into their understanding of the soul and the pursuit of wisdom. They viewed fate as a natural law governed by cause and effect, which could be reconciled with virtuous living to achieve *eudaimonia*, or flourishing. This perspective emphasized personal agency, suggesting that by aligning with rational principles, individuals could attain inner peace and fulfillment.

Neoplatonism expanded the dialogue on fate and free will by introducing celestial forces as benevolent guides. Platonists saw planets as spiritual entities emanating goodness, influencing emotions, thoughts, and actions positively. Plotinus, inspired by Plato's *Timaeus*, described the soul as being influenced by two forces: its yearning for unity with the divine (*the One*) and its temperament, shaped by the stars. This integration of celestial influence and individual agency presented fate as an interactive and dynamic process.

Porphyry, a follower of Plotinus and Pythagorean teachings, sought to harmonize astrology with the Platonic view of the soul's freedom. Interpreting Plato's *Myth of Er*, Porphyry proposed that souls pre-select their guardian *daimon* before birth, shaping their destinies while leaving room for personal choice. The daimon represents the soul's innate drive toward fulfilling its unique destiny—the deep impulse guiding what the soul seeks to realize in life. Iamblichus, in *On the Mysteries* (Shaw, 2024, p. 268), critiqued deterministic astrology, asserting its original purpose was to reveal divine cosmic principles rather than predicting mundane events. He argued that celestial bodies were not mechanical determiners of fate but participants in a divine order designed to elevate the soul's higher purpose.

Carl Jung and later thinkers like Richard Tarnas extended these ideas into the realm of depth psychology. Jung noted that unresolved inner conflicts often manifest externally as "fate" (CW 9i, para. 126).

> That is to say, when the individual remains undivided and does not become conscious of his inner opposite, the world must perforce act out the conflict and be torn into opposing halves.

Tarnas (2006, p. 78) elaborated that unconscious archetypal forces drive actions until individuals gain self-awareness, which allows for conscious engagement with these patterns.

For example, identifying the influence of Mars as a warrior archetype might inspire someone struggling with self-doubt to cultivate courage and resilience.

Astrological archetypes like Saturn offer powerful metaphors for navigating life's difficulties. Saturn's associations with discipline and persistence can guide individuals in embracing setbacks as opportunities for long-term growth. This aligns with Stoic ideals of finding purpose amid adversity and cultivating endurance.

Astrology, when approached symbolically, provides a map for understanding internal struggles and external events. By fostering greater awareness of these influences, individuals can integrate unconscious aspects of the psyche, achieving harmony with the cosmos and transforming potential "fate" into meaningful personal evolution. This framework, rooted in ancient Greek philosophies, continues to inspire approaches to self-awareness and resilience.

Consider a client with Mars (representing drive and fighting impulse) in a tense aspect such as a square, to Mercury (symbolizing intellect and communication). This astrological configuration often indicates a tendency toward getting involved in disputes and possibly using aggressive speech to assert oneself. The client might find themselves frequently embroiled in arguments, sometimes abusing their power of speech to dominate conversations or situations.

Understanding this aspect can provide profound insights. By recognizing that Mars square Mercury can lead to an insatiable mind with relentless intellectual energy, the client can learn to channel this force constructively. Instead of engaging in conflicts, they can direct this powerful drive toward intellectual pursuits such as research, writing, or problem-solving tasks. This shift in perspective helps the client see their challenging aspect not as a liability but as a potent asset.

Thus, an astrological understanding of archetypes and their aspects offers a personalized manual of potentials, guiding individuals on how to harness their unique traits and energies for positive outcomes.

Fostering Reverence through the Archetypes

Ancient Greeks thought that tyranny was the height of irreverence, and they described it as forgetting that you are only human and thinking you can act like a god (Woodruff, 2005, p. 6). For them, reverence was a virtue and a strength of character. Reverence, in the eyes of the ancient Greeks, was a fundamental aspect of maintaining humility and respect for one's own limitations as a mortal being.

In *Astrology, Psychology, and the Four Elements*, Arroyo (1975, pp. 76–77) explains that the planets (symbolizing the gods) must be honored and respected. These fundamental life forces cannot be ignored without consequences to the individual. They must be recognized, given due attention, and accepted, allowing their energy to be consciously directed. Without awareness of these forces, one risks being controlled by them. The Greeks viewed *hybris* – the audacity to disregard the gods – as a great sin, inevitably followed by *nemesis*, or the destructive release of pent-up energy that was not channeled properly.

To transcend Fate, Iamblichus taught that theurgists must recognize and honor the presence of planetary gods in their lives. Resistance to these gods resulted in the oppressive experience of Fate, while veneration allowed the soul to perceive Fate as the harmonious movements of the stars. The path to deification required addressing the pathological complexes entangling the soul, which arose from the soul's limited ability to reflect divine wholeness. Confronting and integrating these distortions were essential for healing and achieving unity. These tendencies, when balanced, revealed noetic principles and became vessels for divine presence. This vessel, the *subtle body* or *ochēma-pneuma*, became luminous through theurgical practice. Iamblichus emphasized honoring all planetary gods and their powers, as offering appropriate gifts to each created a complete receptacle (*hupodochē*) for the divine (Shaw, 2024, pp. 263–265).

An example of this principle in a modern context can be found in the experience of Spring, as described in Chapters 4 and 6. After engaging in a guided somatic meditation and entering an expanded state of mind, Spring created a physical symbol of her inner transformation – a clay bowl (see Figure 4.8) – during an active imagination session where she dialogued with dream symbols and archetypes. She reflected on this creation, saying:

> I feel like the clay was representing the holder, the container of life, and the fire was representing the potential transformation. (Spring, in Carod, 2021, pp. 127–130)

Iamblichus taught that honoring the gods and engaging with symbolic representations of inner life create a "receptacle" for divine power. Similarly, Spring's clay bowl, shaped through her work with archetypes and dream symbols, became a luminous vessel for divine presence. This tangible creation mirrored the Iamblichean concept of a divine vessel, symbolizing her psychic journey, transformation, and capacity to hold life's experiences.

As illustrated in Chapter 6, participants frequently used the term "honor" to describe the acknowledgment of their unrecognized archetypal features. It appears that recognizing and establishing a relationship with these inner forces activated a sense of order, providing meaning to their experiences and contributing to a sense of peace of mind.

> Having a name for that, naming it, my Mars, or my Saturn, it gives me less of this thinking process. More of a bigger cosmic process. I need to honor that, because I need to honor the energy of the universe that is coming through me. (Spring, pp. 175–179, in Carod, 2021)

By connecting with the archetypes of the wise elder (Saturn and Jupiter), the nurturing mother (the Moon), the brave warrior (Mars), and the creative artist (the Sun and Venus), individuals can begin to cultivate a sense of reverence for themselves, their relationships, and the world around them.

Ficino: Exploring Duality and the Symbolic Function

It wasn't until the 15th century Ficino, a Renaissance Florentine philosopher who revived Platonic philosophy in the Christian West, recognized again that human beings are themselves gods who can change their relationship with fate.

Marsilio Ficino integrated Theurgy into his philosophical and astrological practices, presenting it as a synthesis of spirituality, magic, and Neoplatonic philosophy. As a priest, Ficino viewed astrological symbols as reflections of the divine mind and poetic metaphors rather than deterministic tools. He emphasized imagination as a means to link concrete symbols with higher meanings, following the Platonic tradition and the guidance of thinkers like Iamblichus. Ficino's astrology uniquely incorporated free will, setting him apart from many of his contemporaries (Voss, 2000, 2006).

Dr. Angela Voss highlights Ficino's transformative influence on astrological philosophy, noting its parallels with depth and transpersonal psychology. Ficino saw symbols as catalysts for connecting with the unity of existence, an idea that resonates with Jungian psychology (Voss, 2006, p. 2). He believed astrological symbols and planetary archetypes could facilitate personal and spiritual development.

Ficino drew inspiration from Pythagoras, Plato, Zoroaster, and Iamblichus. He used music, particularly Orphic Hymns[14], as a medium to engage imagination and explore planetary archetypes. Pythagoras inspired Ficino's belief in music's capacity to evoke specific spiritual states, while Plato's emphasis on rhythm, harmony, and verse informed his approach to prayer.

Ficino's cosmological model drew heavily from Neoplatonic sources, particularly the hierarchical view of the universe. In his framework, the human soul mediated between material and spiritual realms, contributing to the universe's interconnectedness. Ficino described the cosmos as infused with active forces and affinities, linking planets, elements, and human souls (Goodrick-Clarke, 2008, p. 41). Astrology became a tool to navigate these connections and guide spiritual ascent.

Ficino recommended counteracting challenging planetary energies – such as balancing Mars (conflict) with Venus (harmony) or Saturn (restriction) with Jupiter (expansion). In his *Liber de Vita*, Book 3, VI, p. 170, Ficino suggested to keep "mind and body" in active imitation or counter imitation of planetary movements:

When you fear Mars, set Venus opposite. When you fear Saturn, set Jupiter.

These notions likely contributed to the development of the Jungian concept of working with opposites (Voss, 1992).

For example, if someone is experiencing a period of frustration and conflict (Mars influence), they can intentionally bring in elements of harmony and peace (Venus influence) to balance out the energy. Similarly, if someone is feeling restricted and overwhelmed (Saturn influence), they can focus on expanding their opportunities and optimism (Jupiter influence) to counteract the negative effects.

Ficino avoided labeling his practices as Theurgy to prevent conflict with the Christian authorities of Florence, but his work reflected its principles. His synthesis of astrology, music, and philosophy laid the foundation for a Renaissance cosmology that viewed the soul as central to the universe's harmony. This imaginative and symbolic perspective offered an alternative to the fatalism often associated with astrology (Shaw, 2008; Voss, 2000).

Ficino's legacy as a philosopher and spiritual astrologer continues to inspire contemporary approaches that integrate cosmology, psychology, and ritual. His emphasis on imagination, free will, and the symbolic significance of planetary archetypes offers valuable tools for personal transformation and alignment with the cosmos. Techniques inspired by Iamblichus involve creating "receptacles" for divine or archetypal influences, emphasizing embodied awareness (Shaw, 2016, pp. 340–341).

After Neoplatonist Iamblichus, Ficino emerged as the unique proponent of astrology that considered free will. In our Western society today, the influence of

Claudius Ptolemy's Tetrabiblos, a late Hellenistic work, shaped most contemporary astrologers' perspectives, emphasizing an unalterable fate determined at birth. This framework sidelines the spiritual dimension of astrology, neglecting the importance of consciousness and receptivity to access the divine realm.

Following that, what is the essence of theurgian practice that we can adopt in our modern era? Similar to the Greek Theurgists, as therapists and coaches, we can facilitate a gradual alignment with the soul through the use of psychology, cosmology, and ritual. The practice of ritual could be replaced by active imagination with archetypes.

In an archetypal approach that combines active imagination with archetypes and dream symbols in an expanded state of consciousness, the focus is on embodied awareness and somatic engagement. This aligns with Iamblichus' concept of preparing "appropriate receptacles" to contain divine influences. As Shaw (2016, pp. 340–341) highlights, both Iamblichus and Hillman emphasize the importance of surrendering control and intellectual grasp when encountering archetypes or gods.

Jung and Astrology

Jung, who was probably the most important intellectual influence on astrologers in the 20th century, considered astrology to represent the sum of all the psychological knowledge of antiquity. He described the natal chart (the picture of the sky from the perspective of Earth at the moment of one's birth) as "a classic mandala containing within its geometry the factors that express the totality of the unique personality, a potential that can manifest in countless ways in the course of a lifetime" (Jung, 1968, p. 206).

According to Tarnas (2006, pp. 61–62), throughout his career, Jung's attention increasingly shifted toward the ancient cosmological perspective of astrology, which posits a symbolic correspondence between planetary positions and human events. Jung's exploration of astrology began as early as 1911, when he mentioned to Freud that he was making horoscopic calculations to uncover psychological truths. His interest in astrology grew over time, eventually becoming a significant area of investigation. Jung once remarked, "Astrology represents the sum of all the psychological knowledge of antiquity." While his published writings presented varying and sometimes ambiguous views on astrology, it is clear that insights from his astrological studies influenced many of his key theoretical formulations, including archetypal theory and synchronicity. Reports from Jung's family and those close to him indicate that in his later years, he regularly used birth chart and transit analyses as part of his clinical work with patients in analysis.

In Jungian terms, the astrological chart is a tool for working with and developing our psyche. In *Psychological Types* (1921), Jung discusses the limitations of modern psychology in comprehending the psyche, describing it as an "infinitely more obscure" entity than the visible body (para. 916). He suggests that in order to approach the psyche, one should begin with external signs and work inward, citing astrology as an ancient method that started "from interstellar space" to trace "those lines of fate whose beginnings lie in the human heart" (para. 917). He equates this approach with other characterological methods such as palmistry, physiognomy, and graphology, all aimed at uncovering psychological insights through external cues. Jung integrated the wisdom of the past with psychotherapy, affirming the importance of spiritual life. Esoteric traditions, according to Jung, contain knowledge that can only be read with a metaphorical and symbolic sensibility (Rossi & Le Grice, 2018).

Jung's notion of individuation implies a universal and interconnected awareness:

> The psychological and spiritual journey of transforming a fragmented state of consciousness into an integrated, non-dual comprehension of oneself and others, establishing a connection with a universal and interconnected awareness. (Jung, 1968, para. 314)

In *Jung on Astrology*, Rossi and Le Grice (2018) explore how Jungian psychology has revived the value of mythological ideas and a sense of cosmological meaning, viewing the celestial realm as a meaningful mirror to the soul. This perspective fosters a sense of alignment with deeper levels of life and a feeling of being a small part of a greater consciousness.

Jung associated individuation with a degree of psychological freedom, comparing the unfoldment of the process with the Platonic myth of the soul's journey through the planetary spheres (Greene, 2018, p. 29). Individuation thus becomes an effort to realize the highest potential of our fragmented soul, as reflected through the various archetypes. It is a process of rediscovering all aspects of the self—both those we consciously identify with and those we deny or project onto others. Jung suggested that by exploring and integrating the unconscious, we gain the power to actively shape our reality and become co-creators of our own destiny. His view encourages us to take responsibility for our lives, break free from the perceived inevitability of fate, and embark on a journey of self-discovery and personal growth.

In Jung's view, astrology is less a predictive science than a mythological language, in which the planet-gods are symbols of the power of the unconscious (Bogart, 2014). His perspective radically challenged the ancient claims that astrology could predict the future and that there were "good" and "bad" birth charts.

Liz Greene, a prominent Jungian analyst and astrologer, has extensively explored the connection between Jungian psychology and astrology. Greene's work links astrological archetypes to Jung's psychological process, providing a robust Jungian framework for integrating astrology with psychological analysis.

> Jung's astrology helped to shape his psychological models [...], and modern astrology has been profoundly reshaped by Jung's psychological concepts. (Greene, 2018, p. 9)

Carl Jung's theory of psychological types, detailed in *Psychological Types* (1921), provides a comprehensive framework for understanding personality. Jung categorized individuals based on two primary attitudes – extraversion and introversion – and four psychological functions: thinking, feeling, sensation, and intuition. These dimensions combine to form eight distinct personality types, each reflecting a unique way of interacting with the world and processing experiences.

Extraverts direct their energy outward, engaging with the external world of objects, social norms, and shared realities. Their conscious focus on objective facts and external adaptation often neglects subjective experiences. Jung (1921, paras. 572, 575) noted that an overly outward focus activates a compensatory response in the unconscious, allowing repressed, archaic aspects of the psyche to influence behavior and emotions. Jung emphasized the role of unconscious as a balancing force, maintaining psychic equilibrium. As extraversion becomes more dominant, the inner, subjective world underdevelops, leading to one-sidedness and unconscious compensations that urge the individual toward wholeness.

For example, an extraverted individual who is overly focused on socializing and external achievements might suddenly experience a deep, unexplained emotional breakdown or a series of intense dreams that highlight themes of isolation or introspection. This emotional disruption could be the unconscious compensating for the neglect of their inner world, urging them to address deeper, unacknowledged aspects of themselves. Such unpredictable manifestations may challenge their rigid outer-focused mindset, ultimately guiding them toward greater balance and integration.

Jung's exploration of these dynamics underscores the necessity of acknowledging and integrating the unconscious. This interplay between the conscious and unconscious ensures a dynamic balance, preventing rigid dominance by one aspect of the psyche over the other.

In *Astrology, Psychology, and the Four Elements*, Arroyo (1975) describes how Jung aligns the four functions – sensation, intuition, feeling, and thinking – with the classical elements of astrology: earth, fire, water, and air. Jung's integration of these elements with his psychological types demonstrates how astrology and psychology are intertwined. The elements are not just external forces but also psychological expressions within the human psyche. Earth grounds us through sensation, fire propels us with intuition, water connects us through feeling, and air guides us with thinking, each offering a distinct mode of experiencing and interacting with the world.

Sensation corresponds to earth, focusing on what is tangible and concrete, similar to the grounded, practical nature of earth signs (Taurus, Virgo, Capricorn). Intuition, linked to fire, represents vision, potential, and inspiration, paralleling the creativity and enthusiasm of fire signs (Aries, Leo, Sagittarius). The feeling function, associated with water, reflects emotional depth and empathy, akin to the fluid and intuitive qualities of water signs (Cancer, Scorpio, Pisces). Lastly, thinking corresponds to air, emphasizing logic, clarity, and intellectual reasoning, much like air signs (Gemini, Libra, Aquarius) which value communication and rationality.

Arroyo (1975, p. 73) explains that, much like modern physics reveals the interconnection between energy and matter, the four elements – earth, water, air, and fire – interweave and combine to form all matter. When life departs from the body at death, these elements dissociate and return to their primal state. It is life itself that holds the elements together in an organized, living whole. Although all four elements are present in every person, individuals are consciously more attuned to some types of elemental energy than others. Arroyo explains that the zodiacal signs, often referred to as "energy fields," "archetypal patterns," or "universal formative principles," represent the same underlying reality. These principles are the living forces that astrology symbolizes, paralleling Jung's concept of archetypes. Both the zodiacal signs and Jung's archetypes refer to primal energy patterns that shape all life, both physical and psychic, although they are invisible to the senses.

Arroyo (1975, p. 105) discusses psychologist Ralph Metzner's exploration of the four elements as they relate to personality types. At Stanford University, Metzner designed encounter sessions between people with different elemental combinations and concluded that each element represents a type of person who "metabolizes experience at different rates" and reacts to conflict in distinct ways. For example, air signs (Gemini, Libra, Aquarius) tend to rise above conflict, avoiding direct confrontation, but may later harbor resentment. Fire signs (Aries, Leo, Sagittarius) confront challenges with intensity and enthusiasm but may benefit from cultivating calm and placidity to manage their energy. Water signs (Cancer, Scorpio, Pisces) respond emotionally, often needing firmness to control their deep feelings. Earth signs (Taurus, Virgo, Capricorn) deal with obstacles through practicality and persistence but could enhance their growth by incorporating generosity. At times, Jung found it necessary to conceal the full extent of his interest in astrology, even from his colleagues – Liz Greene (2018) offers detailed information on how Jung's involvement with astrology was an open secret in analytical circles, causing discomfort among some analysts and Jungian training groups due to its perceived questionable nature. His exploration drew inspiration from historical texts and the work of spiritual astrologers Alan Leo and Max Heindel, who modernized astrology, emphasizing individual psychology and inner transformation and incorporating the concept of reincarnation (Greene, 2018).

Yet, a new phase in the West's cultural and psychological evolution introduces a transformed vision of astrology, aligned with principles of personal freedom and the fulfillment of one's authentic nature and potential, akin to Jung's concept of individuation (Tarnas, 2011). During the last three decades of the 20th century, astrology has progressively abandoned the idea of predestination, embracing the emerging approaches of depth psychology and humanism.

Connecting Deities with Subpersonalities

One of the most fundamental ideas of the Western philosophical tradition is that the universe is permeated by timeless patterns of consciousness and experience, which Jung would later, in their psychological forms, call archetypes. The ancient Greeks viewed archetypes as living gods like Zeus and Aphrodite, while Plato saw them as transcendent forms shaping the world. Hindu mythology's flying vehicles, the Hopi "star-people," and the Sumerian myth of the Annunaki are other examples of stories of gods, visitors with advanced technology descending from the heavens to instruct or create humanity.

Some authors have proposed theories about the concept of a "divine genetic imprint" or a spiritual component inherent in human DNA, reflecting the idea that our essence or soul is encoded in our biology. Lipton's *The Biology of Belief* explores the influence of consciousness and belief systems on genetic expression, suggesting a divine connection in our cells. Braden's *The God Code*[15] suggests our DNA reflects ancient truths, while Oschman's *Energy Medicine: The Scientific Basis*[16] suggests a divine component in our genetic makeup.

According to professor Richard Tarnas (as cited in Butler, 2019, p. 16): "There are three broad ways that the archetypes have been understood in Western civilization: as mythic deities, as metaphysical principles, and as inner psychological structures."

As outlined in the earlier section discussing the history of astrology, ancient Sumerian, Egyptian, and Greek civilizations perceived archetypes as divine entities and metaphysical principles that encouraged contemplation and alignment with the cosmic order. These principles, personified in ancient times as immortal gods and goddesses, are still relevant today because they embody fundamental dynamics of the human psyche. They represent the energies of desire, motivation, willpower, instinct, impulse, thought, emotion, and intuition.

In therapeutic or coaching contexts, exploring archetypes through astrological symbolism empowers individuals to confront challenges as opportunities for growth.

For example, in therapy or coaching, a client may explore their inner warrior archetype to find courage and determination to face past traumas. By embodying the nurturing mother archetype, they may learn self-love and compassion, leading to healthier relationships. Through connecting with the wise elder archetype, the client may gain perspective and insight into their own journey.

Astrology allows clients to contemplate the cosmic metaphorical mirror of myths in search of meaning and inspiration. The astrological archetypes reveal our personal struggles and imperfections, while also pointing us toward the remedy. Their myths encapsulate the lessons we must learn. As we deepen our understanding of the myth along with the theater of archetypes interacting with each other, we naturally become less influenced by their mundane aspects and more capable of embodying their higher qualities.

The Resurgence of the Anima Mundi

Platonism introduced the concept of the *anima mundi*, or world soul (Greek: *psychè kósmou*), as the source of physical forms. In the Timeus, Plato adhered to this idea, identifying the universe as a single, visible, living being, containing within itself all living creatures that are by nature akin to it.

The cosmos was divided into "being" (the unchanging realm of archetypes) and "becoming" (the realm of constant change). This dichotomy informed Platonic and Neoplatonic metaphysics, asserting that all things are interdependent, from human souls to divine realms (Tarnas, 2011).

Professor Richard Tarnas, in his introduction to archetypal astrology[17] (1987, p. 2), claims that "Astrology thus supports the ancient idea of an anima mundi, or world soul, in which the human psyche participates." From this perspective, it can be assumed that a transpersonal approach to astrology implies a dialogue, an inter-action with archetypal forces. This framework is open to a co-creative dialogical participation with the cosmos. In this cosmic perspective, rather than regarding the archetypes as fixed structures waiting to be discovered, the soul can interact with them with imaginative vision and emotion.

Although the idea of the anima mundi originated in classical antiquity, similar no-tions can be found in the philosophies of later European thinkers. Among them are Baruch Spinoza, Gottfried Leibniz, Immanuel Kant, Friedrich Schelling, and Georg W. F. Hegel, especially in his concept of Weltgeist or world spirit (Butler, 2019).

Self-knowledge and awareness of oneself in relationship to the archetypes of the collective unconscious may bring a sense of unity and belonging to the cosmos that can counterbalance a sense of alienation and separateness that many coaches feel. Spring offers an example of how archetypal awareness can develop what is already there. The coaching sessions gave her, she said:

> ... an understanding of that type of energy that is my birthright, surrounding me, influencing me... having a name, naming it, my Mars, or my Saturn, it gives me more of a bigger cosmic process... I need to honour the energy of the universe that is coming through me. (Spring, pp. 175–183, in Carod, 2021)

Through dreams, imagination, meditative states, and contemplation of archetypes, we can gently lead our consciousness into the liminal space, where we can receive intuitive insights and inspirations from the *mundus imaginalis* – what Iamblichus understood to be the sacred ground where the divine and human could meet.

Transpersonal Astrology: Restoring Order in Times of Crisis

Rudhyar (in Bogart, 2014, p. 127) referred to astrology as "threshold knowledge," a tool guiding individuals to step into a transpersonal life. Transpersonal astrology shares common interests and goals with transpersonal psychology, investigating non-ordinary, mystical states of consciousness such as transcendence, wholeness, non-duality, and their possible positive outcomes (Bogart, 2014). This framework posits an inherent order or purpose in the universe that surpasses individual com-prehension, aligning with the notion that life events are not arbitrary but integral to a greater, meaningful plan.

Mary's response to my research question on the effects of archetypal work em-phasized archetypes' ability to establish order and find meaning.

> ... a sense that we are all part of this universe and intelligence, and everything is connected, in some way, and when I need help it's always there, brings a real sense of safety. (Mary, pp. 123–124)

In his work *From Humanistic to Transpersonal Psychology* (1975), Dane Rudhyar viewed astrology as a spiritual discipline aimed at helping individuals realize their divine nature and fulfill their unique potential. Rudhyar, who was contemporary to Jung and influenced by his ideas, focused on personal growth, psychological awareness, and the integration of opposites. He argued that becoming fully actualized involves freeing oneself from unconscious cultural influences and developing distinctive traits (Rudhyar, in Bogart, 2014, p. 127).

Rudhyar believed that astrology, when used as a tool for self-awareness and personal growth, could guide individuals in their journey toward self-realization and the integration of their various psychological components. In this context, the integration of the Moon and the Sun within a person's chart can highlight the need to bring unconscious patterns to light. The Moon in an individual's astrological chart symbolizes automatic responses ingrained in early childhood, which can trap someone into habitual behaviors. These automatic responses, rooted in past experiences and early conditioning, may hinder one's self-realization as symbolized by the Sun, which represents the core self and purpose in life.

Rudhyar's framework encourages a shift from ego-centered consciousness to a wholeness-centered approach, where individuals make what he calls a "self-consecration to the whole." This is the moment when one turns inward to connect with spirit, aligning with the cosmic order rather than resisting it. Thus, astrology, according to Rudhyar, offers a path to self-actualization and participation in the larger spiritual evolution of humanity.

The narratives shared in Chapter 6 demonstrate how self-discovery, facilitated by an understanding of the archetypes and dream symbols, brought about a sense of harmony and connection to the cosmos. Examples include Mary's sense of completeness through embracing her insecurity, Roshani's depiction of the ephemeral touch of butterfly dust, Spring's perception of collective freedom from a transpersonal information field, and Susanne's awakening by embracing polarities within the heart space (see Chapter 6).

In transpersonal astrology, the question is not how we can avoid pain or change but how we can learn and grow in the most creative way possible. As highlighted by Bogart (2009), astrology serves as a valuable tool by providing meaning and order to individuals navigating transformative experiences.

The process of metamorphosis takes us outside of our comfort zone as we receive transpersonal archetypal influences – mediated by Uranus, Neptune, and Pluto, the solar system's furthest planets – that precipitate crises and transformative passages. Making room for the operation of these transpersonal forces often means leaving aside our original plans and attachments to let change happen. By understanding and cooperating with planetary patterns, individuals can shift from a victimized state to an empowered one.

Transpersonal astrology implies a belief in a transpersonal or universal force guiding events and influencing individual actions. Assagioli (1965) described this state as "collaboration with the inevitable," blessing obstacles and transforming them into stepping stones. Similarly, Rudhyar (1975) considers that crises occur so that an individual can become more fully what they are.

This is what what my client Roshani (see Chapter 6) reported. She felt that in some way she had invited her accident into her life:

> I feel I invited this lesson because maybe I reached a point where I was not being very true to myself.

Roshani experienced a spontaneous insight that the accident would serve as a catalyst for personal growth, revealing previously unexplored aspects of her personality.

Engaging with symbols in an embodied state enables the soul to break free from intellectual constraints, allowing for deeper, transformative experiences. By recognizing our "nothingness" and moving beyond the ego's need for control, we create space for divine or archetypal forces to guide us toward a higher order of being, facilitating the soul's transformation.

Navigating the Unconscious with Astrological Archetypes

The coaching process begins by identifying the client's emotional triggers and exploring their significance through astrological and dream symbols. Active participation in this dialogue – not as a passive recipient of astrological insights but as an engaged co-creator – enriches the session.

Through guided meditation, we invite archetypal symbols or dream images into awareness, fostering a dialogue with them. Rather than providing chart readings as static monologs, approaching the process as a dynamic conversation breathes life into the session. This approach not only evolves with the details of a person's life but also involves engaging with planetary archetypes themselves, meditating on their intentions, and considering how to express them.

The coach's role is to foster a safe, supportive space where clients can engage with their unconscious, witness what emerges, and feel nurtured in the process. Gently guiding clients toward actionable steps inspired by their archetypal interactions helps them harness their potential. This process is inherently collaborative. Coaches and clients co-create archetypal imagery, inviting symbols that represent both challenges and opportunities. In active imagination, clients are encouraged to explore these images personally, free from rigid interpretations, discovering their unique meaning.

We guide clients to align their strengths with their archetypal traits, reimagining their life story in a way that brings balance and meaning. This approach harmonizes the competing energies within their psyche and encourages integration. Clients are introduced to archetypes in simple terms before engaging in active imagination. Once unconscious impulses are identified, the next step involves discovering the positive potentials in the client's natal chart and related dream symbols.

These archetypal configurations illuminate the source of inner conflict and can provide flexible, intelligent responses to life's challenges.

For instance, a client struggling with aggression may learn to reinterpret their "Mars" archetype as the energy of a focused warrior, shifting from reactive hostility to assertive goal-setting. A strong Mars placement, in tense aspects to other planets or in a fire sign like Aries, Leo, or Sagittarius, might emphasize initiative and boldness, giving insights into empowering experiences that can be consciously cultivated.

One of my clients presents a striking Mars archetype, shaped by challenging aspects to the Moon, Uranus, and her Sun. These astrological dynamics have manifested in her life as ongoing struggles, particularly in her relationships with relatives and colleagues. However, I noticed a transformative pattern: when she channels her energy into significant tasks requiring both physical exertion and focus, her Mars energy becomes a potent tool for achievement.

Her Mars, positioned in Capricorn, combines the disciplined, goal-oriented qualities of this earth sign with Uranus's inventive and disruptive creativity. This dynamic combination allowed her to start her own business in the arts, a field that requires originality and boldness. While Mars's tense aspect with her Sun often fuels her impulses and bold actions, these traits are now directed toward entrepreneurial success, harmonizing with the stabilizing energy of Mars in Capricorn, providing a structured outlet for her dynamic personality. Her business not only provides a creative outlet for her originality but also allows her to meet demanding goals (Mars in Capricorn), all while expressing her impulses in a constructive manner.

Finding Archetypal Patterns through Questioning

Repetitive patterns in relationships at work, with family, or among friends often signal the influence of an unconscious archetype. Astrological archetypes provide a meaningful lens for understanding the subpersonalities and defense mechanisms within our psyche, helping individuals make conscious choices that align with their potential. To address these patterns, it is vital to recognize them, identify their nature, and build a new relationship with them.

For Jung, a psychoneurosis arises from the suffering of a soul seeking meaning (Pascal, 1992, p. 107). Recognizing a personality trait through an archetype can relieve stress, as it shifts the focus from self-judgment to exploration of unconscious patterns. Astrological archetypes, in particular, facilitate this process by revealing distorted beliefs while simultaneously inspiring new possibilities. Archetypes guide individuals through emotional distress by mediating understanding and offering a symbolic framework for acceptance.

When instincts or complexes are triggered, such as survival drives or feelings of abandonment, powerful unconscious forces can take over, leading to anxiety, depression, or fear. These forces, acting as fragmented subpersonalities, may overwhelm the conscious mind. Archetypes, through their narrative and metaphorical expression, provide a structure for clients to understand and navigate these forces. By bearing the emotional weight of the client's experience, archetypes can be used as tools to anchor the client's journey forward and motivate constructive action.

The coaching process begins by identifying the client's emotional triggers and exploring their significance through astrological and dream symbols. Following Bogart's strategy (2020), clients are asked how specific archetypes manifest in their lives. This dialogue reveals untapped potentials and provides opportunities for deeper self-reflection.

> Rather than giving chart readings that are droning monologues, approaching the work as dialogue makes sessions lively and engaged. Our interpretation evolves as we learn the details of a person's life. The process also involves dialogue with the planets themselves, meditating and considering, what does this planet want? How can I best express it? (pp. 25–26)

The coach's role is to foster a safe, supportive space where clients can engage with their unconscious, witness what emerges, and feel nurtured in the process. Coaches and clients co-create archetypal imagery, inviting symbols that represent both challenges and opportunities. In active imagination, clients are encouraged to explore these images personally, free from rigid interpretations, discovering their unique meaning.

We guide clients to align their strengths with their archetypal traits, reimagining their life story in a way that brings balance and meaning. Clients are introduced to archetypes in simple terms before engaging in active imagination. Once unconscious impulses are identified, the next step involves discovering the positive potentials in the client's natal chart and related dream symbols. These archetypal configurations illuminate the source of inner conflict and can provide flexible, intelligent responses to life's challenges.

A Tapestry of Rich Meanings

Critics of astrology often highlight the perceived lack of consistency among astrologers when interpreting astrological configurations, suggesting that this undermines astrology's validity. However, such critiques may miss a crucial aspect of astrological practice: its reliance on symbolic and metaphorical language. Unlike rigid, deterministic systems, astrology operates through the rich multivalence of symbols – allowing for multiple layers of meaning that are context-dependent. Astrology's multivalence mirrors the complexity of human experience. Thus, disagreements among astrologers do not necessarily indicate a lack of coherence but rather reflect the richness of symbolic language and its adaptability to diverse contexts.

Goddard (2005) offers a critical response to the claim that astrological multivalence and the principle of indeterminism merely serve as interpretative hedges— suggesting that "anything can mean anything." While archetypes do indeed possess a multiplicity of potential expressions, their core qualities remain distinct and do not blur into one another, even as they interact to form complex patterns and influences. For instance, Jupiter's expressions are inherently expansive and inclusive, and thus cannot dissolve into the separative, contracting qualities of Saturn. Despite their continual interaction, each archetype retains its essential nature, contributing uniquely to the rich and multifaceted palette of manifest experience.

Each archetypal principle contains its own order, balance, excess, intensity, and shadow and can be expressed in the individual life and psyche or on a collective level (Goddard, 2009).

For example, the astrological principle of Uranus correlates with the Promethean archetype, which symbolizes liberation and can manifest itself as a sudden rising to a new level of awareness and consciousness and radical freedom from previous constrictions. Prometheus[18] defied the Olympian gods by stealing fire and gifting it, along with knowledge and civilization, to humanity.

The expression of archetypes in human life is inherently fluid, shaped by the cultural context and the individual's level of consciousness and self-awareness. In his book *Cosmos and Psyche*, Tarnas (2006, p. 87) offers an example of the archetypes' variations through history and through different cultures. For example, the archetype of Venus can be approached as the Greek mythic figure of Aphrodite, the goddess of beauty and love, the Mesopotamian Ishtar, and the Roman Venus. These mythic figures reflect transcultural archetypal patterns of meaning. On the Jungian level, Venus can be viewed as "the psychological tendency to perceive, desire, create, or in some other way experience beauty and love, to attract and be attracted, to seek harmony and aesthetic or sensuous pleasure, to engage in artistic activity and in romantic and social relation."

Prometheus, a Titan, embodies the concept of foreknowledge, possessing the ability to foresee events before they unfold. In the conflict between Zeus and the Titans, Prometheus anticipated Zeus' triumph and chose to support him, aligning himself against his own kind. Individuals whose natal charts prominently feature this archetype may have intuitive insights into the future. A veil is lifted, offering a broader perspective on our lives and a deeper understanding of the lessons embedded in crises and challenges. The shadow side of the Uranus/Prometheus archetype finds its expression in anarchy, eccentricity, and acting out against limitations and laws of any kind.

Prometheus also represents the impulse for progress and the necessity to improve our current circumstances. When this archetype is activated, we may undergo a shift in consciousness, experiencing a revelation that transforms our perception of ourselves and life itself. This transformation may manifest as acts of rebellion against a constraining society, seeking to unleash creativity within an environment of freedom.

Another archetype, Jupiter, the mighty Roman deity, stood as the most powerful and highest among the gods, presiding over the great Roman games. Revered as the guardian of law and protector of justice and virtue, Jupiter shares similarities with the Greek Zeus, the Nordic-Germanic Thor, and the Babylonian god Marduk.

In his book *Exploring Jupiter*, Arroyo (1996) says that an essential aspect of Jupiter's nature in both mythology and astrology is the profound connection to what was often referred to as the "higher mind" or "divine mind." The archetype of Jupiter, when well placed, signifies growth and a healthy optimism and vitality. However, when negatively expressed, Jupiter can lead to over-optimism, poor judgment, and scattered energy. The generosity inherent in Jupiter may evolve into extravagance or making excessive promises. Similarly, idealism can turn into self-righteous judgmentalism, and nobility can become inflated egocentricity.

For example, in the case of the Jupiter archetype, to manifest its beneficial and ennobling vibrations, a balance between its enthusiastic approach to life and Saturn's prudent, cautious perspective is essential. It's crucial to harmonize visions of infinite possibilities with the realistic assessment of what experiences have shown to be likely achievable.

The Basics of Astrology

The natal chart is founded on the fundamental concept that the positions of the planets at the moment of a person's birth can reveal a meaningful archetypal pattern, which in turn influences the individual's personality, values, and beliefs.

In his book *Astrology's Higher Octaves: New Dimensions of a Healing Art*, Professor Greg Bogart (2020, p. 55) elaborates: "Every interpretation of a birth chart is a hypothesis, an attempt to read an unknown text, revealing the wisdom of a superior organizing intelligence."

The natal chart offers an endless number of interpretations. In coaching or therapy, we focus on the key theme that the client has presented and do not pretend to provide a thorough chart interpretation. It is not practical and would overwhelm the client. Knowing the nature of the particular archetypes that are seeking to manifest can play a significant role in positively influencing the outcome, helping the client align more consciously with the energies at play in their current life situation. The client can be familiarized with these patterns and their polarities and work with his or her own archetypes in a co-creative way—drawing on the archetypes' potential value as a source of guidance in the process of whole-making and liberation from compulsive, unconscious patterns of behavior that may be blocking personal goals.

To understand the birth chart, it is important to have a general knowledge of planets, signs, aspects, houses, and cycles. Imagine three roulette wheels in the sky at the moment of birth, each spinning at their own pace: the signs, the planets, and the houses. The furthest wheel encompasses the constellation of stars that make up the signs of the zodiac. The ten planets embody the archetypal forces and are positioned in a constellation of stars from the perspective of the Earth, and the 12 houses depend on the daily rotation of the Earth on its axis. Each planet is located in a constellation of stars (symbolizing the qualities with which the planet expresses itself: Aries, Taurus, Gemini…) and in a specific house (domain of life such as career, family, health, relationships). In this context, the planet represents the actor, the sign represents the role they play, and the house represents the theater stage and the various scenarios in our lives (our personality, possessions, neighbor-hood, family, house, self-expression, creativity, job, health, relationships, aspira-tions, ideals, ambitions, and goals, projects, friends, and our spiritual life, or how we transcend this reality).

Planets and zodiacal signs represent mythical, recurrent patterns of experience, universal human situations, and motivations.

The personal planets are the Sun, Moon, Mercury, Venus, and Mars. We awaken the Sun to express an identity, our individual will. Through the Moon, we connect with feelings and caring; through Mercury, we learn and communicate; Venus describes how we express joy through relationships and pleasures. What I like or dislike (Venus) can be a source of great harmony or tension in our close relationships. Mars is the archetype that injects us with energy, vitality, and self-assertion. The social planets are Jupiter and Saturn. Jupiter represents our beliefs, goals, and aspirations, and Saturn shows us how we can stabilize our lives through focused, sustained effort. Uranus, Neptune, and Pluto are called the transpersonal planets. They are the furthest planets and bring great transfor-mation through changes in personal life structures (career, family, relationships, health, and so on).

Although every planetary archetype plays an important role in one's chart, the most personally significant are the Sun and Moon. The Sun represents the center of personal identity, the conscious ego – the autonomous willing self, and is associated with one's sense of individual self-directedness and self-expression. The Moon, by contrast, corresponds to one's feelings and unconscious psychological patterns established deep in one's past. To awaken the Sun, which represents our feeling of dignity, healthy pride, and joy in being ourselves, it is essential to examine our automatic mind and emotional reactions. This self-examination involves delving into our thought patterns, emotional responses, and underlying beliefs.

Disturbing emotions such as anxiety, anger, or fear can often cloud the bright-ness of our inner Sun. When these emotions arise, they may overshadow our sense of self-worth and confidence. The term "emotion" comes from the Latin verb *emovere*, which means "to shake, or stir." Emotions, therefore, imply movement; the state of tranquility is shaken, and the balance is broken. Everything in life is in motion, and emotions are meant to flow like a river running its course. Instead of blocking or ignoring these emotions, it is crucial to acknowledge and understand them. By embracing the ebb and flow of our emotions, we can develop maturity, resilience, and adaptability in the face of life's challenges.

To discern archetypal patterns in human experience, astrologers examine plan-etary alignments measured along the ecliptic, the apparent path the Sun traces on the celestial sphere over a year as viewed from Earth. These alignments, known as aspects, are defined by the angular distance between planets. The nature of these aspects influences the quality and dynamics of the interaction between the archetypal forces represented by the planets. Every planetary alignment represents experiences that are happening or trying to happen. The more people understand the emotional-archetypal impulses that are operating in their psyches, the more consciously and responsibly they can work with those tendencies, helping them to manifest in the most constructive and life-supporting ways possible (Butler, p. 17).

When two planets are in aspect, their energies dynamically interact, creating experiences that reflect the archetypal themes associated with those planets. The nature of their interaction depends on the type of aspect and the planets involved. The most important aspects are based on divisions of the 360° circle by the whole numbers 1, 2, 3, 4, and 6 – to form the conjunction (two planets 0° apart in the sky), opposition (180° apart), the trine (120°), square (90°), and sextile (60°) aspects respectively. The conjunctions, squares, and oppositions are sometimes referred to as dynamic aspects, while the trines and sextiles are considered as flowing aspects.

Arroyo (2004, p. 135) offers the following tip for the interpretation of aspects:

> The planets in the signs indicate the basic urges towards expression and needs for fulfillment, but the aspects reveal the actual state of the energy flow, and thus how much personal effort is needed in order to express a particular urge or to fulfill a particular need.

This interplay shapes how the individual perceives and responds to life events, offering opportunities for growth, challenge, or integration of opposing forces.

The interplay between Mars and Venus, particularly in challenging aspects like squares or oppositions, often reveals profound insights into the dynamics of passion and conflict within the psyche. Mars, associated with assertiveness and anger, brings unyielding energy, while Venus, symbolizing love and values, seeks harmony and connection. When these planets clash, the resulting tension may manifest in relationships, creative endeavors, or personal conflicts, often reflecting the houses they occupy in the natal chart. For clients experiencing such dynamics, a coaching approach rooted in creative redirection and emotional awareness can offer a pathway toward growth and balance.

Imagine a client who frequently finds themselves torn between their desire for self-assertion and their yearning for harmony in relationships. The Mars-Venus conflict might emerge in their interactions with others, leading to feelings of frustration or misunderstanding. The goal of coaching in this context is to help the client explore this tension, understand its underlying patterns, and find constructive outlets for these powerful energies.

The first step in this process involves guiding the client to reflect on how this planetary aspect manifests in their life. Through thoughtful dialogue, the coach might pose questions like *when you feel a surge of frustration or passion, how do you usually respond?* Or *how do you balance your need for independence with your desire for connection?* Such inquiries encourage self-awareness and illuminate patterns that might otherwise remain unconscious.

As the client begins to uncover these patterns, the coach helps them reframe the conflict. Rather than viewing the tension between Mars and Venus as a problem, the client is encouraged to see it as a dynamic interplay of energies – one that holds the potential for creative and relational growth.

One effective technique is anchoring the intense energy of Mars in activities that channel passion and drive. If the client enjoys creative pursuits, they might be encouraged to explore dance, painting, or writing as a way to express Mars's assertive force while engaging Venus's aesthetic sensibilities. For instance, improvisational movement or dance can provide a physical outlet for Mars's energy, fostering spontaneity and connection in the moment. Similarly, creating art with bold, dynamic strokes might allow the client to feel both empowered and connected to their inner world.

The process also involves cultivating social skills and emotional regulation. When the client faces real-life challenges that echo the Mars-Venus dynamic, mindfulness techniques can help them pause and respond thoughtfully rather than reacting impulsively. The coach might also introduce role-playing scenarios where the client practices asserting their needs with grace, ensuring their Mars-driven directness is tempered by Venusian tact.

If we have a hard aspect between Mars and our Moon, instead of suppressing or acting out on our anger, we can learn to channel this energy in constructive ways, such as setting healthy boundaries or advocating for ourselves. A client with Saturn in a Retense aspect to the Moon may struggle with emotional expression and self-nurturance, often feeling they must earn love and care through hard work or self-denial. By addressing this myth of unworthiness, the coach can help the client explore and affirm their right to emotional needs and self-care.

Similarly, if Saturn squares Venus, issues around self-worth and relationships may come to the fore, with the client feeling unworthy of love or fearing rejection. The coach can work with the client to identify and challenge these beliefs, encouraging them to engage in activities that build self-esteem and foster healthy connections. This might include exploring past experiences that contributed to the myth of unworthiness and reframing these experiences in a more empowering light. By embracing the constructive side of Saturn's energy, we can develop self-discipline and face our fears with courage and determination. Techniques such as journaling, mindfulness, and self-compassion exercises can be integrated to support this process, gradually helping the client to rewrite their inner narrative.

The teachings of Rinpoche Thulku Thondup about unconditional love, for example, could be very beneficial for those suffering from Saturn's challenging aspects to personal planets. Thulku Thondup explains the Buddhist practice known as loving-kindness meditation, which aims to find unconditional love in our own hearts, in our relationships, and in our perceptions of the world around us. He also offers helpful tips, such as the practice of magnifying your progress, which can balance the Saturnian tendency to undervalue our actions.

In his book *The Healing Power of the Mind* (1996, p. 40), Tulku Thondup says:

No matter how small our progress, if we celebrate it as something significant and valuable, it becomes a powerful achievement. So recognize your positive qualities and the small steps you take. Say to yourself: 'How wonderful, I made this progress!' and then spontaneously the progress will be magnified and the obstacles minimized.

We focus on the archetypal configurations that address the specific needs and concerns of each individual, offering practical advice and support that are directly relevant to their current situation. For example, if a client discusses feeling overwhelmed by work and struggling to find balance in their life, a therapist/coach might focus on exploring the themes of responsibility, boundaries, and self-care expressed by the planet Saturn and the earthly houses of the chart, especially the sixth and tenth houses. Understanding a client's sixth house can reveal insights into their work habits, approach to health, and how they manage their day-to-day life. It also encompasses physical health, wellness, and the care of the body. The tenth house, also known as the Midheaven, represents career, public life, and societal status. It is associated with one's ambitions, achievements, and the legacy they wish for. By honing in on these key areas instead of attempting a comprehensive analysis of every aspect of the client's natal chart, the therapist can provide more targeted and effective support for the client's current challenges.

Understanding Attachment Styles through the Moon

The Moon represents the subconscious mind and tells us about our automatic reactions and natural disposition toward the environment. It speaks to our basic need for safety and survival. If this basic need is covered, we can express our feelings constructively and develop our capacity for caring and empathy toward others. If it is not sufficiently satisfied, it causes us anguish or anxiety. For some people, this anguish is lifelong. Recognizing these subconscious responses is crucial for helping clients work with their shadow aspects, those parts of themselves they may not fully acknowledge or understand.

In practice, this means paying attention to the Moon's house placement, sign, and aspects with other planets.

In his book *Chart Interpretation Handbook, Guidelines for Understanding the Essentials of the Birth Chart*, Arroyo (2004, p. 148) points out that the Moon is "the key to objectivity about oneself":

> The challenging aspects to the Moon show that one will have to work to gain the sort of objectivity that comes naturally with harmonious lunar aspects. A harmoniously aspected Moon has a natural objectivity about the self and often therefore a fairly accurate self-image, but when the Moon is stressfully aspected, one tends to take everything personally with no detachment about oneself. In that case, one is not able to adjust easily to changing circumstances, and one's self-image is often quite inaccurate in the areas indicated by the planets, signs, and houses involved.

This is why it is essential for a therapist or coach to carefully examine the client's Moon placement and its aspects, as it offers valuable insights into emotional needs, nurturing patterns, and core vulnerabilities. The Moon offers us clues about how the client can feel secure and have their needs fulfilled. Understanding the Moon's placement and aspects can help the therapist or coach create an environment that nurtures the client's emotional well-being. This information allows for a more personalized and empathetic interaction, ensuring that the client's unique emotional landscape is respected and supported.

For instance, a client with a Moon in a challenging aspect to Saturn might struggle with feelings of inadequacy and emotional restraint. Recognizing this pattern, the coach can support the client in strengthening self-esteem and fostering emotional reassurance, helping them develop a more nurturing inner dialogue. Conversely, a client with a harmoniously aspected Moon may naturally possess a stable self-image and emotional resilience, allowing the coach to leverage these strengths in their personal growth journey.

By looking at the Moon's position by sign (the stars behind the Moon seen from the Earth at birth), house (area of life where it will manifest), and aspects (significant geometric relationship with other planets), we also gain information about the attachment style that conditioned our early years, for better or worse (Bogart, 2020). The exploration of archetypes influencing the Moon offers valuable insights into our automatic emotional mind, helping us understand our reactions and uncover the needs of our inner child.

If any major aspect is formed between the Moon and another planet in one's birth chart, this second planetary archetype will tend to channel itself through one's emotions and moods, one's infancy and childhood, one's mother and early familial environment, and one's intimate relationships and domestic life. Tense aspects of the Moon can generate automatic reactions that challenge the ability to be true to oneself, which is represented by the Sun.

Depending on the quality of the relationship we had with our early caregiver, the fulfillment or frustration of our needs, we developed a secure or insecure attachment style, which became a template for our future relationships. Life is not safe if, in our childhood, we had experiences of dissatisfaction, insecurity, threats of abandonment, or changes of environment.

Ainsworth et al. (1978) identified three major styles of attachment: secure attachment, anxious-insecure attachment, and avoidant-insecure attachment.

Secure attachment is the result of feeling secure, understood, and comforted by caregivers from childhood. Caregivers were emotionally available and aware of their own emotions and behaviors and valued their interactions with the child. When growing up, these children tend to be generally positive, trusting, and loving to their partners. Positive contacts of the Moon with the Sun, Venus, and Jupiter typically correlate with secure attachment. A reliable, warm, responding, nurturing caregiver provides feelings of safety and well-being for the child (Bogart, 2020).

Insecure attachment styles develop when the child cannot rely on his caregivers to fulfill basic needs and feel safe. People with an insecure attachment style generally have trouble making emotional connections with others. They can be dependent, needy, aggressive, or unpredictable toward their loved ones. These are behaviors rooted in the lack of consistent love and affection they experienced in their childhood.

Conditioning that fostered an insecure attachment style can threaten our authenticity through defensive psychological mechanisms such as denial, projection, or idealization. If we do not know how to identify our innate lunar wisdom, that is, the things that can offer us security, our Moon will act indirectly through defense mechanisms that act unconsciously when we are distressed.

Unconscious lunar needs may be met through a compulsive relationship with food, addiction, status, or a fixation on the accumulation of money or material goods. Instead of normal preoccupation, anguish is manifested at any threat of change. Nevertheless, as grown-ups, we can change our attachment style as long as we are willing to identify it, understand it, and act in ways that will feed our inner needs. Here is where the information decoded in the natal chart can provide valuable knowledge.

A good relationship with the moon will not prevent us from suffering from distress or anxiety from time to time, but it will show us possibilities for handling distress creatively. This understanding allows us to care for ourselves with the same compassion and attentiveness a nurturing mother would provide. The more we learn to nourish ourselves emotionally, the less dependent or resentful we become when life doesn't meet our needs in the ways we expect. When there is a conflict, for a Moon placed on an Earth sign (Taurus, Virgo, and Capricorn), the first step is to cover the practical needs of the material domain and physical body, the temple of the soul. This could be done through healthy eating, massage, aromatherapy, spending time in nature, or practicing body-awareness movements such as yoga and qigong. A Moon in an air element (Gemini, Libra, Aquarius) needs clarity and is analytical and evasive when threatened by too much intimacy; to balance itself, it needs communication without emotional confrontation. On the contrary, a Moon placed in a water sign (Cancer, Scorpio, Pisces) will need emotional proximity to merge with the environment and to investigate the hidden motivations in themselves and others. Moons in fire (Aries, Leo, Sagittarius) will feel good by connecting with their spontaneity, reacting with direct action and enthusiasm.

In *Astrology, Psychology, and the Four Elements*, Arroyo (1975, p. 98) explains that in Jungian psychology, the trans-Saturnian planets (Uranus, Neptune, and Pluto) represent the functional modes of the Collective Unconscious, while the Moon and Saturn represent the structural patterns and subconscious needs of the Personal Unconscious. The Moon symbolizes intangible emotional security needs associated with the mother (inner support), whereas Saturn symbolizes tangible material security needs linked to the father (outer support).

I will offer examples of transpersonal influences by describing aspects of Uranus, Neptune, and Pluto to the Moon.

When there are hard aspects between the transpersonal planet Uranus and the Moon, the child often perceives coolness, aloofness, and unavailability on the part of the caregiver and develops an avoidant attachment style. Such children perceive that their parents rejected their emotional needs and stop expecting any response from them. One consequence of this is that they become self-sufficient and independent as adults. Their strategy is to repress their emotions because of a subconscious belief that other people will reject their emotions anyway. The unconscious fear that closeness will drive the attention figure away is why people with an avoidant or dismissive attachment style are not comfortable in intimacy and have difficulty asking others for help.

The planet Uranus symbolizes a force that manifests as sudden changes in routine and shifts of consciousness, flashes of intuition, and new ideas, providing a strong impulse toward change and freedom. When the archetype Uranus is strong in a chart, it electrifies and magnetizes the areas of life symbolized by the planets and houses with which Uranus is in contact.

One of my clients, whose Uranus is forming challenging aspects to her Sun and Moon, experienced extremely stressful events as a young child. She was the only one in her family capable of calming his father's temper. Growing up in the midst of this unpredictability has caused her unconscious to continue manifesting this unpredictable environment through her relationships and jobs, where she is the one to relieve tension among unpredictable people. She is now aware of this factor and seeks innovative ways to express her Uranus characteristics. She writes poetry, paints watercolors, and creates very unique artistic activities for children. Through her creative outlets, she is able to channel her Uranus energy in a positive and constructive way, allowing her to break free from the cycle of unpredictability that once defined her life.

In Spring's example (see Chapter 6), Uranus is strongly placed in her first house (her personality) and aspects her natal Moon harmonically. Spring needs to communicate freely, feel emotionally free, and not depend on anyone. Her speech distills her need for freedom in her family relationships as well as in her work environment. Her love for change and freedom (Uranus) has helped her to adapt easily to changes of residence and country (Moon), including other continents.

Children with anxious (or ambivalent insecure) attachment lived with unpredictable or neglecting parents. Because of a lack of attention from early caregivers, they require constant validation and can be seen as clingy or needy. For example, hard aspects of Neptune (the planet that symbolizes altered states of consciousness) to the Moon can indicate a caregiver who was not responsive to the child's needs. Maybe the mother was suffering from depression or had an addiction to alcohol or drugs. These aspects can produce long periods of confusion and low energy levels. However, Neptune also represents high sensitivity and a longing and capacity for emotional harmonization with higher levels of existence. If constructively addressed, Neptune allows us to contact a larger field of existence through art and spiritual practices.

Marguerite's story illustrates the Neptunian longing for a spiritual path, as detailed in Chapter 6. The close aspect of Neptune to her Moon makes her highly sensitive to her environment, rendering her a hyper-empathic person who keenly perceives the needs of others. This sensitivity has led to tendencies toward escapism and the idealization of affectionate figures in her life, resulting in disappointment and disillusionment in relationships. Driven by a deep longing for peace and a strong connection to a higher plane of existence, she left behind a structured professional life in France to pursue a more holistic way of living. This journey led her across continents, where she embraced spiritual practices such as participating in ayahuasca retreats.

The conjunction of her natal Moon with Neptune also manifests as artistic creativity. Marguerite channels her spiritual and emotional experiences into tangible forms through creative practices such as crocheting, playing the ukulele, and regularly drawing her dreams.

Another type of insecure attachment is caused by parents who act as figures of both control and comfort to a child. When the Moon aspects Pluto (the planet that symbolizes power control, death, and rebirth), the emotional relationship with the mother or other caregivers is usually deep and intense. In some cases, the mother may be controlling or intrusive, a domineering presence. Pluto is often feared as an agent of death and emotional turbulence, yet it is through Pluto that we can confront our shadows and undergo regeneration, transforming what no longer serves us.

Roshani (see Chapter 6) exemplifies the transformative power of Pluto's contact with the Moon through her ability to address her shadow and repressed emotions. The recent death of her mother left unresolved issues. Her dog also passed away and, to top it off, she broke her wrist. These sudden losses and the accident forced her to confront feelings of vulnerability she had repressed since childhood and to accept loving care from her partner, which was a challenge for her, as she had always struggled not to find herself in the situation of needing help.

> Pain is a very important reality toward any kind of movement into growth, evolution, progress… it was like a fire. There was this pot, and I was inside being cooked slowly. I feel I invited this lesson because maybe I reached a point where I was not being very true to myself. Transformation is not just about change, it means being able to look at things that you don't want to look at, being able to resolve stuff, not pretending that all is okay. (Roshani, pp. 91–124, in Carod, 2021)

Transits: Divine Timing

It would be beneficial for coaches to be somewhat informed about transits or the planets' positions in the sky at the time of the consultation and how they are aspecting the client's natal planets. Transits provide insight into the type of energy being activated for the client at that moment, reflecting the areas for potential learning and growth.

Professor Richard Tarnas research (2006) showed correlations between particular planetary alignments (transits) and what appears to be the simultaneous activation of corresponding archetypal meanings, experiences, and psychological tendencies in specific individual lives and historical periods.

Since each planet or luminary has a unique orbital speed, the duration of their transits varies accordingly. The Moon's transits are brief, typically lasting only a few hours, while those of the Sun, Mercury, Venus, and Mars span several days.

In contrast, Jupiter and Saturn exert their influence over several months, and the slower-moving outer planets—Uranus, Neptune, and Pluto—have transits that can extend over several years. For a comprehensive understanding of basic astrology and transits, reputable sources include psychologists and astrologers like Greg Bogart, Richard Tarnas, Liz Greene, Howard Sasportas, Robert Hand, and Stephen Arroyo. These authors offer detailed insights into how transits mirror our inner processes and help us navigate our paths of personal growth and self-realization.

Arroyo (1979) emphasizes that transits, while often associated with visible events, are fundamentally processes that reveal inner trends. He explains that these transits can either culminate a process or act as a catalyst initiating change. Transits may manifest as inner urges or feelings without any apparent external events, or they may provoke external experiences that compel the person to confront underlying issues, particularly if they are unaware of these internal dynamics. In such cases, external events often force the individual to look inward.

This is evident in Roshani's story. Her accident, which dramatically impacted her life, compelled her to explore her emotional depths. During this time, the transits she experienced were particularly significant, emphasizing her Moon (emotions and relationship with her mother), urging her to confront and integrate these aspects of her psyche.

Most of my clients' transits showed Saturn, Uranus, Neptune, and Pluto aspecting personal planets or important points of the chart like the ascendant (personality and self-image), the fourth house (house, family), the descendant (relationships), and the tenth house (career, status).

The transiting location of Saturn in our charts highlights the area that presents the greatest tension in our lives, demanding our full focus. It points to behavior patterns that need examination. Depression, melancholy, and physical or emotional loss are symptoms of not effectively addressing the issues associated with Saturn's transits. It is crucial to inform our clients that these reactions are common and can be mitigated through conscious self-work.

Saturn provides valuable information about specific areas where the client needs to put in consistent effort. This information is crucial for determining the next steps in coaching. We should carefully consider both Natal Saturn and transiting Saturn in a chart to suggest practical steps for our clients to release the heaviness and feelings of inadequacy and frustration that this planet often provokes.

According to Bogart (2012, p. 306):

> Hard work is always involved. But work isn't as hard if you have focus and a sense of purpose. The transits of Saturn mean we have to face that area of life (house) or that part of ourselves (natal planet) with clarity and realism. The current transiting position of Saturn shows us where we need to get organized, focus on our responsibilities, and get things done.

A common personal myth encountered in coaching and therapy is the myth of unworthiness. When Saturn is in a challenging aspect to a personal planet, it can manifest as self-doubt, feelings of inadequacy, and a fear of failure or success.

By uncovering and working through this personal myth, the coach can assist the client in developing a new narrative that empowers them to achieve their objectives. For example, a client with Saturn squaring the Sun might feel an inherent pressure to prove themselves, often setting excessively high standards and being overly critical of their achievements. Through the positive representation of the archetype facilitated by the coach, the client can learn to recognize and challenge these limiting beliefs, understanding that their worth is not solely defined by external accomplishments. They can be guided to see the value in their efforts and intrinsic qualities, fostering a healthier self-concept.

Saturn helps identify areas where the client can become an active agent of their destiny, aligning well with Stoic values such as detachment, resilience, practicality, and realism. For instance, a client exhibiting patterns of self-sabotage and doubt may have a personal myth revolving around unworthiness and fear of success. If this client has Saturn in a tense aspect to the Sun, Moon, Venus, or Mars, it can reflect deep-seated beliefs about their value and capabilities. The Sun represents one's core identity and sense of purpose, and the Moon governs emotional security and inner life. Venus rules self-worth and relationships and Mars represents our self-assertiveness and how we pursue our goals. When Saturn challenges these planets, it can create internal narratives of not being good enough, deserving enough, or lovable enough.

Rudhyar (in Bogart, 2009) viewed the transits of Uranus, Neptune, and Pluto as key moments in the process of spiritual development.

Uranus transits mark moments of sudden awakening, where individuals embrace innovation and change. Uranus symbolizes the urge to break free from cultural norms, facilitating decisive acts of self-liberation and encouraging us to act as agents of transformation.

In *Planets in Therapy*, Bogart (2012, p. 307) says:

> If we're not ready for Uranus it can manifest as disruption, surprise, shock. These transits can bring sudden and unexpected changes. On the other hand, if we're living in alignment with our true selves, if we're individuating, then Uranus transits bring an air of excitement, freedom, exhilaration, and the feeling of sudden awakening, or being swept up in a wave, a strong wind, a ripple of change. Uranus is the catalyst of changes that thrust us into a new experience or a new attitude toward an area of life.

An important role for the coach is to help the client find healthy ways to manage the new life energy they are experiencing. Our task is to highlight the positive, transformative potential of their current transit. For example, if a client is under a significant transit of Uranus, feeling restless, impatient, and rebellious, we can guide them toward living their inner truth with more authenticity. The powerful energy channeled from Uranus provides with the courage needed for breaking free from obstacles that hinder them from experiencing something new that aligns with their core values.

Neptune transits invite individuals to transcend the ego and align with a higher spiritual purpose. Rudhyar (in Bogart, 2011) described Neptune's influence as fostering compassion, stillness, and a selfless attitude. By responding to Neptune's energies, individuals become more in tune with the spiritual needs of the moment, cultivating a visionary imagination that connects them to the greater whole. It's about becoming a vessel for light and consciousness.

Neptune can be a challenging planetary influence that can cause confusion, ambiguity, and ego-denying feelings, while also introducing beautiful ideal influences.

In his famous book *Planets in Transit*, Robert Hand (1976, p. 425) explains how Neptune dissolves our sense of reality, leaving us confused and with doubt:

> Neptune dissolves whatever Saturn builds, such as your ego, your sense of duty and responsibility, your sense of definite reality, and everything else about the world that is definite, clear, and predictable. Neptune works against all these structures; it dissolves or threatens to dissolve your ego so that initially you feel lost, confused, or defeated, but this effect can also make you feel exhilarated and at one with the entire universe. It depends on your level of consciousness.

We can recognize Neptunian energy among the Platonists, particularly the Theurgists, and their desire to connect with the One, or our divine nature. This impulse is also evident in Plato's glorification of beauty and goodness.

However, under a transit of Neptune, clients might engage in self-destructive escapism, such as drug or alcohol abuse, or over-idealizing a relationship. Developing a spiritual practice or committing to an ideal, while also being mindful of not losing contact with reality, can fulfill their need to belong to a greater entity.

In order to counterbalance Neptunian delusions, we can look at Saturn, both in its natal position and in transit. Mixing Platonic and Stoic philosophies can provide a balanced approach. Too much Saturn can make us feel melancholy and disenchantment with life, while too much Neptune can lead to a sense of futility, lack of grounding, and losing contact with reality in pursuit of an unattainable dream.

Astrology can enable us to identify the nature of the crisis, its meaning and purpose, what it asks of us, and its probable length. Transits of the transpersonal planets (Saturn, Uranus, Neptune, and Pluto) to natal Moon can involve an emotional crisis. Transits to Mercury may involve a crisis in our way of thinking or communicating. Transits to Venus can denote a crisis in our way of relating to others, a change or upheaval in a relationship, or a crisis involving money. Transits to Mars signify a crisis involving the necessity of taking action, expressing initiative, anger, or self-assertiveness (Bogart, 2012, p. 291).

Ruperti (in Bogart, 2012, p. 307) says:

> A crisis, however, is not a terrible calamity. It derives from the Greek word krino, "to decide," and means simply a time for decision[,]…a turning point— that which precedes change. In order to avoid a crisis one would have to avoid change itself, an obvious impossibility…

Something needs to be decided for the evolutionary process to take place. This decision is usually painful or involves some degree of suffering, renunciation, or loss.

Another important point is that understanding the duration of specific transits can greatly assist clients in strategic planning. For example, if one is experiencing an aspect of Saturn to their Sun, they can anticipate a period of reduced vitality lasting approximately one year. However, Saturn allows for a sustained effort on long-term projects. If Neptune is aspecting Venus, one can expect a two- to three-year period characterized by a tendency to romanticize reality, over-idealize partners, or engage in escapist behaviors through addictions or spiritual biases. On a more positive side, one can also achieve excellent results in artistic endeavors and connect with their higher self or any kind of spiritual experience that expands consciousness. There is the possibility of connecting with the more subtle aspects of reality and the beautiful aspects of life through art, spirituality, and relationships. Foreknowledge of Neptune's possible manifestations can guide individuals to practice somatic awareness in practices such as yoga, mindfulness, and involvement in creative tasks, helping them avoid the pitfalls of evading reality.

In the case of the feared Pluto, the transit might result in empowerment and enhanced effectiveness, or it can lead to power struggles, antagonism, or control over others. Pluto transits are frequently moments of testing. It could be a period of closure and new beginnings, crisis, catharsis, or release. Compulsive or obsessive behaviors or manipulation of others might be avoided by honestly confronting one's deepest desires, having the courage to transform them or let them go, thereby allowing unhealthy parts of the personality to die.

Pluto's influence can be inferred from Rudhyar's broader philosophy (in Bogart, 2020) which considers astrology as an initiatory process. Pluto symbolizes deep transformation and the destruction of old psychological structures, often requiring us to confront shadow elements within ourselves. This process, though difficult, is a vital part of spiritual rebirth and empowerment.

Knowledge of Pluto's transits can offer valuable information on what is now meant to be transformed. We can help our clients understand both what the personal planet represents and the positive potential indicated by the transiting planet. For example, if Pluto is squaring Venus, we should channel energy into transforming Venus, which represents values such as love, creativity, and our relationship with money. This involves shifting our attitude from resistance to acceptance and finding creative ways to honor the energies of the transit.

For Arroyo (1979), Bogart (2012, 2020), Hand (1976), and Tarnas (2006), the only general rule for transits is that transits manifest according to the level of consciousness:

> The more self knowledge you have and the more subtle your consciousness is, the more you pick up the inner meanings of the experiences in your life, and the more likely the transits will manifest on a subtler level rather than on a gross level. (Arroyo, 1979, p. 161)

The level of consciousness with which one approaches one's own life is not determined by the natal chart. Archetypes inform us about behavioral tendencies and possible areas of learning, but it's only through changes in consciousness and self-awareness that one is able to identify these tendencies and transform old patterns of thought and behavior that hinder one's growth.

Notes

1 The names given to the stars by the Babylonians were for individual stars such as Mul. lugal (Šarru or King), which is identifiable as Regulus, or for stars grouped into constellations such as the True Shepherd of Anu, identified as Orion. The only star groups mentioned by Homer and by Hesiod around 700 BC were the Bear, Arcturus, Sirius, the Pleiades, the Hyades, and Orion.

   Graßhoff, G. (2020). Star-lists from the Babylonians to Ptolemy. In A. Bowen & F. Rochberg (Eds.), *Hellenistic astrology* (pp. 240–246). Brill.

2 The epic, written by an unknown poet at an undetermined date (possibly in the 14th century BCE), begins with the universe as a watery chaos with no sky or land. The goddess Tiamat personifies the sea, while the god Apsu represents the sweet waters underground. In their midst, gods are born.

   https://www.britannica.com/topic/Enuma-Elish.

3 Various natural phenomena such as the movements of clouds, winds, shooting stars, and extraordinary occurrences like the birth of malformed animals or children, lightning, thunder, earthquakes, or floods were considered significant by the Mesopotamians. These events were not viewed as gratuitous but were believed to potentially reveal the desires of the gods. Deciphering these signs correctly offering a brief prediction for the effect upon the kingdom was the responsibility of the diviner (Baigent, 1995).

4 "The Kybalion," a widely embraced text, elucidates Hermetic principles and has served as a valuable source of insight for occult enthusiasts since its initial publication in 1908. The practice of altering the conditions of the universe involves adherence to the principles of matter, force, and mind, along with an exploration of mental transmutation.

   Atkinson, W. (1932). *The Kybalion: A study of the hermetic philosophy of ancient Egypt and Greece.* Library of Congress.

5 Born in 610 BCE, Miletus [now in Turkey] – died in 546 BCE – was a Greek philosopher who was the first to develop a cosmology or systematic philosophical view of the world. Anaximander set up a gnomon (a shadow-casting rod) at Sparta and used it to demonstrate the equinoxes and solstices and perhaps the hours of the day. In his cosmogony, he held that everything originated from the *apeiron* (the "infinite," "unlimited," or "indefinite") rather than from a particular element, such as water (as Thales had held).

   Evans, J. (2024). Anaximander. *Encyclopedia Britannica*, https://www.britannica.com/biography/Anaximander. Accessed 19 November 2024.

6 Anaximenes of Miletus (flourished c. 545 BC) was a Greek philosopher of nature and one of three thinkers of Miletus traditionally considered to be the first philosophers in the Western world. There is evidence that he made the common analogy between the divine air that sustains the universe and the human "air," or soul, that animates people.

   Britannica, The Editors of Encyclopedia. (2024). Anaximenes Of Miletus. *Encyclopedia Britannica*. https://www.britannica.com/biography/Anaximenes-of-Miletus. Accessed 19 November 2024.

7 The ancient Greeks viewed Zoroastrianism as embodying the archetype of dualism, where good and evil engage in an uneven struggle destined to end in the triumph of good. This perspective includes the belief in human free will and the responsibility to

participate in this cosmic battle. Zarathushtra is said to have influenced Pythagoras in Babylon and inspired Chaldean astrology and magic doctrines.

Duchesne-Guillemin, J. (2024, July 29). Zoroastrianism. *Encyclopedia Britannica*. https://www.britannica.com/topic/Zoroastrianism.

8 Heraclitus complained that most people failed to comprehend the *logos* (Greek: "reason"), the universal principle through which all things are interrelated and all natural events occur, and thus lived like dreamers with a false view of the world. A significant manifestation of the *logos*, Heraclitus claimed, is the underlying connection between opposites. For example, health and disease define each other. Good and evil, hot and cold, and other opposites are similarly related.

Britannica, The Editors of Encyclopaedia. (2024). Heraclitus. *Encyclopedia Britannica*. https://www.britannica.com/biography/Heraclitus.

9 Poimandres is the first tractate in the *Corpus Hermeticum*. The *Corpus Hermeticum* is a collection of 17 Greek writings whose authorship is traditionally attributed to the legendary Hellenistic figure Hermes Trismegistus, a syncretic combination of the Greek god Hermes and the Egyptian god Thot. The treatises were originally written between c. 100 and c. 300 CE. The character Poimandres can be considered to be a sort of deity, or attribute of God as nous or "mind."

Bull, C. H. (2018). *The tradition of Hermes Trismegistus: The Egyptian priestly figure as a teacher of hellenized wisdom*. Religions in the Greco-Roman World (p. 186). Brill.

10 Plotinus viewed planets as ensouled beings contributing to cosmic balance (*Enneads*, 3.15). While he rejected deterministic astrology and the notion of malefic planets like Mars and Saturn, he acknowledged the symbolic significance of celestial movements.

11 The hierophant established a connection between initiates and the souls of heroes and gods. This connection reached out to the Creator, Demiurgus, the torchbearer of the Sun, and Hermes, the interpreter of the divine word. Throughout initiations and mysteries, the gods would manifest in various ways, ranging from ethereal light to taking on a human form or assuming different shapes.

Schuré, E. (1913). *Hermes and Plato*. William Rider & Son.

12 The Greek philosopher and astrologer Valens (120–175c) made the readers swear an oath to keep his teaching secret and not to impart it to the unlearned or the uninitiated (Valens, in Brennan, 2017, p. 46).

Brennan, C. (2017). *Hellenistic astrology: The study of fate and fortune*. Amor Fati Publications.

13 At the beginning of book 7 of his *Mathesis,* he makes the reader swear a similar oath. Following the rule of Orpheus, Plato, and Pythagoras he begs the reader to take note by God that these secret doctrines will not be revealed to profane ears but that the entire teaching of divinity will be made known only to "those equipped with pure splendor of mind whom an uncorrupted soul has led to the right path of life whose loyalty is above reproach and whose hands are free of all crime" (Maternus, in Brennan, 2017, p. 47).

Brennan, C. (2017). *Hellenistic astrology: The study of fate and fortune*. Amor Fati Publications.

14 The Orphic Hymns are a collection of 87 short religious poems composed in either the late Hellenistic (C3rd or C2nd B.C.) or early Roman (C1st to C2nd A.D.) era. They are based on the beliefs of Orphism, a mystery cult or religious philosophy which claimed descent from the teachings of the mythical hero Orpheus.

The Hymns of Orpheus. Translated by Taylor, Thomas (1792). University of Pennsylvania Press, 1999. (Current edition).

15 Lipton, B. H. (2005). *The biology of belief: Unleashing the power of consciousness, matter, & miracles*. Mountain of Love/Elite Books.

16 Oschman, J. L. (2000). *Energy medicine: The scientific basis*. Churchill Livingstone.

17 Archetypal astrology has emerged as part of the academic discipline of archetypal cosmology, a new theory that arose from the confluence of ancient Greek thought, depth

psychology, and astrology, which emphasizes the contributions of Jung, Hillman, Tarnas, and Stanislav Grof. A new stage in the West's cultural and psychological evolution
has brought with it a transformed vision of astrology that stems from the principles of
personal freedom and fulfillment of one's authentic nature and potential.

18 In Greek mythology, he and his brother Epimetheus were tasked with assigning defining traits to creatures. When they reached humans, Prometheus granted them fire and
other civilizing skills. As punishment, Zeus condemned Prometheus to eternal suffering,
where an eagle would daily consume his liver. In retaliation for the fire theft, Zeus sent
Pandora, whose curiosity led to the release of various troubles, though Hope remained
trapped. Eventually, Heracles intervened, slaying the eagle and securing Prometheus'
release with Zeus' approval. This tale is detailed in Hesiod's "Theogony."

      Kirk, G. S., & R. M. Hesiod. (1966). Theogony. In M. L. West (Ed.), *The Journal of
Hellenic Studies*. The Clarendon Press.

References

Afonasin, E., & Afonasina, A. (2019). Pythagoras traveling East: An image of a sage in Late Antiquity. *Archai: Revista de Estudos Sobre as Origens Do Pensamento Ocidental, 27*, e02709.

Afonasin, E., Dillon, J., & Finamore, J. (2012). The Pythagorean Way of Life in Clement of Alexandria and Iamblichus. In *Lamblichus and the foundations of late platonism*
(pp. 13–36). Brill.

Ainsworth, M. D. S., Blehar, M. C., Waters, E., & Wall, S. (1978). *Patterns of attachment:
A psychological study of the strange situation.* Lawrence Erlbaum.

Arroyo, S. (1975). *Astrology, psychology and the four elements: An energy approach to
astrology & its use in the counseling arts.* CRCS Publications.

Arroyo, S. (1979). *Relationships and life cycles.* Modern Dimensions of Astrology.

Arroyo, S. (1996). *Exploring Jupiter.* CRCS Publications.

Arroyo, S. (2004). *Chart interpretation handbook: Guidelines for understanding the essentials of the birth chart.* CRCS Publications.

Assagioli, R. (1965). *Psychosynthesis: A collection of basic writings.* Psychosynthesis.

Baigent, M. (1995). *From the Omens of Babylon: Astrology and ancient mesopotamia.* Bear
& Company.

Barker, A. T. (1925). *The Letters of H.P. Blavatsky to A.P.* Sinnett. T. Fisher Unwin LTD.

Bogart, G. (2009). *Dreamwork and self healing.* Routledge.

Bogart, G. (2012). *Planets in therapy.* Ibis Press.

Bogart, G. (2014). *Astrology and spiritual awakening.* American Federation of Astrologers.
Kindle Edition.

Bogart, G. (2020). *Astrology's higher octaves. New dimensions of a healing art.* Ibis Press.

Brennan, C. (2017). *Hellenistic astrology: The study of fate and fortune.* Amor Fati Publications.

Butler, R. (2019). *Pathways to wholeness.* Aeon Books. Kindle Edition.

Campion, N. (2012). *Astrology and cosmology in the world's religions.* New York University Press.

Carod, A. (2021). *The transformative experiences of coaching using archetypal imagery
within a participatory framework: An organic inquiry.* John Moores University.

Clayton, P., & Price, M. (2002). *The seven wonders of the ancient world.* Routledge.

Goddard, G. (2005). Counterpoints in transpersonal theory: Toward an astro-logical resolution. *ReVision, 27*(3), 9.

Goddard, G. (2009). *Transpersonal theory and the astrological mandala: An evolutionary
model.* Trafford Publishing.

Goodrick-Clarke, N. (2008). Marsilio Ficino and the renaissance Neoplatonism. In *The Western esoteric traditions: A historical introduction*. Oxford University Press.

Greene, L. (2018). *Jung's understanding of astrology. Prophecy, magic, and the qualities of time*. Routledge.

Hand, R. (1976). *Planets in transit: Life cycles for living*. Whitford Press.

Jung, C. G. (1921). *Psychological types*. Princeton University Press.

Jung, C. G. (1968). Archetypes and the collective unconscious. In H. Read, M. Fordham, G. Adler, & W. McGuire (Eds.), *The collected works of C. G. Jung* (R. F. C. Hull, Trans.) (2nd ed., Vol. 9). Princeton University Press.

Kahn, C. (2001). *Pythagoras and the Pythagoreans*. Hackett.

Kingsley, P. (1995). *Ancient philosophy, mystery, and magic: Empedocles and Pythagorean tradition*. Oxford University Press.

Pascal, E. (1992). *Jung para la vida cotidiana*. Ediciones Obelisco.

Redondo, J. (2015). The celestial imagination: Proclus the philosopher on theurgy. *Culture and Cosmos*, 19, 25–46.

Rogers, J. H. (1998). Origins of the ancient constellations: II. The Mediterranean traditions. *Journal of the British Astronomical Association*, 108(2), 79–98.

Rossi, S., & Le Grice, K. (2018). *Jung on astrology*. Routledge.

Rudhyar, D. (1975). *From humanistic to transpersonal astrology*. Seed Center.

Shaw, G. (1995). *Theurgy and the soul: The Neoplatonism of Iamblichus*. Pennsylvania State University Press.

Shaw, G. (2008). Astrology as divination: Iamblichean theory and its contemporary practice. In J. Finamore & R. Berchman (Eds.), *Metaphysical patterns in platonism*. University Press of the South.

Shaw, G. (2016). Archetypal psychology, dream work, and Neoplatonism. In H. T. Hakl (Ed.), *Octagon: The quest for wholeness* (Vol. 2, pp. 329–358). H. Frietsch Verlag.

Shaw, G. (2024). *Hellenic tantra: The theurgic platonism of Iamblichus*. Angelico Press. Kindle Edition.

Tarnas, R. (1987). An introduction to archetypal astrology. https://cosmosandpsyche.com/essays

Tarnas, R. (2006). *Cosmos and psyche: Intimations of a new world view*. Viking.

Tarnas, R. (2011). Archetypal cosmology: Past and present. *The Mountain Astrologer* (June/July, pp. 65–69).

Taylor, T. (1891). In A. Wilder (Ed.), *A dissertation on the Eleusinian and Bacchic mysteries*. The Vinne Press.

Thondup, T. (1996). *The healing power of mind*. Shamballa.

Van der Waerden, B. L. (1974). *Science awakening II: The birth of astronomy*. Leyden.

Viglas, K. S. (2013). Chaldean and neo-platonic theology. *Journal Of Hellenic Religion*, 6, 55–76.

Voss, A. (1992). The natural magic of Marsilio Ficino. *The Journal of Dolmetsch Historical Dance Society*, 3(1), 25–30.

Voss, A. (2000). The astrology of Marsilio Ficino: Divination or science? *Culture and Cosmos*, 4(2), 29–45.

Voss, A. (2006). *Marsilio Ficino*. North Atlantic Books.

Woodruff, P. (2005). *Reverence: Renewing a forgotten virtue*. Press Oxford University Press.

Zelinová, Z. (2021). Plato's Socrates and a new interpretation of the kosmos. *Philosophy and Conflict Studies*, 37(1), 53–63. https://doi.org/10.21638/spbu17.2021.105

Zhmud, L. (2012). *Pythagoras and the early pythagoreans*. Oxford University Press.

Chapter 6

Case Stories: Bringing It All Together

Spring: Being a Vessel for the Universal Energies

Spring is a teacher and mother who feels a strong need to be true to her instincts and intuition. She is currently involved in master studies of transpersonal psychology, movement, dance, and expressive arts. Lightning-fast and with a brilliant intellect, she requires a great deal of mental stimulation to keep herself from feeling bored. I shared with her the qualities that I saw, heard, and sensed (confident, inspirational, spontaneous, and idealistic) to support her in feeling seen at her authentic core.

In our first session, she brought a dream about a coach slipping under the water; the dream was pointing to her intense fear of the writing process, a fear of losing boundaries with so much information and so many theories to work with. I resonated with her fear, and my kinaesthetic reactions confirmed that I was getting the essence of her trigger.

We reframed her fear as a fear of losing contact with who she is, dissociating from her essence. Next, we used her dream as a magnifying glass to focus on specific archetypes of her natal chart.

Her discourse distilled some needs in conflict with each other that we could identify through archetypal patterns. Exploring her Mercury and Uranus gave us a bigger picture of her need to express herself with freedom and authenticity, while Saturn gave us tips on ways to fulfill her need to complete tasks efficiently. In active imagination, we embraced polarities through dialoguing and identifying needs and archetypes: her need for persistent effort and concentration (represented by Mars conjunct Saturn) and her need to express herself bluntly and to nurture her insights and intuitions (symbolized by the contact between Mercury and Uranus).

In another dream, Spring described a scene with a wise old man in a big room with balls of clay popping all over the place; she sensed she had to leave this room to avoid being hit by them. We associated these stones to her natal Mars-Saturn conjunction – Mars symbolizing aggression and movement and Saturn the heaviness of the rocks and their force of gravity. I clarified her need for persistent effort and concentration with determination to overcome all obstacles (Mars influenced by Saturn) and her need to be inspired and access her intuitive knowledge (Neptune). I suggested that she do active imagination around these needs and hold them with respect without making one side more important than the other. Through

DOI: 10.4324/9781003627258-7

the dialogue between her dream symbols and her inner Saturn archetype, Spring received an embodied insight about Saturn's role as a detector of what is in the environment as well as a protector, allowing her to set boundaries. As an antidote to feeling overwhelmed, blocked, or frustrated, her inner Saturnian archetype was suggesting sacred action, creating from a more mindful space. She was inspired to listen to the advice of Saturn whenever her Mars energy is charging ahead at full speed, and she started to use these archetypes to help her focus more on the way she approached her studies and creative projects. The written reflective exercise helped her name what was emerging in the sessions.

Saturn will help me limit myself to new projects until I can complete others. I will tap into my contact Uranus-Mercury for the depth of creativity it affords me and for a unique approach to how I can put ideas together and venture into new ways of thinking and synthesizing information (Carod, 2021, Appendix H, p. 1).

I encouraged her to engage in a creative work incorporating the archetypal qualities of her personality in a unifying symbol as an anchor to focus her attention and manifest her vision. Spring's artwork was prospective and anticipatory, revealing what was emerging for her. For the representation of her inner Saturn (structure in the physical world), she decided to build a container with clay and burned some sage as a symbol of her potential transformation.

She described her experience as "journeying into Saturn" and named the integration of her opposed needs – freedom and efficiency – "centered freedom." The visual image of this integration acted as a powerful anchor, helping Spring approach her tasks with greater focus and balance, allowing her to harness her creativity while staying disciplined in her intellectual pursuits.

Self-knowledge through awareness of the archetypes of the collective unconscious and dream symbols brought Spring a sense of unity and belonging to the cosmos, as well as a sense of collective freedom coming from a transpersonal field of information.

I feel bigger. I feel way bigger than this body. My body is like a vessel for these energies that want themselves to be known in the world. (pp. 96–98, in Carod, 2021)

Her conscious elaboration of a larger field of change concurs with Jung's archetypal theory (1960) of the collective universal unconscious present in all of us.

The following two examples illustrate how the research participant and I engaged in active imagination with the most significant archetypes in the natal chart: the Sun, representing conscious will, and the Moon, symbolizing emotional responses and reactions.

Roshani, the Healing Touch of Butterfly Dust

Born in Mumbai, India, Roshani is a brilliant filmmaker and teacher with a powerful personality who was going through a tough period. Pluto, the planet of death and transformation, was contacting her natal Moon, which represents the maternal figure, emotional reactions, and childhood conditioning. Roshani's mother passed away two years ago, leaving unresolved issues. A year later, her dog died, and on top of all this, she was knocked over by a dog and broke her wrist. "… it was like a fire. There was this pot and I was inside being cooked slowly" (Carod, 2021, pp. 91–92). She described pain as a "very important reality toward any kind of movement into growth, evolution, progress."

During our first session, Roshani shared that she felt her old structures were breaking down. While she sensed a need for change, this realization also triggered anxiety. She even expressed the feeling that, in some way, she had invited the accident into her life. The emotional turbulence that the sudden losses had caused her, in addition to the physical pain produced by her broken wrist, forced Roshani to come into contact with unconscious fears and emotions. The transit of Pluto was bringing to light these fears and emotions so that she could accept them, process them, and let them go.

Many of the dream symbols that Roshani brought to the sessions before the accident were about not being able to fulfill her will: the elevator not stopping at her floor, being late, missing the bus, or standing in the wrong queue for the wrong train. It seemed that she was in the process of making an effort to trust the unknown and accept imperfections in her life.

She reflected on a dream in which she was a small child being fed by her daughter, while her mother listened attentively. "In these last few years… I think my feminine aspect has been wanting to surface." (p. 153). Roshani realized that the accident had given her the opportunity to embody feelings of vulnerability. Rather than viewing vulnerability as useless or ineffective, she began to recognize its value and transformative potential. After this acknowledgment, she dreamed of three butterflies, which were fluttering and standing in alignment, symbolizing her inner child at three different ages.

> I had a dream of three butterflies fluttering, and in the meditation I felt them on my skin, the ephemeral butterfly dust from my childhood. (pp. 45–46, in Carod, 2021)

Archetypal knowledge of the Moon's placement by sign and aspects provided Roshani with valuable information about her automatic emotional mind and the reactions associated with it. I suggested that we practice a dialogue between her Sun and Moon archetypes in order to explore the relationship between her self-power and conscious will on the one side and her unconscious reactions linked to her early emotional needs on the other. In expanded awareness, I encouraged her to voice what her Moon needed as a symbol of her inner child. The answer included three messages for her three inner children and their needs at three different ages; the two-year-old child needed to be held, the five-year-old child needed to be joyous and laughing, and the twelve-year-old needed to feel secure.

Roshani's embodied experience with the three aligned and fluttering butterflies of her dream was associated with the three inner children that appeared in active imagination. She created the painting in Figure 6.1 that encapsulates our work together.

Figure 6.1 The three fluttering butterflies. Illustration by Roshani

We invoked the butterflies in guided meditation, and Roshani felt them caressing her face, fluttering, and leaving their color on her skin. This subtle, embodied experience provided her with a profound sense of peace. For Roshani, transformation is something very ephemeral and very delicate.

There's a lot of healing that comes about. Like I told you, this information is very delicate, and it's like the butterfly dust. You can miss it if you don't look carefully (Roshani, pp. 75–77 in Carod, 2021).

Marguerite: Focusing Effort to Manifest My Truth

Marguerite, 36, was born in France, close to the Swiss border, and was brought up in a traditional Catholic environment in a very loving family.

After ten years of experience in management consulting in the corporate world, she embarked on new adventures, traveling, becoming an entrepreneur, and exploring both the outer world and her own inner world. She embarked on a spiritual journey, diving deep into different spiritual practices. She studied yoga, meditation, astrology, holotropic breathwork, shamanism, plant medicine, intuitive writing, and dream work.

Marguerite had spent the previous six years traveling and verbalized her current need to ground; her values related to committing to a place and its inhabitants. She was then creating a permaculture project for her community in the Philippines and leading meditations based on Moon cycles.

When I talked to her, she transmitted an ancient wisdom to me; she has the presence of an old shaman soul. Marguerite records her dreams daily and lets herself be guided by her intuition; she knows how to tune into the rhythms of nature and be attentive to synchronicities. We connected her dream of giving birth alone with her Sun archetype, representing the focus and strength that she was putting into her permaculture project for the local community.

We also elaborated Marguerite's dream, where she saw a Merkabah (two three-dimensional opposing triangles) next to a tree. Through archetypal amplification of the dream image, we found that the word *Merkabah* comes from a Hebrew

Figure 6.2 The Moon meditation ritual. Picture by Marguerite

Figure 6.3 The tree archetype. Illustration by Marguerite

word that means "chariot" or "light, body, spirit." As Bogart (2009, p. 101) points out, natural elements are archetypal. The tree is a key archetype that represents the process of becoming awake, the desire for individuation, and the eventual realization of potential (Figure 6.3).

Marguerite's drawing expressed her need for a deep connection with nature. The client spent her last six years traveling and verbalized her current need to ground. Settling in a place taking care of plants represented an outlet for her need for grounding and connected her to the value she places on committing to a place and its habitants.

As a next small step, Marguerite resolved to ask permission to start her project to plant trees for healing purposes and to hold ceremonies. Her artistic creation served as an anchor to focus her attention and embody her desired vision.

She had the potential to be a leader in her community but felt insecure about speaking publicly. I asked her to formulate a question starting with *how* that described what she wanted to achieve with regard to her fear of speaking publicly. She asked, "How can I release the fear of showing myself to the world?"

Before diving into her fears and exploring them through her natal Saturn, I pointed to the prominent position of her Jupiter as a neutralizing factor. Jupiter is the archetype of expansion through education and ideals. In her natal chart. Jupiter is the most elevated planet in the sector of professional status and public image in the sign of Aquarius, a placement that suggests expansion and opportunities with like-minded groups of people. Regarding Jupiter, she addressed this archetype as "an inspiration to cultivate greater trust in life and in her coaching opportunities." This work helped her align herself to a resource state and also provided her with inspired actions and practical steps to follow her vision or desired outcome (guiding others to heal). As a next step, she resolved to ask permission to start her project of planting trees for healing purposes and to hold ceremonies.

I guided her to anchoring to a resource state with the aid of qualities expressed by her Jupiter, Sun, and, Saturn, archetypes that we had been commenting on in this and previous sessions.

We searched for archetypal meaning and made the connection to Saturn and Mercury: Saturn likes to build, structure, and organize, while Mercury rules communication, thinking processes, and learning. This inspired her to put more effort into her studies and focus on her professional development. As a practical step she started to build her own website.

Mary: Resting in Stillness through the Centered Man

> To be able to use my own motifs and archetypes to work with shadows. I feel much more in the driver's seat of the experience, able to be with it how I choose.
> —Mary, journal entry, March 17, 2021

Besides integrating unconscious aspects, another significant role of dreams is assisting the process of transformation through a fusion with transcendent qualities. The next example shows how Mary is lifted to a higher state of consciousness and can bring those magical qualities into waking physical reality.

Mary is a mother and mindfulness teacher for adults and kids who had a spiritual awakening during a silent retreat in Thailand. Her initial trigger was her relationship with her husband and kids.

She had been inquiring more deeply into fear over the previous few years. But she felt she was still in the grip of fear rather than being a witness to it. I asked her to formulate a question starting with *how* that described what she wanted to achieve from her current situation. She said: "How to relate with more authenticity."

She brought several dreams that revealed root patterns that were triggering her in her current relationships. The themes of self-protection and her fear of people around her rejecting her were identified through her dreams and also through exploring her Saturn archetype. She then elaborated another dream in which she felt she wasn't good enough to be out there with the angels. Revisiting the dream and dialoguing with them in active imagination, she observed that she had feelings of anger. The dream helped her acknowledge that, and we worked on how to accept those feelings with compassion and stop judging herself. The golden angels brought Mary a sense of warmth and safety, a sense that we are all part of this universe and its intelligence and that everything is connected in some way. She felt uplifted, awakened, and a lot lighter and luminous. I also felt within myself the qualities she described. She identified a need to feel accepted and concluded that the core of it was self-acceptance. Mary defined her inspired action as a movement toward freedom from fear.

Another day, Mary dreamed of "centeredness," an image of an 18th-century masculine figure who kept peaceful and calm while being attacked by a crowd of people (see Figure 6.4). This dream provided her with clarity, serenity, and compassion for the different aspects of herself. It also offered her another way to be with and accept all parts of herself: the parts that feel helpless in the face of her own inner conflict, and the part that feels centered and is allowing the reactivity and

Figure 6.4 The centered man. Illustration by Mary

feeling of helplessness. The active imagination exercise with the symbols of this dream offered her the possibility of letting it all be while holding it all in compassionate love. The centered man acted as a tool of integration for different parts of her personality.

After she had led a guided meditation group one night, Mary had a sinking feeling and felt fear and rejection. When she meditated the next morning, she became conscious of her discomfort. She then embodied the centered man and was curious to view the discomfort from this position, resting in the stillness while allowing the reactivity:

> And then offering a loving presence as a parent would do to an angry child (as if to a lynch mob). Then, just resting in the stillness, while allowing the reactivity, and offering a loving presence as I embody the person being accused, the centered entity. (journal entry, 17th March 2021, in Carod, 2021)

In active imagination, she embraced polarities that appeared to be in conflict, holding them with respect, without making one side more important than the other. The centered man image of her dream montage awoke her to the fact that she gets stuck in the moment when reactivity has her, rather than her watching reactivity. Mary concluded that the key to being free of this pattern was to continue on her spiritual path, which consists of self-acceptance and self-compassion through integrating polarities.

Embracing both the feminine and the masculine, the conditioned and the luminous—not as separate dualities, but as integral aspects of a unified whole (journal entry, 17th March 2021, in Carod, 2021).

Susanne: Making Questions and Accepting the Gifts

Susanne was brought up as a Catholic in a relatively conservative Irish environment. She specialized in language teaching at university, founded a language school, and also set up a volunteer teacher-training project in India.

Her desire to experience something out of the ordinary led her to encompass a wide range of spiritual practices and studies, in particular, self-inquiry, meditation, spontaneous drawing, shamanic journeying, yoga, and hypnotherapy. Susanne described her life story through the metaphor of sleeping beauty:

"My own religious involvement was very out of body, and I would say that in many regards I was totally asleep, even though I appeared to be very spiritual" (pp. 210–214, in Carod, 2021).

Susanne has a youthful personality; she is very talkative and curious and is able to invest a lot of passion and enthusiasm in her profession. Her work situation was severely impacted by COVID. She missed her job as a teacher very much.

The issues she brought to the first sessions were self-criticism and overthinking. Susanne had a feeling that her overthinking (symbolized by the planet Mercury) was blocking her on her spiritual path. In active imagination, we used her

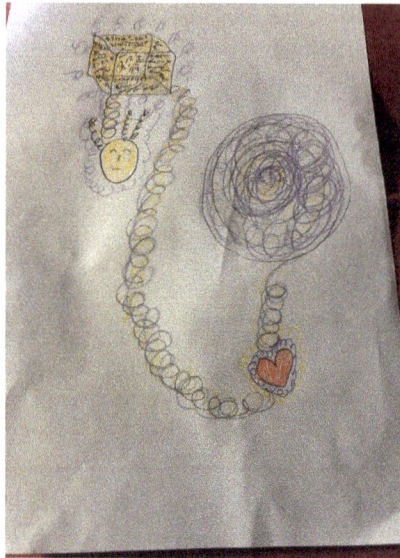

Figure 6.5 Connecting mind and soul through the heart. Illustration by Susanne

recent dreams to focus on specific archetypes. I encouraged a dialogue between her Mercury (communication and thinking process), Uranus (intuition, impulse to be free and express her own creativity), and Neptune (her mystic side).

Mercury suggested using her ability to ask questions instead of engaging in self-criticism. She achieved a resolution by means of a visual metaphor that connected her Mercury and Neptune through the heart (see Figure 6.5).

"The thing was how to find a bridge between my mind and my soul. One of the things that I did was to draw that, and I discovered that what could actually help was if the heart could connect these two things" (Susanne, pp. 75–80, in Carod, 2021).

Another day, Susanne brought a dream of looking at herself in a mirror after her hair had been cut. She wasn't comfortable with this hairstyle – it was alien to her and done against her will. But then a voice came to her saying "accept." The dream suggested to her that she should accept the new hairstyle and embrace her feminine side. The moment the acceptance was felt, the dream scene changed, and she found herself in the desert, carrying a tray with gifts, food, and incense cones. We elaborated on her self-criticism and unmet needs through archetypes and dreams. Through dialogue with her dream symbols, Susanne received a message that suggested the need to accept change. "I felt that everything has its place. Everything is okay, I can embrace all of it" (pp. 89–90).

In active imagination, we used dreams as a loop to focus on specific archetypes. Following Mercury's suggestion of using her ability to pose questions instead of engaging in self-criticism, Susanne asked herself: "How is this confusion and lack of clarity serving me?" The answer she received was: "opening up to possibilities."

We linked this to her dream about gifts, and she asked, "What gifts are there in this current situation?" We developed the message of acceptance and the tray of gifts. She referred to accepting unwanted changes that her current job situation brought, renouncing control, trusting, and surrendering.

Rose: Looking Up

Rose grew up surrounded by beautiful hills in Scotland. She was academically "bright" and good at sports. "But in reality, I was more like a dead person until I found breath…"

She realized she had been disassociated from her body since she was abused by her stepfather and had participated in ayahuasca retreats to purge, transform, and leave behind the trauma. She was in the process of learning to love herself and trust people.

> I married at 18, had three children, divorced at 28. I never loved him, though. I just didn't know how to say "no" essentially. I only realized a few years ago that love has to start from inside.

A single parent of three, she decided to learn accountancy to earn a decent living for her kids. The universe was certainly on her side, and a multinational organization sponsored her and paid her to wander around the globe with her kids through a series of exotic expat postings. While she was working for an oil company in the Middle East, Rose suffered a mountain-bike accident that seriously affected her spine. She subsequently healed herself through daily exercises of conscious breathing.

Rose came to realize that she had lived the first 40 years of her life in a disconnected state; her mind and body were two quite separate entities. Basically, she could think and act without feeling, quite literally.

In more recent years, Rose has studied transpersonal psychology, mindfulness, functional medicine, and literature. She meditates regularly, does breathing exercises, and generally "looks within." She is very satisfied with her current job, in which she teaches people how to breathe.

Gentle, sociable, and kind, Rose has a light, fun, curious, and chatty quality. She was in the process of learning how to love herself and was open to meeting new people. She likes to live dynamically and to benefit from as many cultural choices as possible. She needs variety and a chance to share ideas or concepts with others. But the situation during COVID made it difficult for her to have social interactions.

Supporting others gave Rose a lot of pleasure, but underneath was a hidden belief of not deserving love, care, or appreciation. She brought a dream about a root vegetable that was old. She associated this dream with not "skimping" on things by being cheap and realized "I am worthy and can afford good food." The dream brought up her tendency for self-neglect and made her reflect on her worthiness and her right to enjoy the pleasures of life. As a next step, she bought a lovely sourdough bread, and that led to a conversation with a lady from India with interests similar to hers.

Rose was very open to using archetypal energies to support herself in her projects. We focused on Venus and how she could embrace the qualities it promotes: joy, beauty, passion for life, art. As a next step, to express her creativity and nurture her Venus archetype in the sign of Gemini (symbolizing communication, writing, and talking), Rose enrolled in a writing course.

In our last session, she felt empowered:

> I'm creative, I'm strong, I have a lot of wisdom. The main insight is that I have these abilities and I can do something with them. There's a lot of potential… and it's encouraging me to reach out to do these breath workshops in the Middle East on a much bigger scale. (pp. 50–53, in Carod, 2021)

As a creative exercise, Rose wrote the poem "Looking Up":

Too numb to think	Patterns broken latent potential
I would have been better underground	Crashing through
Hidden archetypes had kept me safe	No more no self-made exclusion zone
And now…	Head held high looking up to the sky
Venus shining in full Moon's light.	My plan… to follow the stars,
Love is calling	The Sun, Venus, and the Moon
Wandering, wondering time to be home	Basking with Jupiter all as one

Summer: Dream Symbols as a Call to Creativity and Authenticity

My client Summer is a multifaceted and bright woman who requested a coaching session to help her decide on her career path. She earned a bachelor's degree in reflexology but is also interested in music therapy and coaching. She writes poetry and journals her dreams as a routine. However, her psychological health is fragile. She had been taking medication pills for trauma recovery for many years, and she was unsure if she could manage the many daily hours required to continue these studies.

She recalled the following dream:

> In the dream, there was a tall woman there who was also named Summer. Another woman asked me what she should buy for her elderly mother, who was in an institution. She was torn between getting her mother a Remi computer game or a painting, but she was leaning more towards the painting. I told her that while the computer game would engage her mother for hours, it would take her into the virtual world and away from real life, whereas a painting would keep her present in the world. I shared that I have many drawings and paintings on my walls, and they make me feel good. I offered to show her a recent painting I was proud of. As I looked through my paintings, I found a beautiful painting of

flowers, but I couldn't locate the one I had mentioned. I suspected that I might have given it away to someone.

After completing a reflective exercise where she practiced active imagination, she began to understand the dream more clearly. She realized that the tall woman, also called Summer, might represent another aspect of herself.

"Perhaps a twin aspect or my higher self, as she appeared taller. The suggestions I gave to the woman about her mother, in hindsight, seemed like advice I needed to give myself. The Remi computer game symbolized my tendency to get lost in distractions like my phone or the internet, while the painting represented creativity and action in the real world. The message was clear – I need to be more in touch with life. The fact that I didn't want the woman to see my messy room reveals how I hide certain parts of my life. The painting of flowers likely symbolizes my connection to gardening and perhaps more deeply to my role as a therapist or caretaker, nurturing others."

During another session, she described a dream about an injured university student whose face was like a mask, with the skin beneath the mask pulled off. We associated the mask to the previous dream where she was hiding certain parts of her life.

The mask gets to tell Summer's story, which is framed, like a painting. Legend is the name she gave to this drawing. She associated it with "the whole content of a story and a life not lived".

Reflecting on the archetypes related to this dream, we found that Saturn, symbolizing the skin and the mask, was a focal point in her natal chart, squaring (a challenging aspect) to her Moon (emotions) and Mars (desires and impulse toward action). This Saturn square symbolizes a blockage of Summer's energy and spontaneity, causing delays and frustration of her desires.

However, we also connected her Saturn to the acceptance of limits and the need for grounding to compensate for her highly intellectual and fast-paced mind. Saturn in Virgo emphasizes the importance of taking care of one's own physical needs and limits and is also related to mastery in health and service to others. She was

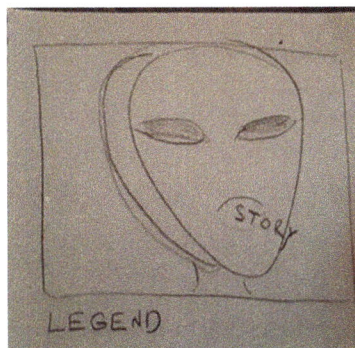

Figure 6.6 A framed mask. Illustration by Summer

considering volunteering to support cancer patients and we discussed the possibility of guiding others while doing reflexology.

In active imagination, we invited Saturn and her dream symbols for dialogue. Through kinaesthetic sensations, she received the message that practicing reflexology would be beneficial for her. It felt good in her body, enabling her to embody the grounded essence of Saturn.

References

Bogart, G. (2009). *Dreamwork and self healing.* Routledge.

Carod, A. (2021). *The transformative experiences of coaching using archetypal imagery within a participatory framework: An organic inquiry.* John Moores University.

Jung, C. G. (1960). The transcendent function (R. F. C. Hull, Trans.). In H. Read, M. Fordham, G. Adler, & W. McGuire (Eds.), *The collected works of C. G. Jung* (Vol. 8). Princeton University Press.

Appendix I

Practical Guidelines for Archetypal Coaching: Steps and Exercises

General Steps for Archetypal Coaching

Step 1: Create a Safe, Mindful Space

Begin by establishing a calm, open environment where the client feels seen and understood.

Invite the client to choose the topic they want to explore and pay attention to key words and to repeated phrases.

Listen for what is not working and invite the client to reflect on what is important there and what is at the center of their issue.

Use empathic resonance to connect, staying curious and attentive. Pay attention to what is showing up: the tone of voice, rhythm, pauses, body posture, facial expression.

Guide willing clients through a mindfulness exercise, like Dängeli's Open Awareness, to foster a grounded, non-reactive state. From this state, encourage them to share their observations and feelings.

Step 2: Identify the Trigger and Clarify the Client's Goals

Show curiosity and help them rephrase their trigger without pressing through questions like: "so, you are stuck, what is that like for you?"

Assist the client in formulating a "how" question that clarifies what they want to achieve in relation to their current situation. For example, they might ask, "How can I develop the ability to act steadily and confidently toward my goals without fear?" This question helps direct their focus toward actionable steps and growth.

Step 3: Informing Clients' Triggers through Archetypes and Dream Symbols (Refer to Sections "Practical Guide to Coaching with Dream Symbols" and "Practical Guide to Coaching with Astrological Archetypes")

Introduce archetypes and dream symbols relevant to the client's experience. For example, if the client feels stuck we will explore how Saturn is displaced in their natal chart. If this client dreams of being a passenger in a car and they're currently dealing with power dynamics, this could signify a struggle with control and agency. This image might prompt a deeper examination of Mars (self-drive) in the natal chart and any significant transits to Mars that could influence the present situation.

Help clients rephrase words like "I must" or "I should" by analyzing their natal chart's archetypal patterns. For example, a client with a challenging aspect between Mars and Saturn might initially experience blocked action due to fear or excessive caution. However, this aspect also holds potential for channeling energy and focus into achieving concrete goals through steady, progressive actions. By recognizing these latent strengths, we can guide clients toward empowering language, such as "I choose to concentrate my energy on specific goals."

Encourage the client to keep a dream journal so that they note any symbols that evoke archetypal themes (i.e. mountains, stones, or elders for Saturn). These images can provide clues to how they can work with their issues.

Encourage the client to explore these archetypes and symbols as resources to set intentions and to highlight positive aspects that align with their goals (i.e. Mars's drive and Saturn's lessons in discipline).

Step 4: Anchoring through Creative Integration

Encourage clients to channel these symbols into creative expressions, such as art, journaling, or building a vision board.

They might design a symbol that encapsulates their challenges and path forward. This creative process provides a physical representation of the issue and potential transformations, helping to solidify new perspectives and growth.

Step 5: Deepen Exploration with Active Imagination

In guided meditation, help clients anchor a symbol that encapsulates their journey, focusing on the emotions and insights it evokes. Using active imagination, encourage them to interact with the symbol in an expanded state of mind, allowing insights to surface. This process provides a supportive space for unconscious images to communicate directly, fostering clarity around underlying issues without heavy reliance on interpretations.

Incorporate somatic awareness meditation to deepen engagement with archetypes and dream symbols aligned with the client's purpose. This embodied interaction creates a space for inner alchemy, facilitating shifts in understanding and perspective.

Step 6: Engage the Client in Reflective Exercises

Finally, provide personalized reflective exercises for the client to complete after the session (see Appendix II). These exercises help anchor insights, allowing clients to explore their personal narrative and reshape beliefs.

Practical Guide to Coaching with Dream Symbols

To develop a holistic approach to working with dreams, this method integrates classic Jungian analysis, Hillman's imaginal psychology, and a contemporary embodied perspective. The process is structured into clear steps that honor the dream's symbolic and autonomous nature, allowing it to "speak" to us while fostering deep engagement with both the body and imagination.

Step 1: Establish Intention and Foster Embodied Engagement with the Dream

Encourage the client to approach the dream with openness, inviting whatever insights the dream holds. Emphasize curiosity over analysis to foster a receptive mindset.

Capture Dream Details: have the client record the dream's scenes, symbols, and sensory details immediately upon waking. The goal is thorough, unfiltered recall.

Engage in Somatic Exploration: guide the client to visualize the dream and pay attention to physical sensations linked to each symbol or character. These bodily responses can provide insights into the dream's emotional tone.

Step 2: Association, Archetypal Amplification, and Imaginal Engagement

Explore Spontaneous Associations: prompt the client to note initial thoughts, memories, or feelings about each dream element. Encourage associations without attempting logical interpretations.

Amplify with Universal Symbols: guide clients in linking personal symbols with broader archetypal figures (mythological, astrological, or cultural) to expand perspective and uncover collective themes.

Invite the Dream to "Speak": following Hillman's approach, encourage clients to approach the dream without seeking specific answers. Prompt them to experience the dream as if listening to an ancient story, allowing it to unfold.

Step 3: Dialogue and Symbolic Exploration

Engage in Symbol Dialogue: use active imagination techniques, prompting clients to converse with dream characters in an expanded state of consciousness. Ask them to be open to what each symbol "says" or represents, helping them uncover unconscious guidance.

Focus on Emotional Resonance: if a powerful feeling arises during exploration, encourage the client to stay with it, acknowledging this as a potential core message of the dream.

Step 4: Creative Expression and Ritual Integration

Encourage Artistic Expression: have clients represent dream elements through art, writing, or movement. This physical act helps grounding and deepens the experience, as Jung suggested.

Design Rituals for Integration: suggest small, symbolic acts that embody the dream's insights. Examples could include:

- Building a Dream Altar: encourage clients to gather objects that represent key symbols or insights from the dream. This space can be used for ongoing reflection.
- Acting in a Way That Honors the Dream: suggest behaviors or choices that align with the dream's message, such as embodying courage, compassion, or patience.
- Creating a Personal Ceremony: this could involve lighting a candle, speaking aloud to honor the dream's insights, or performing a symbolic act like planting a seed to represent growth.

Step 5: Reflection and Continued Engagement. Return to the Dream over Time

Encourage clients to revisit the dream and notice how interpretations evolve. Repeated engagement often uncovers new perspectives.

Practical Guide to Coaching with Astrological Archetypes

Step 1: Identify the Client's Initial Trigger

Begin by exploring the client's current issue or emotional state.

Step 2: Explore Astrological Archetypes

Provide clients with a basic understanding of the archetypes at stake. Astrological archetypes offer rich insights into complex dynamics, such as the tension between personal drives for assertion (Mars) and the desire for harmony (Venus), or the balance between emotional needs (Moon) and the aspiration for self-expression and visibility (Sun). Clients may also explore contrasts like the urge for expansion and idealism (Jupiter) versus the impulse to build structure through sustained effort (Saturn). This exploration fosters greater self-awareness and clarity about inner conflicts and growth opportunities.

Use astrological symbols to frame their trigger, helping the client understand how archetypes represent unconscious instincts or complexes (e.g., survival, social dominance, or abandonment) are influencing their behaviors.

Ask the client how they embody the astrological archetypes connected to their trigger. Their narrative will illuminate whether their potential is being fully expressed or remains untapped.

Assist the client in recognizing their subpersonalities and archetypes with openness and without judgment. Guide them to identify the unique needs and tendencies reflected in their astrological chart.

Step 3: Exploring Positive Potentials in the Natal Chart

Explore the client's archetypal potential that directly relates to their initial request (how they want to feel or be).

If a client struggles with anger management and their Sun forms a conflicting aspect with Mars, this suggests their behavior may be driven by a strong desire for action, recognition, and creative expression. While this configuration highlights leadership potential, it can also lead to aggression if not balanced. The Mars archetype can be redirected into assertiveness or goal-setting, while exploring the Venus archetype fosters balance and harmony in relationships.

Use these potentials as anchors for personal growth. As they become aware of archetypal meanings and images, guide them toward practical, constructive actions that align with their values and goals.

Step 4: Active Imagination

In this step, we'll encourage dynamic interaction between the client's dream symbols and archetypal images while they are in an expanded state of mind. Invite the relevant archetypes worked in previous sessions. During the session, avoid offering interpretations; instead, hold space for the images produced by the unconscious to communicate directly.

Example Scenario: Archetypal Anchor

Step 1: Identify the Negative State and Related Archetype

For instance, someone with Mars in Capricorn in a challenging square to Saturn may face amplified self-doubt and obstacles that inhibit their assertiveness. Saturn's restrictive energy, when negative, can manifest as self-criticism, procrastination, and fear of failure, often taking the form of an Inner Critic or Overseer.

While Mars in Capricorn values disciplined, goal-oriented action, the Saturn square can introduce fears of inadequacy, making decisive action more difficult. Helping clients recognize this archetype allows them to understand these feelings as part of a broader, impersonal pattern rather than personal flaws, enabling them to address and release these negative states.

Step 2: Identify the Positive Resource States

We seek resourceful aspects of both Mars (strength, resilience, courage) and Saturn (discipline, patience, mastery). From the Mars archetype, we anchor a sense of focused action and fearlessness. From Saturn, we anchor qualities of stable discipline, mastery, and wisdom.

To navigate this restrictive influence constructively, it can be helpful for individuals with this placement to channel their energy into structured, achievable goals. This can build confidence and provide a sense of accomplishment, reinforcing their ability to assert themselves without feeling overwhelmed by self-criticism.

Step 3: Guide the Visualization and Anchor the Positive States

We guide the client to imagine scenarios where they embody these positive traits, such as handling their business with assertive confidence or tackling their thesis with steady discipline and commitment.

During this visualization, anchor the feeling of courage, determination, and self-trust for a few seconds, making it stronger each time.

Step 4: Reinforcement and Future Visualization

Guide the client to embody the positive qualities of Mars (courage and action) and Saturn (wisdom and discipline) as inherent strengths they can now access with ease. Encourage them to mentally rehearse future scenarios where they apply these strengths, envisioning themselves taking action on their goals with confidence and stability, free from fear or self-doubt.

Connect specific future triggers, such as managing positions or preparing a business plan, to their new resourceful responses, ensuring these associations are automatically activated in similar situations.

Integrating Archetypal Astrology into Subpersonality Work

Step 1: Recognize and Identify Subpersonalities

Notice recurring thoughts, emotions, or behaviors that may indicate the presence of a subpersonality.

Encourage clients to "converse" with these aspects of themselves as distinct personalities, using techniques like placing opposing parts in separate chairs to facilitate dialogue. For instance, one client may recognize an "Inner Critic" that emerges in stressful situations, while another might identify with a childlike aspect of themselves that resists responsibility and craves constant attention and care.

Step 2: Discover the Purpose and Value behind Subpersonalities

Use open-ended and reflective questions to uncover each subpersonality's motivations. For instance, ask, "What does this part want to achieve?" or "What role does this part play in your life?"

Link each subpersonality to a planetary archetype that represents its core values and traits. For example, the Inner Critic could be linked to Saturn, representing a drive for security and self-discipline, and the inner child could be associated to the Moon.

Step 3: Dis-Identification Exercise

Guide the client through affirmations, such as "I have emotions, but I am not my emotions" and "I have desires, but I am not my desires."

Incorporate planetary symbolism to support dis-identification. For example, the Moon, representing emotions, can help clients recognize that their feelings, while meaningful, do not define them entirely.

Step 4: Archetypal Substitution Technique

Help the client recognize a limiting pattern associated with a planetary archetype. For example, a self-critical thought pattern could be linked to Mercury's analytical nature.

Substitute the limiting aspect with a constructive quality of the same planet. For instance, Mercury's energy could be redirected from overanalyzing to insightful awareness.

Encourage the client to hold an image of this positive expression, allowing it to gradually replace the limiting thought or behavior.

Step 5: Cross-Planetary Substitution

Recognize when one planetary archetype is too dominant (e.g., Mercury's over-thinking). Introduce the influence of another planet to balance the challenging expression. For instance, invite Jupiter's expansive qualities to offset Mercury's critical thoughts by encouraging a broader perspective.

Guide the client in visualizing this new planetary energy to replace the original limiting behavior. If Jupiter is chosen, the client might imagine themselves feeling confident and connected to a larger purpose, counteracting Mercury's narrow focus.

Appendix II
Reflective Exercises

These exercises are designed for clients to complete both before and after sessions: a dream work exercise to be done pre-session and a reflective exercise with archetypes and story reframing to be done post-session.

Dream Work Exercise

1   Incubate a dream to receive guidance for integration of the polarities or conflicting energies addressed during the archetypal work. Before going to sleep write in your journal the theme or question you want to incubate and say it out loud three times before falling asleep.
2   Next day, recall the dream when you wake up before moving your head. Then, start to write (or record) the image or scene that you remember, trusting that this is what your psyche wants you to elaborate. Write without expectations, not wanting to transform it into a strictly defined meaning but having a rich reflection on it.
3   After writing the dream as faithfully as you can, first sense the meaning more in your body than in your mind. Write down these embodied perceptions and feelings.
4   You can later practice active imagination through dialoguing with the parts of the dream. Again, leave your rational mind aside, bringing awareness to your breath and body and feel free to ask the symbols/images any questions that you feel inspired to ask. A figure from your dream may rise up, continuing where it left off, or a new image might appear, one you've never seen before. You might wonder who this is and why they've appeared in your imagination. The simplest and most direct invitation is to ask:

- *Who are you?*
- *What do you want?*
- *What do you have to say?*

Your dialogue begins here. Once you initiate the inner conversation, it's essential to relinquish control and allow the process to unfold naturally.

Reflective Exercise with Archetypes

1 *Inspired Action*: where do you want to go (Sun, Mars)? What are your aspirations and long-term goals (Jupiter, Saturn)?
2 *Identifying Blockages*: where are you feeling stuck or restricted (Saturn)?
3 *Emotional Security*: how can you feel more secure and nurtured in your life (Moon)?
4 *Improving Communication*: how can you enhance your communication skills and learning abilities (Mercury)?
5 *Finding Joy*: how can you experience more joy and connection with others (Venus)?
6 *Support and Action*: how can each archetype or dream symbol support you on your path? What steps are you going to take to move forward?

Reframing Your Story

I invite you to work with your latent potential story to help you shift your story about yourself, about others, and about life itself. To do so, you will address the symbols and archetypes that came out in the coaching sessions for meaning and inspiration.

1 Imagine the challenge you presented unfolding successfully. Envision associating the trigger with a positive outcome, drawing on the archetypal traits you've discovered within yourself. Allow these qualities – such as resilience, diplomacy, strategic thinking, vision, charisma, empathy, wisdom, or courage – to guide the scene, reinforcing a sense of capability and confidence as you visualize the best possible outcome.
2 Take note of the positive qualities and gifts that make you unique. What defines you now?
3 Describe how they are merging with your past self and if they are changing you. What new perceptions (sensations, thoughts, feelings), values, and purposes are you noticing?
4 To solidify this emerging narrative, articulate these qualities through a creative medium. This could involve creating a mandala, collage, or vision board; sculpting or drawing; or even writing a story or poem that embodies your new self.

Index

Note: *Italic* page numbers refer to figures and page numbers followed by "n" denote endnotes.

For Product Safety Concerns and Information please contact our EU
representative GPSR@taylorandfrancis.com
Taylor & Francis Verlag GmbH, Kaufingerstraße 24, 80331 München, Germany